Michael Rothery, PhD
George Enns, MSW

Clinical Practice with Families
Supporting Creativity and Competence

Pre-publication
REVIEWS,
COMMENTARIES,
EVALUATIONS . . .

"This is an excellent resource for frontline social workers who wish to enhance their skills in family-centered practice. It will help generalist practitioners better understand key elements of family assessment, and will serve to strengthen their interventions with families in distress. Rich case material is interwoven with important theoretical material throughout, which helps bring sharp clarity to some of the more abstract practice concepts."

Barry Trute, PhD
Fisher Chair and Professor,
School of Social Work,
McGill University,
Montreal, Quebec

"This book offers a refreshing sense of connection to the families we work with and a unique mix of clinical ingenuity. Starting with the personal frameworks of clinicians and families, the authors then devote considerable discussion to the nature and function of boundaries—examining family beliefs and interpersonal behaviors and the contribution of these processes to family functioning. The authors have skillfully blended the ecological perspective with the strengths and solution-focused views in clinical applications."

Barbara Thomlison, PhD
Professor and Acting Director,
The Institute for Children
& Families at Risk,
School of Social Work,
Florida International University,
Miami

"**C***linical Practice with Families* provides practitioners, students, and instructors with a rare gift: a text that keeps the baby and the bathwater together. Rothery and Enns succeed brilliantly in striking a tone of 'enlightened pragmatism.' They outline a series of theoretical frameworks, ranging from structural to solution-focused approaches, as possible and overlapping lenses through which the practitioner can view the struggles of family life and develop effective means of helping. What is even more helpful is the inclusion of themes, conversations, and associated reflections from the therapy room itself. As the reader is carried along from lens to lens and case story to case story, the possibility of an integrated, inclusive, and fundamentally respectful approach becomes increasingly tangible. *Clinical Practice with Families* will no doubt find a home in the kit bag of practitioners and on the reading lists of family therapy and clinical social work courses."

Arden Henley, MA, RCC
Director of Canadian Programs,
Faculty of Human Services
and Applied Behavioural Sciences,
City University,
Vancouver, British Columbia

"**R**othery and Enns have written an important book that has much to offer students, teachers, and practitioners. Students especially will appreciate the clear explanation and elaboration of key clinical concepts and their illustration through case transcripts. Teachers will value the integrative and open stance that transcends adherence to a particular practice model,

while providing guidelines for respectful, strength-based efforts to facilitate change. Practitioners will recognize the usefulness of a book that confirms much of what we already know by presenting it in a new light and expands their knowledge by adding important concepts from models that they may not be familiar with. As both a teacher of clinical practice and a practitioner, I have been waiting for a book like this."

Harvey Frankel, PhD
Associate Dean,
Faculty of Social Work,
University of Manitoba, Canada

"**S**tudents of family therapy are always looking for texts that clearly articulate the theory and process of family intervention. There are numerous examples of family therapy books that espouse one model or another of family therapy, but seldom link theory to practice and/or provide an integrated approach that allows the student to understand the complexity, challenge, and excitement of family healing. Rothery and Enns accomplish exactly this in their new textbook on family practice. Although their book is written for social work students and practitioners, anyone interested in a compassionate and hopeful view of family intervention will discover abundant ideas on how to be helpful to families in crisis."

David S. Freeman, DSW
Author,
Multigenerational Family Therapy
and *Family Therapy with Couples:
A Family-of-Origin Approach*

"**T**his book makes a number of significant contributions to the field of family therapy and should prove to be a valuable resource to students, educators, and practitioners. First, in a field too often dominated by competition among and rigid adherence to theoretical approaches, Rothery and Enns offer an integrative framework consisting of an ecological perspective and key concepts that cross theoretical divisions. Their discussion of boundaries, traditions (patterns of thinking, feeling, and acting that are influenced by family of origin and broader culture), and family development integrate consideration of multiple theoretical perspectives. Second, the authors' discussion of the artistic and creative nature of practice and the need to adapt theoretical frameworks and techniques to each unique family reflects an appreciation for the complexities of practice that is often missing in books on family therapy. Third, toward demonstrating how general theoretical principles can be translated into interventions that are sensitive to the uniqueness of families, extensive case examples and transcripts of family sessions are employed usefully throughout the book. Finally, the book includes a chapter that focuses on special considerations in helping vulnerable families whose stability and safety are particularly fragile."

Nick Coady, PhD
Associate Professor,
Wilfrid Laurier University,
Waterloo, Ontario

The Haworth Social Work Practice Press
An Imprint of The Haworth Press, Inc.
New York   London   Oxford

Clinical Practice with Families
Supporting Creativity and Competence

Clinical Practice with Families
Supporting Creativity and Competence

Michael Rothery, PhD
George Enns, MSW

The Haworth Social Work Practice Press
An Imprint of The Haworth Press, Inc.
New York • London • Oxford

Published by

The Haworth Social Work Practice Press, an imprint of The Haworth Press, Inc., 10 Alice Street, Binghamton, NY 13904-1580

Cover design by Marylouise E. Doyle.

Library of Congress Cataloging-in-Publication Data

Rothery, M. A., 1945-
    Clinical practice with families : supporting creativity and competence / Michael Rothery, George Enns.
        p. cm.
    Includes bibliographical references and index.
    ISBN 0-7890-1084-4 (hardcover : alk. paper)—ISBN 0-7890-1085-2 (pbk. : alk. paper)
    1. Family social work—United States. 2. Family psychotherapy—United States. I. Enns, George. II. Title.

HV699 .R67 2000
362.82′8′0973—dc21   00-040783

Our parents are not here to read this book,
but in a sense they were reading over our shoulders
as each sentence was written.

We dedicate it to their memories.

ABOUT THE AUTHORS

Michael Rothery, PhD, MSW, has taught clinical social work practice and research for two decades, prior to which he practiced for many years in child welfare and mental health settings. As a professional and academic, he has a special interest in vulnerable families, the hard-to-serve groups that social workers engage with more frequently than other professions. His research has focused on ecological understandings of child mistreatment, and, more recently, family violence. Dr. Rothery is currently a professor on the faculty of social work at the University of Calgary in Western Canada.

George Enns, MSW, began clinical social work practice with families over twenty-five years ago. His specialized family therapy training was completed through the Post-Master's Training Program at the Philadelphia Child Guidance Clinic, where he participated in workshops and training seminars with renowned therapists, including Peggy Papp, Salvador Minuchin, Jay Haley, and Braulio Montalvo. He is an approved supervisor with the American Association of Marriage and Family Therapy. He is Adjunct Professor on the faculty of social work at the University of Saskatchewan's College of Medicine and Department of Educational Psychology and Special Education. He is coordinator of the Youth and Family Team for a district mental health service, and was honored, in 1987, to receive a Distinguished Service Award from his provincial government's Mental Health Services Branch.

CONTENTS

Foreword

In general, the course of graduate study in the human service professions involves the acquisition of knowledge and skills derived from various theoretical perspectives seminal to a particular discipline. For social work students, this is a two-step process. The foundational focus areas include human behavior and the social environment, social welfare policy, research, and practicum. Integrated into these areas is a consideration of such key themes and issues as social and economic justice, values and ethics, diversity, and populations at risk. Following the completion of their initial course of study, students move to a more advanced level relative to a specific concentration of interest.

As students elect clinical work with individuals and/or families for their area of concentration, they find themselves challenged by more in-depth exploration of the frameworks of a number of theorists and therapists. Along the way, specifically focused practicum placements give them the opportunity to implement and hone newly acquired skills. Upon graduation, they suddenly find that they are deemed ready to enter the professional realm.

However, even at the point of graduation, very few students are equipped with a fully integrated model of practice. Often there has been little opportunity or encouragement to think about the process of developing an individual model of therapy and/or delineating the underlying assumptions upon which it is based. What is more, students rarely have had exposure to such a framework, one that has been informed by and tested in the real world of practice over a period of many years by experienced and seasoned clinicians. Rather, all too often advanced study involves immersion in one or two approaches to clinical work, generally the favorites of the instructors. This despite the fact that, as we have noted elsewhere (Becvar and Becvar, 2000), a concern for integration and the development of metaframeworks has reached the proportions of a movement within the realm of clinical practice today.

According to Held (1995) three major approaches to this process of integration generally are utilized by theorists and therapists. The first is pluralism, in which models are assumed to coexist peacefully and there is an understanding that something meaningful and useful may be found in each. In the second approach, theoretical integration, an umbrella theory or metatheory that captures the central aspects of a variety of theories created. According to the third approach, labeled technical/systematic eclecticism, the focus is on various strategies and techniques whose effectiveness with specific problems or clients has been demonstrated.

It is a manner consistent with the second approach, theoretical integration, that Mike Rothery and George Enns offer the articulation of their perspective. That is, they have provided a model that enables students to understand how one's approach may be created through the meshing together of a variety of theories found to be useful while at the same time remaining flexible enough to accommodate both change in perspective on the part of the creators and differences in clients and the situations with which they may be dealing. Further, the approach has emerged and taken shape through the application of theory in the real world of practice.

In addition to focusing throughout on the importance of frameworks, lenses, and process, the authors urge readers to recognize that "Every person we meet professionally or otherwise has a unique story to tell and each tells that story from a particular position or perspective." They also continually remind us that there are always many ways in which a particular phenomenon may be viewed. Thus, although they have been chosen to weave particular theories into the unique fabric that is their theoretical perspective, there is implicit acknowledgment that this perspective is not necessarily either the best or the only one that may be utilized. What is more, numerous illustrations of what may or may not work are included, as well as recognizing that each client must be understood and responded to in a way that is appropriate for that client.

With this book, students have the opportunity to see into the minds of their mentors: to understand what story on the part of the therapists informed particular strategies and interventions, and to hear their reflections, in retrospect, on what did or did not take place. What they may learn is the process involved with the development and ongoing creation of a model of practice. Included is the way in which practitioners may select from a variety of perspectives those concepts which they find most useful and then adapt them to fit their particular orientation to the world in general and the world of therapy in particular. In sharing their approach, Mike Rothery and George Enns make a valuable contribution to the movement within the realm of clinical practice of theoretical integration and the creation of metaframeworks.

Dorothy S. Becvar, PhD
Founding Partner, President, and CEO
The Haelan Centers™
St. Louis, MO

REFERENCES

Becvar, D. S. and Becvar, R. J. (2000). *Family therapy: A systematic integration.* Boston: Allyn & Bacon.
Held, B. S. (1995). *Back to reality.* New York: W.W. Norton.

Acknowledgments

Authors are inevitably obligated to a host of people who have influenced them and contributed to their work. In acknowledging those who have helped us along we feel an unexpected affinity for the victors at the annual Academy Awards. Struggle breathlessly though we might to make sure everyone gets his or her due, we can do an inadequate job at best.

The clients who appear in our book will always attract our admiration and gratitude. In the face of daunting challenges, they tapped their capacities for creativity and courage. The opportunity to have been there sustains us, and it is precisely this that makes our work more rewarding than any other vocation could possibly be.

Our partners, Leslie and Joyce, have influenced us deeply. Inevitably, their voices are present in this book—we hope that they like what they read, and we thank them for their forbearance and support as we wrestled with words, our computers, and those blank sheets of paper. Writing may be a solitary exercise, yet it is also a family affair; more thanks are due our children for the space and time we took from them to get this job done. Galen, Nathan, Heather, Jason, and Evan have taught us much about the practicalities of family life—sometimes more than we wanted to know.

Our students have helped by keeping us honest, and several have made useful comments about early drafts of this material as it was "field tested" in the classroom. Colleagues have also been generous: we would like to especially recognize Nick Coady, Francis Turner, Lorraine Wright, Bryan Barker, and Tim Greenough. Mike received the support of a Killian Foundation Fellowship to complete his part of the work. This support was vital to our success, and is gratefully acknowledged.

George thanks the many workshop participants and interns who have learned and worked with him over the years. Their questions and discussion invited reflection and clarity. George also is grateful to the members of his team past and present: Joyce Tremmel, Karen Derian, Bryan Woods, Paul Doerksen, Jeannette Ambrose, Marj McKinnon, Margo Couldwell, and Sherry Heidebrecht. Their competence and creativity have expanded his vision, while their friendship and support have nurtured and challenged him, and made work a lively, fun-filled place to be. George owes a special debt of gratitude to his brother Henry, whose creativity, determination, gentleness, and persistence have been, and continue to be, an ongoing source of inspiration.

Mike owes a further debt of thanks to his friend, colleague, and former dean Dr. Ray Thomlison, a challenging thinker with a generous spirit. Such qualities are not always properly celebrated in an imperfect world, but they are essential if a faculty is to be a context supporting creative work. Others have recognized the importance of Ray's leadership in the past, and Mike's voice is added, enthusiastically, to theirs. Dr. Glen Edwards' humanity, intelligence, and skill were an important influence at critical times as well; one wishes one could do more than simply say "thanks."

Introduction

Creativity and Frameworks

*How many things people notions we bring with us into the world,
how many possibilities and also restrictions of possibility!*

Salman Rushdie, *Midnight's Children*

OUR PURPOSE

As authors, we bring to the task of writing this book experience in two worlds: the social work agency and the classroom. Each of us has invested a good part of his life in practicing clinical social work as well as in teaching it.

This work began with informal discussions about our difficulties in finding a book for advanced students and beginning professionals that would provide an integrative treatment of contemporary clinical theory. Books that proselytize for one model or school of therapy are fine for professionals who may be interested in such a focus. On the other hand, books that simply survey a range of schools or models often leave practitioners and advanced students dissatisfied because they do not take their discussions deep enough to develop a subtle understanding of theories and their practical implications.

There is a growing interest in integration in the clinical practice world, setting aside a competitive spirit that may have exhausted its usefulness. Welcoming the new integrative agenda, we do not promote a particular therapeutic school or the very latest new innovations. Instead, we present ideas that have been developed by various

1

important clinical thinkers over the past several decades, which we think are key—ideas that are important to most if not all seasoned clinicians. While competition between models can become heated (and there are many important issues that should be vigorously debated), there is also an accumulation of shared wisdom that supports workers from different schools, and this is what we are interested in exploring. We set as our goal to identify those key insights and present them as complementary elements in a foundational framework: substantial enough to support practice but also something to be built upon, and open to further elaboration and growth.

Although this book has a family focus, the line separating family therapy from work with individuals, groups, networks, and other social units is not as sharp as it once was. The reader will find that we have not been constrained by our family orientation, either with respect to the sources of the ideas we explore, or the applications to practice we discuss. Since we are social workers, we have written with clinical social workers in mind. Disciplinary boundaries are not a preoccupation of ours, however, and we hope that students and practitioners in cognate professions—especially clinical and community psychology—will find much of interest in these pages.

CLINICAL THEORY
AND THE ECOLOGICAL PERSPECTIVE

Social work emerged as an effort to provide a professional home to people with a range of practical social concerns: how to ameliorate the effects of poverty, rehabilitate criminals, overcome the devastation caused by substance abuse, support families uprooted by economic or political forces, reach out to marginalized people, prevent the mistreatment of children, and so on. What brought the first social workers together was a shared commitment to make things better by helping clients change as well as by advocating for a more humane and responsive society.

Social work, therefore, did not begin with a coherent theory explaining people's difficulties and methods of facilitating change. It began with problems and shared values about helping people and society improve. In retrospect, it is surprising that this was enough to hold people together, but despite significant differences in goals and priorities among those who identify themselves as social workers, the profession has survived for over a century.

The clinical arm of the social work profession has always been most strongly interested in facilitating change at the personal and familial levels. These professionals have been prominent in charity organizations, child welfare agencies, mental health clinics, and child and family guidance centers. Faced with the need to respond effectively to some of the most intractable problems imaginable, they have always been acutely aware of the need for good theory to guide their efforts. They have borrowed freely from medicine, psychology, sociology, and wherever else it seemed useful ideas were to be found. At the same time, the profession made important contributions of its own. Family systems theory originated in the child guidance clinics (Wood and Geismar, 1989), for example. Knowledge of the essential skills of interviewing and the components of a helping relationship was likewise highly developed by social workers (Young, 1935) before being embraced and disseminated by clinical psychologists and others, notably Carl Rogers and his followers (Rothery and Tutty, in press).

Currently, clinical social workers continue to utilize theory from a vast and growing body of ideas about how problems develop and how people can be helped to solve them. They do so, however, within a very general unifying framework or perspective. This perspective is ecological in nature, emphasizing the "goodness of fit" between people and their environments (Rothery, in press). There is good support for the ecological perspective (see Cameron and Vanderwoerd, 1997 for a detailed discussion of theory and research germane to claims made in this section), and its adoption is not unique to social work; related disciplines have acknowledged its potential, community psychology being an important example.

Clinical and research evidence is conclusive on the point that our well-being is affected by the stresses we have to cope with. We all constantly adapt to pressures from our social and physical environment, as well as to the internal demands posed by our individual and familial needs. When we adapt well to such demands, our needs are met and we (as individuals or families) may flourish as a result, working creatively to compose lives that are gratifying for us. When the demands that confront us exceed our ability to respond effectively, creative options recede and we tend to become more rigid or disorganized as a result.

Considerable evidence also indicates that our ability to respond creatively to demands is largely a function of the resources available to us. As individuals and families, we are more or less fortunate in our ability to access goods and services, information, safe opportunities to share our feelings and have them understood, and roles in which we are recognized as important and competent.

An ecological view, stressing goodness of fit between individuals, families, and their social situations, can be partly understood in these terms. When our personal and familial resources are plentiful enough that we have what we need to cope with the demands in our lives, we will tend to live productively and well. When the balance is not favorable we will be less creative and will tend to care for ourselves less effectively. Clinical social workers are encouraged by their allegiance to a person-in-environment orientation to pay careful attention to demand and resource factors because of these considerations.

However, as Rothery (1999) indicates, demands and resources are not the whole ecological story. There are considerable differences between people and families with respect to vulnerability and resilience (see Gilgun, 1996a, 1996b). The same balance of demands and resources that proves debilitating to family A will be easily manageable by family B. These differences are attributable to mediating factors, primarily personal and familial beliefs, values, competencies, and skills. They are also powerfully influenced by context.

Context includes a very complex mix of environmental, cultural, and social factors that cannot really be diagrammed in a comprehensive way. Commonly emphasized contextual variables (elements we will address frequently), however, include culture, gender, and development.

Clinical social workers, along with other ecologically oriented therapists, cannot neglect the importance of context and the balance of demands with resources as ever-present influences in their client's lives—concerns they share with community workers, policy developers, and other colleagues who work at a more general level. However, they also have a primary interest and expertise in working toward change in the mediating factors, intervening at the level of clients' beliefs, values, and competencies.

Beginning with the next chapter, we argue that clear, safe structures (boundaries and identity) are an essential springboard for creative living (and therapy). Subsequently, we give full recognition to the ways in which history and culture work with our families of origin to support and constrain our lives. Despite our constraints, we all remain authors of our lives, working the themes we are given into unique variations. Throughout the life cycle, we confront common issues in inventive ways. It is this creativity, always observable (no matter how unhappy the story), that is the single most important theme in the pages to come.

CLINICAL THEORY:
AN EMBARRASSMENT OF RICHES

One of the more striking developments facing professional helpers in the 1990s was the proliferation of models or practice theories to chose from. Some estimates count over 600 schools of therapy to which one can pledge allegiance. On one hand, this suggests a richness of choice and opportunity—a diversity of ideas and approaches that must contain something for everybody. The situation is also daunting: How can we make sense of so many different approaches to understanding problems and setting about solving them?

A common solution to the problem of too many competing schools is to simply chose one, declare it to be the best, and become an expert in its beliefs and techniques (to the exclusion of all others). Another way of coping with too much choice is to choose nothing—declare theory to be irrelevant, and conclude that as long as you are a caring person your clients will benefit from a warmly empathic and genuine relationship with you.

Our own solution is an eclecticism that seeks to identify and integrate key ideas embedded in the overabundance of theory. These ideas are offered as a framework for organizing our thinking about how to understand clients' situations and help them plan changes. Such a framework is necessary if we are to respect the diversity of clients' problems and maintain an integrationist stance toward practice theory as it continues to proliferate. Rothery (1999) has suggested that such a framework should meet three criteria (among others):

- It should encourage a sufficiently broad or comprehensive perspective.
- It should provide a sense of direction and focus.
- It should be open rather than closed.

The key concepts that we have elected to include in our suggested framework form the body of this book, beginning with the next chapter. Such key ideas are offered in the hope that the framework they form will be an open one: open to new ideas and fresh, creative approaches to each unique challenge that presents itself in our work.

CASE EXAMPLE: THE DOYLES

To keep the theory we discuss grounded in practice, we will make frequent use of relatively few examples. Our readers will become especially familiar with a family of four (George Enns was their therapist), whose pseudonym is Doyle.* The mother, Anita, is thirty-seven years old; the father, John, is forty; Maria, thirteen, is the daughter whose difficulties led to their referral; Maria's younger sister is Carla, age ten. Here is the intake information that was filed at the time their physician referred the family, with changes to identifying details.

> Dr. Clement has recently seen Maria (age thirteen), who disclosed suicidal thoughts and plans. She has thought of various means to commit suicide and ways it would create the least stress to her family.

Disclaimer: In class and at workshops, it is not uncommon for students or participants to feel they recognize the clients we use as examples. "I know that person," they say, even when they cannot possibly have met. Everyone's story is unique, but none is entirely so.

We have taken considerable care to disguise the people discussed in this book through changes of name and other details, and we are confident that any reader's experience of déjà vu in response to our examples is just that.

Maria feels like a failure and expresses a very low sense of self-worth. She is protecting her family from her feelings of sadness, etc. She has tried drinking and glue sniffing to deal with her sadness but this only contributes to her negative self-image. She views her parents as "perfect" and feels she can't achieve the academic standards her parents achieved. Her father is an engineer and her mother has advanced qualifications for teaching Spanish (and English as a second language to Latino immigrants).

Maria attends a Spanish school, where she obtains C- and B-level grades. Apparently Mrs. Doyle (Anita) kept both her daughters back in kindergarten because she didn't feel that they were emotionally ready for grade one. Now Maria feels she failed.

Maria is very reluctant to share her feelings with her family. She is protecting them.

This appears to require urgent attention. This girl is very depressed and has formulated suicide plans, without having made any attempts to date.

CREATIVITY

The creativity that exists in everyday life is one of this book's constant themes. Without achieving the public success of a novel in print or a commission to compose an opera, each of us is continually involved in creating meaning, identity, our families, our networks of friends, and plans to achieve the goals we value. We write our lives, and it may be because this is so commonplace that we do not always appreciate the energy and intelligence that goes into the stories we and other people create.

The Doyles are unintentionally and unfortunately authoring what could become a tragedy, and a similar story could be unfolding next door to any of us. Even the most seemingly homogeneous neighborhood contains a rich mix of drama, humor, triumph, conflict, betrayal, generosity, and courage.

Self-authorship is never a solitary accomplishment, but a collaboration of many people—as individuals, we may be fortunate enough to have a large say in who we are and what our families, friends, and work mates are like. However, it would be misleading to deny the pervasiveness of cultural, social, familial, and other influences (even dumb luck) that simultaneously nurture and limit our growth. We compose ourselves and our families within a context that is at once supportive and constraining; the limitations culture or other circumstances impose may be stultifying, even destructive, but they are also essential.

Mozart

In recent years, new insights into human creativity have been achieved through advances in cognitive psychology. Applying ideas from this study of intensely creative people not only helps us understand how they achieve their extraordinary accomplishments, but also sheds light on what conditions are optimal for the rest of us. What circumstances enable us to create lives rich in accomplishments and gratifications, and what deficits in our environments are likely to make this move more difficult? Gardner (1982, 1997) suggests that using cognitive insights to understand (albeit only in part) the genius of someone such as Mozart sheds light on the creativity of "ordinary" people.

Dead at the age of thirty-five, Mozart left a body of work that hundreds of scholars across intervening generations have spent lifetimes studying, without exhausting our interest. He is a mystery to people who want to understand the creative process, not only because he produced so much, but also because so much of what he created was fresh and powerful.

Though his accomplishments are uniquely his, Mozart did not work in a vacuum. In the ecological language introduced earlier, the goodness of fit between him and his environment was unusually fortuitous. His personal musical gifts were unparalleled, but he also grew up in Austria in the eighteenth century. There, he was able to immerse himself in a rich and highly evolved musical tradition, with the work of earlier geniuses such as Haydn and Bach to inspire and guide him. He was part of a culture to which music was important and a society in which being an accomplished musician brought with it the possibility of substantial recognition and material rewards. Also, he had a father (an accomplished musician himself) who recognized the son's talent and was willing to dedicate much of his own life to making sure that talent was developed properly, and profitably marketed. His creativity, driven by his enormous personal abilities, flourished in this context; in another time and place, the outcome could have been entirely different.

Among the personal abilities contributing to his creative productivity were extremely high musical intelligence, an extraordinary memory, and an ability to mentally order a host of disparate though related ideas. In addition to these, however, Gardner (1997) stresses the extent to which Mozart utilized schemas, which are a kind of mental blueprint. The schemas Mozart employed consisted of the rules and conventions governing composition in his day, approaches he had learned in his own development, his knowledge of the capacities of the instruments he was scoring for, and so on. Mozart's approach to any given new task was shaped by a highly evolved set of tools and rules—a substantial framework within which he worked.

FRAMEWORKS

Apparently Mozart evolved his ideas using his rich preexisting frameworks as a starting point. New themes, their development, and their relations to one another were invented with the schemas in mind, supporting and guiding the enterprise. An important point for future discussion, however, is that these schemas or frameworks were not, in Mozart's case, rigid. Just as they shaped his approach to new musical problems, they could be altered to accommodate fresh solutions; rules could be broken and new tools invented, often with startling effects.

At once, Mozart was a consummate master of the rules of his craft and he was always ready to rework those rules in a creative pursuit of his musical goals. In some ways, composition was an activity in which preexisting schemas and new problems were brought into interplay with each other. One outcome was work that was recognizably his at the same time that it was always somehow new; another was increased complexity and richness in the schemas that would inform his future work. Contemporaries of Mozart were masters of compositional theory, and many wrote substantial amounts of competent music within the conventions of their day. One reason they are largely forgotten while the fascination with Mozart has not abated two centuries later is that his understanding of composition as a discipline was complete, but open to brilliant revisions and elaboration as new possibilities and demands were accommodated.

Mozart's achievements are history, and this book is about clinical social work, not music. Sometimes, however, a bit of distance helps us see more clearly, and part of the reason cognitive scientists such as Gardner want to understand people such as Mozart is for what we can learn about ourselves. In this case, the lesson we would draw is that the strategies Mozart employed are used by us all—within the limits of our endowments we develop schemas and then use them to meet the creative challenge of composing our lives. The schemas we work with to create our selves and our families are far richer and more complex than we know, coming to us through our society and culture, our friends, our work, the histories of our families of origin, and the ever-growing body of experience that we as individuals with families of our own accumulate.

Clients' Frameworks

For most of us, the lives we compose are a mixed accomplishment, some of which we value and some of which is a source of pain to others and ourselves. People such as the Doyles, whose stories are painful enough that they come to share them with a therapist, have often run out of creative options. The frameworks (schemas) that guide them are inadequate, or are so rigidly held that pressing tasks and problems cannot be addressed. Hopefully, therapy will help Maria and her family rediscover the nurturing and supportive aspects of their schemas while reassessing aspects that are blocking them from finding new tools and options.

The Clinician's Frameworks

In our discussion of frameworks we need to move back and forth between two types, somewhat different though not entirely so. *Personal* frameworks support all of us through the creative challenge of composing our lives, while we as clinicians have *professional* frameworks, a more specialized subset of beliefs and techniques that guide us in our work with clients.

The information in the intake record quoted earlier is sparse, but it is enough to trigger ideas in the mind of the clinician. Although we would resist leaping to premature convictions about what has brought this family to such a critical state, we may well form tentative hypotheses regarding the family's needs and the reasons for Maria's despair. The creative interaction of the data in the report and our framework of ideas regarding people, families, and problems generates these ideas. For our purposes, we have identified two aspects of our professional frameworks: those we employ in the service of *understanding,* and those we employ in the service of *change.*

Our human desire to ameliorate Maria's suffering and self-destructiveness is informed by professional knowledge about adolescence, families, and depression. We use our frameworks (as do our clients) in the service of understanding, to explain why Maria is on her unique, disturbing path. Not everyone agrees that explanations matter, but people seem driven to look for them, in part because feeling able to master situations is caught up in our ability to explain them.

Further, our beliefs about how people change will suggest conditional ideas about what we can do for them. Our explanations as to why Maria's family is in pain and our understanding of how they might change are certainly related, but they are not entirely the same thing.

Our frameworks are very powerful influences on the service we provide client families. Consider brief sketches of three out of a host of possible examples:

- Therapist A believes that depressions such as Maria's are a consequence of inherited biochemical imbalances affecting brain functions; therapist B assumes that an adolescent's emotional pain signals a struggle in her family system; therapist C has been trained to focus on how Maria's internal dialogue—her "self-talk"—has become irrationally harsh, devastating her self-esteem and leaving her feeling depressed and hopeless.
- While working with the family, therapist A may develop an explanation of the problem by asking about a history of depression in the parents' and grandparents' generations, seeking to educate Maria and her parents about the medical issues involved. Therapist B will respectfully explore the problem, alert to evidence that Maria's troubles are a symptom of unresolved conflict, or a sign of family stress ("She is protecting them," says the referring physician, and this is an important clue).

cognitive

Therapist C will want to help Maria understand how her accusations against herself (a "failure" and a disappointment to her "perfect" parents) are irrational and self-defeating.

- With respect to change, therapist A may well work to establish a friendly but authoritative "expert" role in relation to the family, to enhance the probability of their compliance with a recommended trial of antidepressant medications. Therapist B might be very concerned with the balancing act of forming a relationship with the family members without aligning with their definition of Maria as the problem, and thereby colluding with them in continuing to avoid confronting the family's unresolved loyalty conflicts. Therapist C could be more focused on using high levels of empathy and support to help Maria share and change her sense of herself as a failure, perhaps with help from other family members.

All of these clinicians will have evidence and experience supporting the validity of their analysis, and each will have used the preferred framework successfully with other depressed clients. Past successes and clinical evidence notwithstanding, it is also true that any therapist holding rigidly to one favored framework runs a risk of misreading Maria's case, possibly with tragic consequences

The Dangers of Frameworks

A dilemma regarding frameworks (or models, or theories) is that they are at once both dangerous and beneficial. The dangers have to do with reductionism, and the risk of attempting to impose an agenda poorly matched to the client's needs. Another important concern has to do with power: if the therapist takes on the role of the expert who is most qualified to define clients' problems and find solutions to them, it disempowers clients and reduces their opportunities to discover their own competence.

Some influential writers about therapy have been so concerned about the dangers of frameworks that they have looked for ways of working which eliminate them. Psychoanalytic therapists several decades ago used the metaphor of the "therapist as mirror" to suggest that we should reflect clients' realities for them, free from distortion by our own preconceptions (Greenson, 1967, pp. 271-272). In the 1950s and 1960s, the humanist Carl Rogers evolved the position that the job of the therapist is simply to provide a relationship within which the client feels safe to self-explore (Rothery and Tutty, in press). A relationship that is warm, empathic, and genuine will be a springboard for growth, without any direction from the therapist regarding ways of understanding problems or discovering their solutions. More recently, in the family therapy field, the concept of neutrality has been developed with the same agenda—to eliminate the risk of therapists imposing their preconceptions, to the detriment of the family (Selvini Palazzoli et al., 1980; Tomm, 1984).

Despite the Risks, Frameworks Are Necessary

Therapists who are overly confident in their understandings can do harm, but the solution is not to attempt to eliminate frameworks altogether. In fact, there is evidence that we are driven from birth to organize our experience of ourselves and the world by searching for patterns, defining things, ordering our experience by framing it (Stern, 1985). The labels, categories, and models that make up our frameworks exist because our neurology insists on it—and the idea that we can approach clients in a state of theoretical innocence, totally open and without preconceptions, is self-defeating because it is impossible. Openness to client experience does not require that we set aside our frameworks, but that we use them creatively. Mozart's schemas increased his ability to innovate and invent; our frameworks, when we use them well, can do the same for our clients and ourselves.

Why Frameworks Are Helpful

The professional frameworks that inform us in our work with clients can be a barrier to understanding, but they are helpful because when we use them well they have the opposite effect—understanding is enormously enhanced. When understanding is enhanced, two of the most basic requirements for effective therapy are met: the establishment of an empathic relationship and support for a sense of hope.

Some of the earliest attempts to understand the essentials of a helping relationship were carried out by social workers, and their conclusions have since been supported by outcome research. Mary Richmond (1922) emphasized the importance of "understanding of individuality," which evolved into Young's (1935) concept of "sympathetic insight," an idea that is exactly congruent with the modern idea of empathy. Empathy has since been recognized as important in counseling psychology, through the work of Carl Rogers and others, and, more recently, psychodynamic self-psychologists (Kohut, 1977; Stern, 1985) have emphasized how important the experience of empathy is to our development and emotional well-being. Reviews of studies of marital and family therapy (Gurman, Kniskern, and Pinsoff, 1986; Miller, Hubble, and Duncan, 1995) also report accumulated evidence that certain core skills, empathy prominent among them, are essential for positive outcomes—much more so than ideological commitment to a popular model.

Among the various definitions of empathy that exist, we would suggest that the essence is *shared understanding* coupled with *acceptance* (cf. Nichols, 1987). If Maria and her family think that George understands their situation in a way that is congruent with their own experience of it and does so in an accepting way, that is empathy. George does not need to pretend to feel what they feel or to believe what they believe, but he does need to communicate to them a "sympathetic insight" into their plight and what it is like for them to be in their situation.

Empathy is possible because there are commonalities in human experience, and one function of a professional framework is to help us draw on patterns that tend to be shared by people so we can understand them more quickly, accurately, and deeply. The more we know about families, families with adolescents, depression in adolescence, the meaning of suicidal temptations, and other issues, the more attuned we will be to issues affecting the Doyles. The Doyles, in turn, will be reassured if George is able to tune in to their issues with quick accuracy. If they learn in the process that they are not entirely unique, they are not likely to take offense, since they are also discovering that they are not alone.

However, if our issues are usually to some extent shared by others in our society, this is never the entire case. Thousands of commonalities exist, but every person and family enacts and experiences them in unique ways. For example, children in families require nurturing, without exception, and every family must feed, stimulate, clean, entertain, and in other ways love their young—failure to do so can have disastrous consequences. But no two families experience and perform these tasks in the same way. The Doyles may well feel offended and misunderstood if George uses his knowledge to try to pigeonhole them, assuming his professional knowledge is all he needs to understand their experience. Effective empathy is possible when we can invoke appropriate frameworks (addressing the commonalities in our clients' experience) at the same time as we hear and respond to the unique aspects of their stories.

Change, of course, occurs only if our clients are willing to make it happen, and this is unlikely unless families and their members have (or can develop) motivation, hope, and a sense of their own power (Frank and Frank, 1991). When professional frameworks are effectively used, empathy is one outcome. Equally important is the fact that a framework which helps us understand why a problem exists should also suggest avenues to explore in the search for relief; this enhances focus, a sense of hope, and motivation to change.

Frameworks and the Competitive Tradition

A tradition in the world of therapy that has been influential for many years, involves developing frameworks in an adversarial, competitive spirit. Family therapy, for example, began as a rebellious movement, defining itself against the therapeutic establishment that had prevailed through the 1950s and early 1960s. As part of the process of earning credibility and attracting adherents, early writers offered a fresh and highly critical analysis of the beliefs and practices that had preceded them—Jay Haley's (1963) classic *Strategies of Psychotherapy* is a brilliant example. Along with their critique of earlier traditions, authors often offered a new approach, and promised increased effectiveness. Frequently, the promise was supported by an abundance of case examples where previously intractable problems were resolved, magically, through powerful new interventions.

Many schools of therapy have pursued the same strategy of discounting other models and inflating their own claims to therapeutic potency. This competitive tradition is, in fact, a venerable one—in 1775 Anton Mesmer assured his personal fame and profits from a wealthy clientele by defeating a famous predecessor, Johann Gassner (Ellenberger, 1970, pp. 57-61). Gassner's framework was Roman Catholicism, and his technique was exorcism. Mesmer worked from a secular framework, the keystone of which was "animal magnetism," an early precursor to modern hypnotherapy. Convinced of his beliefs and personally charismatic, Mesmer allied with the revolutionary spirit of his time and initiated changes that continue in their effects today. Since then, hundreds of psychotherapeutic models have emerged (and disappeared), many marketed with the same message: "The work of our predecessors contains nothing of value. Embrace this new approach and you will be able to work miracles" (see Miller, Hubble, and Duncan, 1995, for recent examples).

Frameworks and the Integrative Stance

Undoubtedly, there has been value in the periodic critical self-appraisal and introduction of new ideas that have been generated as a result of the competitive tradition, along with the costs. The primary difficulty with the competitive approach is that it promotes rigidity in practitioners' frameworks, since adherence to one set of beliefs is linked to rejection of others. True belief in a systemic epistemology, for example, was said to require the uprooting and rejection of any regressive tendency toward linear thinking; more recently, it is argued that a proper understanding of narrative theory requires us to set aside an interest in pattern or system (White, 1995, pp. 214-215). Openness to new ideas may exact a very heavy price if it requires a rigid rejection of everything that has gone before—as if clinical wisdom painstakingly developed over decades of hard work should be simply abandoned whenever an attractive new philosophical fad seductively beckons.

Unfortunately, the competitive approach is still prevalent, probably for reasons that have more to do with marketing than helping clients—to be new and better (improved!) is good for sales, and the proponents of models often have books and workshop subscriptions to sell.

Although competitive allegiances to alternative models will continue among therapists, we have emphasized our hope that it will increasingly be tempered by a more integrative attitude. Clinical social workers and other ecologically minded therapists should not be pressured to declare themselves adherents to a school or disciples of a popular mentor. Instead, one's framework needs to be regarded as open and continually evolving. Professionally obligated to master as much as we can of the knowledge and clinical wisdom that has accumulated regarding how to work with our clients, we need to place this expertise within a framework that is open. If we do so, we will be freer to incorporate new ideas from the broadest possible range of sources, more able to respond to clients whose needs suggest modifications to our frameworks, and more creative in our responses to new knowledge and new problems.

PART I:
ESSENTIAL THEMES—
A FRAMEWORK
FOR UNDERSTANDING

Chapter 1

Boundaries

Then she says, out of nowhere, "When I was seven, my father said 'Who remembers the opening of the *Aeneid?*' as he stood at the end of the table, carving the Sunday joint. 'Anyone?' They were all better scholars than me, but I *knew. 'Arma virumque cano. . . .'* Everyone cheered—Leo, the cook, Margaret, Charity, George, even Mother. My father slowly put down the knife and fork and just stared at me. I wasn't supposed to be the clever one."

There is some hurt this story is trying to name, a tomboy's grief at never being taken seriously, never being listened to, which has lasted to this moment next to me in the darkness. But her emotions are a secret river. She has her pride, her gaiety and her elusiveness. She will not put a name to the grievance, and silence falls between us. It is dark and we both feel the chill of evening. She gets up, drains her glass and then says, "Mother always said, 'Never make a fuss.' That was the family rule. Good night." I brush her cheek with a kiss. We will not make a fuss.

Michael Ignatieff, *August in My Father's House*

"No son of mine," says Jason's normally affable father with unusual intensity, "would even think of stealing from his parents." If Jason absorbs this message as it is intended, he learns a rule against stealing, at least from his parents.

Individuals and families operate using rules; some we are aware of and can easily articulate, while most are taken for granted and we tend not to think about them.

Rules work by permission (what is encouraged), and prohibition (what is discouraged), and this is bound to identity—rules help us decide "this is me (or my family) and that is not me." When a friend attempts to talk him into stealing some of his parents' vodka, to enliven a planned social event, Jason refuses. His sense of who he is and what his membership in his family means cause him to reject his friend's influence. His friend says "Do this"and Jason says, "That is foreign to my sense of who I am, and I must decline" (or words to that effect).

This commonplace example illustrates something basic about people and their families. In his narrative, Jason is writing themes that are, in essence, common to all of us—rules that prescribe and constrain his choices. A basic thread in every human story is one of the most important ways we use such rules, which is to establish and maintain boundaries. Our success with this narrative task affects us at a very deep level. In fact, it is critical to our sense of who we are.

As we argued in the introduction, we are free to be creative in authoring our lives when we have a secure context. For all of us, boundaries are a basic part of such a context, a primary element out of which personal and familial frameworks are built. Understanding how people use boundaries to organize and structure their lives is critical for clinicians; this is why we have devoted a full chapter to exploring what boundaries are, what we do with them, and how they affect our ability to adapt creatively to life's demands.

THE NATURE OF BOUNDARIES

Definitions of "boundary" in the family therapy literature have tended to emphasize issues such as the exchange of information between subgroups of people. To return to the family we discussed in our introduction, John and Anita, as a "parental subsystem" within the Doyle family, have a life to which their children—another subsystem—have limited access. This is a boundary: "a set of rules governing who is included within [a given] subsystem and how they interact with those outside it" (Nichols and Schwartz, 1995, p. 97; see also Becvar and Becvar, 1993, p. 72). According to the traditional view, the main reason we need boundaries is for regulation of intimacy: "The nature of the family's structure is determined by emotional boundaries which keep family members close or distant" (Nichols and Schwartz, 1995, p. 54).

In this chapter, we expand on the idea of regulation of distance, suggesting a relatively complex view of what boundaries are and the purposes they serve in our lives. Understood broadly, the concept is fundamental for most theories of helping, though differences in language obscure how much agreement exists. When we discuss boundaries, we address phenomena that others reference through terms such as *differentiation, identity, autonomy, responsibility, empowerment,* and *individuation.*

How We View Boundaries: Their Nature and Function

Before we offer our definition of boundaries, a few points need to be made briefly:

- Boundaries start with beliefs, enacted through various interpersonal behaviors.
- Boundaries are not things, but processes. There is no fence or row of guard posts to guide us when we observe a boundary. What we see are patterns of relating that serve certain purposes for people.
- In considering the qualities of boundaries, the concept of clarity is critical. Clarity of boundaries exists when people "own" authorship of their feelings, thoughts, and actions. As we will discuss in more depth later, difficulties in this regard have powerful effects on us—if we are angry (for example) and are committed to the belief that our anger is someone else's fault and responsibility, we will make poor decisions regarding what to do. If someone close to us is depressed and we feel obligated to be miserable as well or think it is up to us to help that person find happiness, our ability to think about the problem and find a way to be helpful is diminished.
- Boundaries are dynamic processes involving two different basic themes: attachments and distance, or a rhythm of contact and withdrawal. We balance these themes to afford ourselves

space and safety at the same time as we access the nurturance that close relationships provide.

- Maintaining boundaries involves filtering our experience, while maintaining access to resources and feedback from the people around us. Much as we benefit when we take in other people's ideas, receive their cues about how to act effectively, and let them in on how we are feeling, we also need to manage the extent to which they influence us. We use distance to protect ourselves at the same time as we maintain the attachments we need to survive and grow.

- Boundaries are highly relevant to the ecological notion of goodness of fit discussed in the introduction. Our ability to engage with others determines how well we will access the resources and supports we require, while our ability to claim and maintain distance helps us manage the extent to which the various demands in our lives are allowed to affect us.

- Boundaries are very much tied to the issue of identity, providing an essential framework within which we develop (and elaborate) our narratives about who we are as individuals and families.

- Whatever generalizations we make about boundaries are offered with a caveat always in force: making and maintaining boundaries are critical themes for all people, but the issues are subtle and open to infinite creative variations among individuals, families, cultures, and the genders. They are also revised and elaborated as we encounter new developmental stages and challenges.

Boundaries Defined

With these basic points established, we are ready to suggest a definition for this pivotal concept.

Boundaries are "filters" serving three related objectives:

1. Managing the extent to which other people or events influence what we think, feel, and do
2. Maintaining clarity regarding ownership of and responsibility for our feelings, thoughts, and actions
3. Balancing our needs for involvement and distance in our relationships

Illustration: "More Like a Funeral"

In his first interview with the Doyles, George forms the hypothesis that Maria feels smothered, and begins to explore this idea with the family by asking the parents about their experience when they were younger, separating from their own families of origin. Questions about this time in parents' lives are often useful for introducing the theme of personal space.

Anita was the sixth child in a sibling group of eleven, and did not have to struggle for permission to leave home.

George: So you never learned to live with loneliness, but you were always fighting for space.

Anita: There was a fight for space, but you tended to find your own space, which was not inside the house. We were on the farm and I think things were available there, you'd hop on your bike and find your space somewhere if you needed to be alone. That is usually what I did. I'd take my bike and go off somewhere.

George: Is that right? And that was allowed in your family?

Anita: That was allowed, yes, because we would—my parents considered the area quite safe being on the farm. You could go quite a ways and still be all right.

George: So were your parents quite supportive of you taking your own space?

Anita: They didn't object if we took off and were gone—[though] not for long periods of time.

George: When you left home, was that a struggle for them or had they gone through it enough with other children that they kind of adjusted to it?

Anita: They adjusted to me leaving home. I think it was more of a struggle when the last one left. The empty nest was there then and that was a real struggle for them but for the others it was easier. Maybe it was less for them to struggle through—we were quite poor, our family, and one less [laughs] maybe helped in that way. There were so many children all the time.

Transitional stages (such as starting school, leaving home, or marrying) always require boundary negotiation. Rituals such as graduation ceremonies and weddings are a formalized recognition that a passage is occurring and new rules for relating are required. Demands for changes such as these may evoke good-willed adaptiveness; they can also bring forth hostility and conflict.

For Anita the task of leaving home was smooth, relatively free of conflict, because her family's boundaries were unusually open. Indeed, they were so open that she felt somewhat unwanted in a family so large that she was lost in it, even feeling that her departure could have been welcomed as lessening her family's burden. Because of this, some sadness is associated with her narrative—there are emotional consequences to boundaries that are this open, just as there are costs when boundaries are rigidly closed, as in John's family. John was one of four brothers.

John [interjecting quickly without being invited]: In my family it was different. I was the oldest, and leaving home was very [long pause] traumatic. I felt the time had come. . . . It was right to spread my wings and go to the university. . . . My parents really found it tough. The first year I was at university there [were] some fairly major scenes.

Anita: But I think our backgrounds created conflict in our relationship. John came from a Protestant family and I was Catholic and Latino and we clashed at one time. Me with his parents . . .

John [interrupting]: But I think it would have been really hard anyway. There was conflict because I was Irish—Protestant Irish. They used to put up signs saying "No dogs and Catholics allowed." I grew up listening to my uncles talking against Catholics, and we would do stuff to show how much we hated Catholics— and so there was a double thing with Anita and I . . .

Anita: There was a double thing.

In contrast to Anita's family, John's responded to his leaving home by attempting to keep their boundaries rigidly closed. The "double thing" referred to by Anita is that John's family did not want him to leave home at all, and they especially did not want him to do so while violating their boundary separating Protestants from Catholics, and Irish Americans from Latinos.

Boundaries are choices strongly influenced by cultural and familial rules. John and Anita had to set their desire to marry against powerful rules embedded in John's family of origin and its cultural heritage—they were challenging beliefs about boundaries that were deeply entrenched. To accomplish their own goals, they had to establish a strong boundary of their own as a couple in relation to John's family, establishing the distance they needed in order to commit to each other.

As a process note, John's interrupting suggests he is anxious as his boundary issues with his family of origin are being discussed. In effect, he invades Anita's space and blocks her from elaborating on her relationship with his parents. Although they have done much to establish the space they need for themselves and their children, his behavior is evidence that the issue is one about which he still has unresolved feelings.

George: So how did your parents respond to your wedding?

John: Oh, it was more like a funeral.

Anita [interrupting]: Yes. There is still hostility. Many topics we do not discuss and there is a fine line. . . .

John [interrupting]: Language and religion is taboo.

Anita [interrupting]: When they visit, we go through formalities, where I am polite to my in-laws, but that's about it.

George: You are still not accepted by them?

Anita: No. . . . It's to a polite level. I don't insult them.

John [interrupting]: It's past the hostile . . . the first few years were hostile. Now its where we have managed to not talk about these areas and so there is kind of a truce. Could you say a truce?

Anita [interrupting]: But there's cold—a wall, and no warmth. Like a coolness—an accepted cool type of relationship. I would not call it warm.

John: No. . . .

Anita and John are interrupting each other continually, further evidence of the stress they feel when discussing John's family of origin. This represents a boundary problem for them as a couple, in that their interruptions constitute a lack of clarity (at this point) for the two of them. Unclear boundaries impede problem solving, and this example shows how—because their anxiety drives them to interrupt, the range and effectiveness of their discussion is restricted.

There is also, in this segment, a certain invitation to George to step in and reduce the Doyles' tensions somehow. An important boundary problem at one level will normally have reverberations at other levels, including the client-clinician relationship, and this is something we are alert to in an ongoing way, since clear boundaries between our clients and ourselves do much to keep the helping relationship functional.

Another process note regarding this segment of dialogue is that the boundary difficulties John and Anita are exhibiting create confusion. The conversation is restricted, and it is difficult to determine whether they see the issue they are talking about (the cool truce) belonging to the relationship with John's parents, or to them as a couple, or both. A lack of boundary clarity affects us behaviorally, and also reduces our ability to be clear about what we think and feel.

Anita and John have adapted to his family's anger by hardening the boundary that separates their family from his: there are topics they do not discuss, and the emotional tone of their relationship is constricted. This is the successful use of boundaries to contain conflict, and it works well. However, a cost is associated with this degree of distance between people who ideally would be exchanging so much more with each other.

Not surprisingly, when George changes the focus from John's to Anita's family of origin, the tension decreases, the interruptions stop, and the conversation becomes more effective and free flowing.

George: And how do your parents accept John?

Anita: They were happy with him because he was a good boy. Well, he turned Catholic too when he became bilingual, so in a way these were all pluses.

George: So they felt more . . . they were more accepting of him.

Anita: He was a good person. A lot of my sisters married non-Catholics and non-Latinos. Well, the religion part for my mother was very, very important though. If they were Catholic then it was acceptable. Whether they were Latino or not, it didn't matter that much.

John: I think the fact that I know Spanish is important to you and that I took the time and effort to learn Spanish meant something, really.

George: It made a difference to Anita and also to her parents.

John: And her parents, to know I cared enough.

John's encounter with Anita, her family, and her culture has been creative: he has been willing to change, learning a new language and embracing a new religion. Unfortunately, what works well for him on one front requires distancing on another.

George: Sure. What was your parents' response to you becoming Catholic?

John: Well, they couldn't understand it . . . to show you where my family came from . . . I have an uncle who used to pound on the table and say "Goddamned Chicanos and Catholics are genetically inferior to the rest of the world." So that kind of shows you where my family came from, and so if I lived three lifetimes I could never convince them that I chose for me and didn't do it for anybody else.

George: So marrying Anita was not just a matter of challenging your family, it was also a real sign of independence for you—you were making a very independent choice here.

John: Oh, I did, yes. They used to, you know . . . I remember she had a white scarf and if it got a little bit gray because it got a little dirt on it, it was a reason not to marry. . . . Everything about her was bad and awful and terrible and all that kind of stuff and so I don't think I went with her to spite them—I would like to think that it was because we were good friends. But it was something I had to do consciously because the easiest thing would have been to say, well, they don't like her so I'll find a good white Irish Protestant, so they'll be happy.

George: Carving out independence and carving out space in your family was a real struggle.

QUALITIES AND FUNCTIONS OF BOUNDARIES

The comment we made in the introduction regarding frameworks bears repeating with respect to boundaries: they are both good and bad news. They are fundamental to the construction of identity and relationships, and are therefore essential to us in a basic sense. However, if they are too rigid, they can restrict our growth and options in myriad ways. Also, if they lack clarity, we may find ourselves investing huge amounts of energy in an ongoing struggle to define who we are. Thus, the following pages are about aspects of boundaries as they affect us for better or worse—protecting and facilitating a narrative richness in our stories, or restricting our ability to engage creatively with life and its challenges.

In the early family literature, a major clinical concern had to do with situations in which boundaries were too weak (Nichols and Schwartz, 1995), and some therapists felt that virtually all problems involved overly open boundaries—children being inappropriately "triangulated" or engaged in parental conflicts being a favorite example.

An exclusive concern with overly open boundaries was supplanted by a view that suggested a continuum: "When boundaries are too open, relationships are described as enmeshed or fused, and when boundaries are too closed, relationships are disengaged or cut-off. Therapists informed by these ideas are interested in who is close to or distant from who in families, and how to reorganize those alliances or coalitions. [In the range of possibilities between these two poles,] there is an ideal level of permeability" (Nichols and Schwartz, 1995, p. 107) associated with boundary clarity.

This way of describing boundaries has problems, missing some of their complexity and dynamic nature. We can be misled by the use of biological models—as if boundaries are like the membrane around a cell, possessing rigidity or permeability as physical qualities. We can also make the mistake of thinking that there is a standard of health for boundaries, an "ideal level of permeability" which is valid independent of individual differences, gender, culture, development, or circumstances.

This definitional issue has stimulated very important debates. Feminist critics have suggested that the ways women normally relate to family and friends have been pathologized as enmeshment by therapists applying a male standard regarding how much closeness is healthy. Another concern has to do with the potential for cultural bias, whereby norms viable in one culture are considered problematic from a different cultural vantage point (Bateson, 1994, is recommended for her compelling examples of this).

Developmental stages also provide a context within which boundaries must be understood. An obvious example is the pervasive dependency of infants, which is healthy at that age but would be problematic in an older child or adult. Throughout life, we face developmental transitions that (whatever our age) can deeply affect our boundaries. Sapolsky's (1995) essay on the death of his father is an eloquent narrative about the fluidity of personal boundaries during a period of profound change.

The most sensible determination as to whether boundaries are functional is a pragmatic one: Do people and their families tell stories in which it is clear which issues belong to whom? Can they engage sufficiently well with others to meet their needs? Are they negotiating the space they need for safety and the chance to compose their lives creatively?

Given this position regarding what constitutes healthy (or problematic) boundary narratives, some generalizations are possible regarding the qualitative aspects of boundaries and how they relate to our well-being.

Clarity

After exploring with Maria, the Doyles' troubled daughter, her need for more space and greater ownership of her own life, George turns attention to John's similar relationship with his mother.

George: What would it take for you to talk with your mother [about your right to be treated like a forty-year-old rather than a twelve-year-old]?

John: I don't know. It would be a pretty earthshaking event because she has a pre-fixed opinion on how she sees the world. And any times in the past when I have attempted to state a view that was contrary to popular belief, it was an earthshaking event and it often came back to haunt you thirty years later kind of thing.

The boundary John is describing is a very rigid one, and it is easy to appreciate how painful his dilemma is. If he challenges his mother she may react with explosive anger and recriminations that never die. If he does not challenge her, he cannot demand that she treat him and his family more appropriately—she will continue to treat him like a child and he will continue, to some extent, to feel like one.

George: Thirty years later.

John: So, and maybe we all adopted the pattern of my father which was, he really had, well, maybe he had more choices but I guess he perceived it as either he had to live with it or leave and . . .

George: And he chose to live with it?

John: He chose to live with it.

me too

John's way of dealing with his mother, conflict avoidance, was a pattern in his parents' marriage, where he perceived it as serving a stabilizing function.

George: Do you have any idea of what happened in your mother's life to make her respond this way?

John: Uh, she was the youngest of the family and I can only see her world through her eyes because she was youngest and all the older aunts were a lot older. They were pioneers, they came out and built the farm from nothing. She felt her family took advantage of her because she was the umpteenth kid and her parents were old and she got taken advantage of. She fell in love with a Mexican guy, and her older brother told her, "You can't marry one of those people" and so she dumped him and married my dad. Probably spending the rest of her life regretting it and so I don't think she really truly loved my dad where I think he truly loved her. And she couldn't tolerate having somebody having a different opinion. It sounds to me—like from her point of view as when she was a little kid she was so much younger that her opinions didn't count. That she couldn't tolerate and so to think and say something differently was taken as a personal affront, was threatening to her.

George: So she was bossed around . . .

John: That's what I gather from her.

George: And when she got older she decided no one would tell her what to do.

John: Oh God, no.

George: And have you ever talked to her about that? Does she realize what she is doing? Does she understand?

John: We have got close to this topic and started talking about things but [hesitates] and there's been some real scenes, and I guess I took the coward's way out and [falters] and through . . . there's only been one member of the family that has ever been able to talk to her. When I was . . . ah, when we were all little we were poor as well and my mom didn't get around to vaccinating one of my brothers for whooping cough [very emotional and having difficulty talking], and he got whooping cough and then he got pneumonia and was within an inch of dying. And he has been the only brother that somehow can say, "Mom, I disagree with this, I disagree with that" and she doesn't take it as a personal affront for some reason or another where all the rest of us, you know if you disagree [John stumbles again, searching for words] . . . The brother that is younger than me, he has disagreed with her in the past and, you know, years later, Christ, you still hear about it. So, no, Maria is miles ahead of where I am because she's been able to do what I can't do at forty.

George: She is breaking the generational pattern.

John: That's right.

George: Now have you ever asked your mother, instead of disagreeing with her, have you ever asked her why she finds it so hard to disagree? Have you ever asked her how she thinks about her life and how she thinks about why she treats you as though you are children?

John: I think she thinks she had a bad life.

George: She thinks she had a bad life [John breaks down crying]. Now you're kind of getting in touch with some pain there [George hands tissues to Anita, who is comforting her husband [who is now sobbing]. Can you tell us what you are getting in touch with?

John now unfolds a tragic story of prejudice and pain, explaining his mother's resentment and bitterness, and helping us to understand her rigid boundaries. It is not clear whether Anita and Maria have heard this story before.

John's turmoil, and his rambling, unclear speech at this point are a consequence of a lack of boundary clarity. Cognitively, he vacillates between different explanations for his mother's rigidity (sibling position or a forced, unhappy marriage). Emotionally, it is hard to know if he is identifying with his mother, feeling her pain and unhappiness; his father, feeling his sadness over being married to someone who did not love him; Anita, feeling her hurt at having been rejected by her mother-in-law; Maria, feeling the sadness of her lack of acceptance by her grandmother; or himself, feeling his own grief over not being validated and supported while growing up. Also, he seems to be feeling guilty, as if he should have been able to do something to make his mother happy.

What is clear is that he lacks the emotional distance to put the problem where it belongs—in the previous generation—and challenge his mother over her treatment of his present family.

John [continues crying, and is in obvious pain]: Just recently we had . . .

George: Take your time.

John: We had a family reunion picture taken and divided all the pictures up. She had a blow-up made of her wedding picture, and when you looked at the blow-up you could see her face—you could see the happiness [starts to cry again].

George: You could see the what?

John: Happiness. And then, afterwards, she made a bunch of comments about the horrible life that she's had since then.

George: Can you help us understand what it is about those comments now that is so painful for you?

John: Oh, I think . . . I think she'd have been happier with the guy she first married [catches and corrects himself]—the one she was engaged to . . . don't want her to suffer . . .

George: Can you help us understand how that's so painful for you? Are you somehow feeling that you contributed to this? Are you somehow feeling that you are responsible for her suffering?

Because John's dilemma is complicated, it is easy to understand why he is confused. First, his ability to think independently is compromised. His mother's belief is that when her children claim their independence they are betraying or abandoning her. It is on this basis that she refuses to negotiate change, and John accepts her position and its rationale. If his boundaries were clearer, he could do his own thinking rather than being controlled by his mother's point of view. With greater clarity, he might well come to a more independent position, reasoning that his desire to be treated as an adult is appropriate. He could recognize that his mother has confused her children's growth with disloyalty, an unfortunate misconception that is causing her pain, but which should not block him from insisting that she relate to him appropriately.

Similarly, John experiences a lack of clarity regarding feelings: which are his responsibility and which are his mother's? If he asks for what he wants she will become explosively upset. While her anger is hers to deal with, John is unclear about this: he feels frightened and guilty when she becomes upset, and this indicates that he has accepted responsibility for her feelings. Imagine an alternative situation in which he recognizes her pain sympathetically, but also sees that she is able (and obligated) to find options for dealing with it other than imposing inappropriate constraints on his growth. Arguably, he would be disinclined to continue seeing her as powerless. He might also decide to stop perpetuating her pain (and his) by protecting her, sparing her the healthy demand that she relate to him as an autonomous adult.

Lacking clear boundaries respecting beliefs and feelings, a lack of boundary clarity is also present with respect to behavior. John is not deciding what to do based on his own cognitive assessment of his situation and emotional needs. Rather, his behavior is dictated by his mother—he does not challenge her and does not ask for what he wants.

John has accommodated to a family tradition (the concept of traditions is the topic of Chapter 2). While he has been willing to defy a taboo against marrying outside his religion and culture, he continues to accept that growing up is disloyal, which prevents him from building the boundaries he needs. He accepts responsibility for his mother's pain, and her view of what restrictions he must adhere to out of loyalty to her. He is prevented thereby from seeing the legitimacy of his own needs, and also from adequately protecting his present family against destructive treatment. Both his wife and daughters are treated poorly by his parents and uncles at times, and he has not been clear and effective in demanding that they behave otherwise.

It can be seen in this discussion that clarity issues are very much circular. If John had clearer cognitive boundaries, this could help in other domains. His ability to assert authorship of his feelings and behaviors would be clearer to him as well. To the extent that he is clear about his feelings (which are his own and which have been prescribed for him?) he will have a more succinct and confident cognitive understanding of his situation and his options. If he knows he is acting out of his own needs, values and priorities, the turmoil regarding his thinking and feelings will abate.

Rigidity

In interpersonal affairs, rigidity is often taken to mean a type of determined disengagement, an adamant rejection of influence. We say our friend is rigid if he adheres to a point of view despite all our compelling arguments and evidence to the contrary. Our friend accuses us of rigidity if we adhere steadfastly to a course of action despite his well-founded warnings that the consequences are certain to be unhappy. Paranoid people are said to be rigidly suspicious—no argument or evidence will convince them their "enemies" are ordinary people with no special wish to do them in. The common thread is inaccessibility to influence.

Some people and families display boundary issues of this sort. They have a chronic pattern of rejecting input, of refusing to be influenced by it. The word "chronic" is important, however, to remind us that rejecting influence is not in itself a bad thing. It is likely to be problematic to the extent that it is favored as a strategy above all others, even in circumstances where it works against our getting needs met. Another form of rigidity, of course, is determined attachment, and a refusal to let go easily even when distance would clearly be beneficial.

With respect to rigidity, there are grounds for concern when we see relationships that seem fixed on either distance or engagement, but where the rhythmic appearance of both behaviors is not evident. What we look for is not the discovery of an ideal position (permeability) between distance and closeness so much as evidence of a flexible selection of those options in response to changing needs and circumstances.

THE RHYTHM OF CONTACT
AND WITHDRAWAL

We have noted that the process of boundary creation and maintenance involves balancing two needs: the need for contact and the need for distance. The balance, however, is not a fixed arrangement so much as a dynamic one—with a rhythm of contact and withdrawal, engagement and disengagement, attachment and distance characterizing relationships. The rhythm may be more constricted in some relationships than others, but it is always true that when we describe boundaries we are not identifying an unvarying arrangement. Terms such as "enmeshed" or "disengaged" sound static, but are really making summary statements about a process changing in time.

A useful comparison can be drawn with the attachment theorists' concept of the secure base (Bowlby, 1988), which emphasizes that we engage with others to reinforce our sense of safety and to build up emotional reserves, then disengage when our curiosity draws us away, to explore our world. This point has also been made by Byng-Hall (1995), who suggests the concept of the "secure family base [which] provides a reliable network of care that gives every member, of whatever age, a sufficient sense of security to explore and develop" (p. 19). We establish autonomy and personal power through the dual operations of attachment and withdrawal, and without good enough opportunities to learn both types of behavior, an essential developmental task is rendered much more difficult.

Maria's parents engage her constantly out of their need for closeness and validation, and out of anxiety for her future. At the same time as she needs this involvement, she has a pressing need to control the extent to which they influence her. This is a complex balancing act.

If our readers could view Maria on videotape as the initial interview unfolds, they would be struck by her need for distance: she sits in a closed posture, head down, arms crossed, knees together, and her hair covering her face. This distance is something she needs if she is going to be able to engage her parents at a new level of honesty.

> **George:** Maria, can you help me understand what was your understanding of why your mother put pressure on you?
>
> **Maria:** Well, I guess she wanted me to get good marks and do well at school.

Maria is answering as her mother would, not with her own thinking.

> **George:** And how did you understand that? What was her motive?
>
> **Maria:** I think . . . she used to be poor, right? She had to work really hard, for her, she had to work . . . she worked for her money so she could be not poor, and I guess I can't remember but maybe she wanted me to do well, I guess, at school.

Maria is very agitated at this point. She is moving her feet rapidly back and forth, and her speech is fragmented. The issue is an emotionally laden one, and a hard one for her to distance herself from (even though *her* family is not poor).

George: For what reason?

Maria: She didn't want me to be poor.

George: So she wanted kind of to prevent some pain for you that she went through? So you understood that in some way she was kind of trying to help you in ways that she hadn't been helped when she was growing up? [Maria nods] You understood that even at your age?

Maria: Yes!

George: Now what was your response to that?

Maria: Sometimes I didn't want her to, because I thought I could do it by myself.

George: Did you ever share that with her?

Maria: No.

George: How come?

Maria: Because if I told her that she would stop. And if it made her feel better to do it then I didn't want her to stop.

George: So you were kind of struggling with, do you share this with her so that she backs off a little and you have a little more space, but then the alternative was that it might hurt her feelings?

Maria: Yes.

George: So you kind of were willing to hurt yourself in order to protect her?

Maria: I guess so.

Like her father, who sacrifices his own needs to avoid being held responsible for his mother's pain, Maria would rather suffer than hurt Anita by being clear about her needs for space.

George: Were you aware of that?

Maria: Yeah, but it didn't matter.

George: Help me understand that.

Maria: Well, it didn't matter if I was going to hurt.

George: So your information was that it would be better to hurt yourself than hurt your mother.

Maria: Yes.

George: Now what has given you the courage here then to be so frank and so honest with her?

Maria: Because I am not looking to her and I am not talking to her.

George: So are you worried that her feelings might be hurt by what you are saying?

Maria: Yes.

George: But you have got the courage to speak about it. What has given you that courage?

Maria: Not looking at her.

George: That helps you?

Maria: Yes.

George: And have you felt sometimes kind of closed in and smothered?

Maria: Yes.

George: What has that been like for you?

Maria: Sad.

George: Sad. So that has made your space quite small, right?

Maria establishes the link between her depression and the boundary issues in her family, and George anchors this important insight.

Maria: Yes.

George: And, is that how you understand your sadness?

Maria: Partly, yes.

George: Are there other parts to it?

Maria: Yes. Sometimes I wish my grandma would like me more.

Maria shows us, with unusual clarity, the steps in building a stronger boundary and how this enables her to be open about difficult issues she has previously kept to herself. Perhaps because of George's respect and understanding of the importance of personal space in her life, she also risks sharing a new area of vulnerability, rejection by her grandmother.

A BOUNDARY DYNAMIC

We have already alluded to the fact that boundaries operate in cognitive, emotional, and behavioral domains, and we find it useful to formalize this observation by conceptualizing a "boundary dynamic." In this dynamic (see Figure 1.1) the domains are highlighted (with the addition of "method of problem solving"), and so is their circular relationship to one another.

The narrative (cognitive) aspect is a story or explanation. Inevitably, this narrative is linked to an emotional experience. Narrative understanding and emotional experience contribute to choices of response, in part a general method of problem solving comprising familiar strategies for managing the situation. The behavioral expression of the dynamic comprises all the specific things we do as we pursue our favored problem-solving strategy.

FIGURE 1.1. A Boundary Dynamic

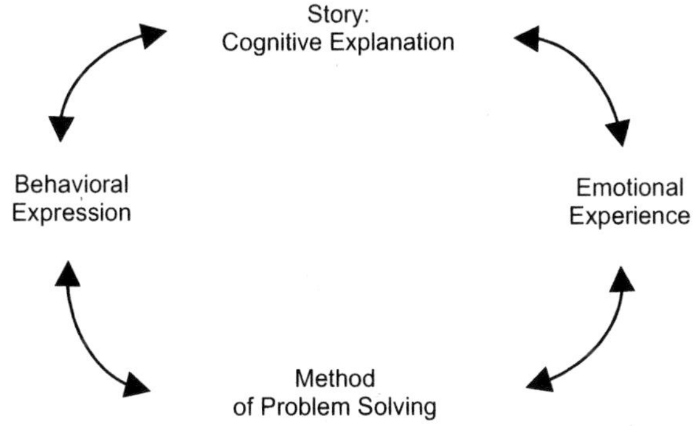

John Doyle's situation illustrates the elements of the boundary dynamic:

1. His story or cognitive explanation is that he has to protect his mother, and that to upset her would be disloyal.
2. His emotional experience is that he feels sorry for her, feels guilty, and buries his unresolved anger.
3. The method of problem solving he has adopted is one of nonconfrontation.
4. The behavioral expression evident is the varied ways he restricts his interactions with her, the taboos observed in what may be discussed, the many compromises of his own priorities accepted in order to buy peace.

The cyclical nature of the dynamic is important. The behavioral expression of John's general approach to managing this problem is such that its continuance is guaranteed. Maintaining rigid distance and refusing to challenge his family of origin with clear and appropriate demands, John creates events that feed back into the unhappy narrative, reinforcing its themes and advancing the plot along predicable lines.

Each element in the boundary dynamic may offer insight into how clients have become stuck, but each also suggests possible avenues for change, for thinking about new options. If John decides to change his relationship with his family, he has several general areas to consider:

1. Reevaluating his story, he may give weight to the observation that his mother's efforts to control him are extreme and are damaging to his own family.
2. Emotionally, he may accept his anger as appropriate and as a healthy push toward taking better care of himself and his family.
3. Alternative methods of problem solving may emerge for him as options. He can determine to be more assertive regarding his rights and the rights of his family in relation to his mother and uncles.
4. Behaviorally, rather than avoiding contentious issues, he can make clear demands as to how he and his family are to be treated, and can refuse to withdraw when recriminations result.

Filters and the Boundary Dynamic

Earlier, we used the metaphor of a filter in offering our definition of boundaries. This function of boundaries is important; we need to control the impact of stimuli in which we are awash, lest we become disorganized. In fact, some types of difficulty, such as attention deficits, are partly a matter of being unable to filter experiences sufficiently well, so that control is threatened.

The boundary dynamic concept highlights different essential ways in which we use boundaries to mediate the effect stresses and stimuli have on us:

1. In maintaining a story or cognitive explanation, we develop some narratives while denying others.
2. With respect to emotional experience, we allow ourselves to acknowledge and express some feelings about situations to a greater or lesser degree than others; and we distinguish whether feelings are ours or someone else's. Also, we make constant choices about the impact the emotional experience of others in our lives is allowed to have on us.
3. In maintaining a particular method of problem solving, we acknowledge the viability of some options, while we are less comfortable recognizing others and may deny or minimize them.
4. Similarly, we exercise choices over the kinds of actions we admit to our repertoire, and reject other behaviors as somehow foreign to us.

The Boundary Dynamic and Boundary Clarity

In stuck families (or other systems), people are not free to develop new stories or behaviors; their narratives become repetitive and uncreative. It is then that problems evolve into symptoms, and function becomes dysfunction. Anita provides an example concerning the third element, her problem-solving strategy in relation to Maria.

George: What is your understanding of why you feel the urgency to have your daughter do well?

Anita: I see my daughter thinking that she is not very intelligent, and I see her as a very intelligent child, and at the back of my mind I am always worrying that she will undervalue herself.

George: And have you thought in the past that by putting pressure on her it would help her to recognize that she is bright and that she is important?

Anita: I guess that is the reason I was doing it. I was trying to tell her, yes you can do that.

George: I am just wondering whether you have, you know, as you have more opportunity to think about your method, have you felt that it has been helpful?

Anita: I am questioning whether it is helpful at this time. In the past I thought it was helpful but now I am really questioning. Yes.

George: Your goal was to convince your daughter that she is bright and that she is worthwhile and that she is competent.

Anita: That's right.

George: And your method was to kind of put pressure on her.

Anita: That's right.

The extent to which Anita has taken responsibility for her daughter's success and self-esteem supports a problem-solving method that is self-defeating. Maria will never feel like a competent, successful person if Anita continues to think for her, worry on her behalf, and attempt to supply her with the motivation to achieve by applying pressure. Anita's method of problem solving results in Maria using her energy to resist the pressure and cope with her confused feelings of guilt and resentment. She would benefit from help redirecting that energy to her schoolwork and other developmentally appropriate tasks. Given greater clarity about Maria's responsibility for her own success and happiness, Anita would be much better able to determine ways to be legitimately supportive as her daughter works out these issues in her own way, and on her own terms.

THE BOUNDARY NEGOTIATION PROCESS

Boundaries are never permanent, but require reworking as people grow and their relationship needs change. Such negotiations involve tensions in the best of relationships, though they are also opportunities for discovering new possibilities. In less positive situations, complications such as accusations of disloyalty, threats of abandonment, even physical intimidation and abuse can block or impede the process.

An ongoing awareness of boundaries and how they define the terms of our relationships is neither usual nor necessary; in fact, when a relationship is going well, such issues properly recede into the background. When inevitable conflicts or demands for boundary change arise, the people concerned may discuss them with enough honesty (and courage) to stay clear about their situation. Conversely, if they retreat into vagueness, over-abstraction, or ambiguity, a loss of clarity can result.

What happens in families when members try to negotiate changes in boundaries? In some this is understood as part of life, an inevitable by-product of growth and adaptation. In others, an effort to redefine boundaries is felt as a threat and is vigorously resisted. John Doyle's decision to marry Anita was not welcomed as an expression of a young person's independence and assumption of adult responsibilities. It was regarded as a betrayal: the wedding was not a celebration, but was "more like a funeral." Anita and he have been strong in their determination to make space for their own family, but the negotiations with John's parents and relatives have been adversarial and have left a residue of pain.

In a previous section, we discussed John Doyle's lack of clarity regarding his boundaries with his mother. One of the reasons this lack of clarity persists is that negotiations are so difficult to initiate. In fact, they are prohibited, as Anita and John explain in another segment:

Anita: Even when we go visit, it is not [an] adult-to-adult relationship with the parents. We all become the children.

George: They have never adjusted to the two of you and to the other children becoming adults.

John: My dad can but my mom can't. My mom absolutely can't. I'm sure if I was one hundred I would still be twelve.

George: Have you ever asked her how old you will need to be before she will feel prepared to let you go or . . .

Anita: She would be very upset.

John: There are some real nontalkable topics around my mom.

Anita: She explodes in an emotional reaction. It is not something you can do.

John and Anita are blocked from even attempting to negotiate with John's mother for fear of precipitating an explosion. The result is that John's growth toward independence and autonomy is severely restricted, and this tradition is carried on into his present family.

BOUNDARIES AND IDENTITY

We indicated early in this chapter that a reason boundaries are so important is that our ability to develop and maintain them is intimately bound to our ability to develop and maintain identity. This is a fundamental matter for individuals and their families—a strong and gratifying identity is the foundation on which a satisfying life is built. Thus, the question of how boundaries serve us in authoring our identities merits our special attention at this point.

By filtering experience, we use boundaries to develop and protect our identity. We sort out who we are emotionally, and which feelings belong to us versus which belong to others. Cognitively, we organize and screen information as we develop stories about ourselves and the world around us. Behaviorally, we use boundaries to maintain focus so we can develop the repertoire of behaviors we will use to enact our stories as our lives unfold. Identification with our emotional selves, with an image of who we are and the niche we inhabit, and with propensities to act in certain ways are all basic parts of identity.

Boundaries and the Sense of Self

In a sense, we all have multiple identities—our various roles, our families, and other important groups to which we belong provide different points of reference that we and others use to define who we are. For some people we *are* what we do occupationally. For others, our family roles define us. For yet others, different "parts" of us represent the whole, such as the part that is someone's friend, a customer, a parishioner, and so on. But it is also true that we move in and out of roles and relationships while continuing to experience ourselves as the same person. Our sense of who we are remains with us from context to context. This has limits, in that under intense psychological or physical stress our sense of self may become more fragile (torture, brainwashing, and some forms of domestic violence involve techniques designed to accomplish precisely this). However, if we are lucky we will live most of our lives with a reasonably solid, intact sense of who we are. Similarly, our families change drastically over time in terms of membership and the nature of people's involvements. We nevertheless retain a fairly stable and enduring idea of who our family is and what it means to us.

Of course, when we talk of an "enduring, intact" sense of personal or familial identity, these are not synonyms for "unchanging." We and our families recreate ourselves on an ongoing basis, but we do so (hopefully) with the sense of what some writers have called a "core self" (Stern, 1985)—a sense of continuity over time and across contexts.

Our sense of personal and familial continuity is largely a consequence of effective boundary maintenance. In different roles, groups and places, we change who we are in some ways, but we also maintain a continuous awareness of who or what we are and are not. As we move through different sets of relationships and expectations, we constantly determine that "this is like me" and "that is not like me." Out of this sensing of similarities and differences comes our awareness of continuity and endurance as persons and families (Boszormenyi-Nagy, 1965).

The image and feeling of who we are that evolves is a critical part of identity. Equally important, we learn to experience ourselves as managers of this critical process. A strong sense of self consists of valued stories and images about who we are, but also of the understanding that we are the source of those stories and images. The core self includes an appreciation of our role as self-creators.

If we live with the belief that our boundaries or our ability to manage them are extremely tentative, then our sense of the reliability of our core self is also vulnerable. An ongoing actual lack of a core self may be an experience restricted to people with psychotic illnesses (Stern, 1985, p. 71), but episodic losses of confidence in this basic aspect of our identity are an issue for victims of severe trauma as well. Clinicians who work with torture victims, victims of domestic violence, and survivors of childhood abuse will testify that these clients have often been taught very powerful lessons. Systematic and painful boundary violations have persuaded them that they cannot trust in their ability to set the most basic limits and have others respect them. Not surprisingly, therefore, the consequences of abuse for victims are often in some sense a loss of self. Panic reactions representing fear of painful intrusion, engulfment, or abandonment are an example; another is dissociation in response to threat.

Differentiation and Adaptation

A reliable core identity, based on trust in our ability to manage our boundaries effectively, is not rigidly set. Rather, the identity we create is open to continued thematic variations and can be given fresh interpretations as we develop and grow. Given a core that is at once reliable and open, we become more complex as we grow, meeting our needs, pursuing our aspirations, and adapting to new demands. Given the prerequisites of safe boundaries, access to the resources that family and friendships provide if they are working well, and adequate health and economic provisions—in brief, good enough frameworks and adequate resources—people and their families grow by becoming richer (experientially) and more complex. During times of growth, we discover new facets of ourselves and write these into our life stories: new emotional capacities, new understandings, new competencies and areas of mastery.

Mastery and Autonomy

The structural family therapists' belief about the function of boundaries is clear: "Boundaries serve to protect the autonomy of the family and its subsystems, by managing proximity and hierarchy" (Nichols and Schwartz, 1995, p. 214). At an individual level as well, the ability to protect our autonomy is a prerequisite for developing a sense of mastery and personal power—the belief that we can act competently and claim authorship of our own lives.

In the human adult . . . needs, interests, wishes, the opportunities of circumstance . . . generate interest in the possibilities of action. In the most articulated case, the imagination of possibilities of action culminates in a conclusive wish to act, in a choice or a decision, in an intention. . . . This kind of action is what we call . . . "will." The capacity for such action is the basis not merely of a comparative independence from the immediate environment but of an active mastery of the environment. It is also the basis for the human sense of autonomy. The experience of the imaginative process, the trying on of possibilities, which culminates in an impetus to act, in an intention, is the experience of choosing, of freedom of action, of being one's own master. (Shapiro, 1981, pp. 17-18)

The question of whether true independent choice is possible, of course, has provided employment to philosophers for centuries. Readers interested in this issue at a philosophical level may wish to start with Erwin (1997), Glover (1988), and Shapiro (1981). Alternatively, we can opt to agree with the novelist William Golding (1959, p. 1) and move on: "Free-will cannot be debated" says one of his characters, "but only experienced, like a color or the taste of potatoes." This experience of ourselves as autonomous, self-directing agents who can act competently in the world is critically important to our well-being, and we start working to acquire it very early in life, in part through learning to assert our boundaries:

Infants can assert their independence [their nascent autonomy] and say a decisive "NO!" with gaze aversions at four months, gestures and vocal intonation at seven months, running away at fourteen months, and language at two years. (Stern, 1985, p. 22)

The relation of boundaries to autonomy and competence is clear enough. First, without adequate boundaries our sense of ourselves as separate people is compromised. Second, the necessary basic experiences of self-regulation and self-direction (Shapiro, 1981) presuppose the existence of boundaries, protecting a personal space within which these skills can be developed and their consequences experienced. Third, establishing and maintaining boundaries is a complex and important task—such achievements, in and of themselves, contribute to our sense of mastery. Finally, remembering that clear boundaries involve engagement as well as distance, we note that our identity is enhanced when we have flexible access to supportive help and feedback from others (especially from our families).

BOUNDARIES IN CONTEXT

Earlier in this chapter, we made a point that deserves reemphasis as we close: while boundary issues are important to all people, there are no universal norms regarding what is desirable or problematic. The optimal rhythm of engagement and withdrawal related to various issues is determined pragmatically (are outcomes for the people involved satisfactory?) and is extremely sensitive to context. Context is defined by many circumstances, but we have highlighted culture, gender, and development.

While acknowledging the importance of culture and gender as contexts for boundary issues, we will not be focusing on them as separate issues in the chapters that follow. Books require boundaries as much as people, and these are topics we have elected to recognize without giving them the full attention they deserve (and are receiving from other writers).

We will, however, spend more time and space specifically on development. One aspect of this (Chapter 2) is how people and families develop traditions, writing themes into their lives that affect their ability to creatively adapt. Another (Chapter 3) is common family developmental themes: given that each of us experiences and reacts to them uniquely, what are the common challenges that we confront as we and our families move through life?

Chapter 2

Traditions

Who what am I? My answer: I am the sum total of everything that went before me, of all I have been seen done, of everything done-to-me. I am everyone everything whose being-in-the-world affected was affected by mine. I am anything that happens after I've gone which would not have happened if I had not come. Nor am I particularly exceptional in this matter; each 'I,' every one of the now-six-million-plus of us, contains a similar multitude. I repeat for the last time: to understand me, you'll have to swallow a world.

Salman Rushdie, *Midnight's Children*

Those who cannot remember the past are condemned to repeat it.

George Santayana, *Life of Reason*

I think history is very stubborn. However much we study it, it is going to work hard to repeat itself.

Constance Nissen-Weber, *Essays and Aphorisms*

The only duty we owe to history is to rewrite it.

Oscar Wilde

Throughout life, we adapt creatively to new problems and circumstances, building (if we are fortunate) an increasingly rich sense of who we are. We have described this as an act of self-authorship, with each of us composing a unique story. Of course, such creativity is not accomplished in a vacuum, but in contexts that support and constrain us—frameworks for growth on which we all rely. These frameworks are open, not fixed; in fact, they usually comprise an enormous range of influences.

It follows from this is that a complete understanding of someone's frameworks (even one's own) is impossible, requiring us to "swallow a world." Fortunately, partial understandings are all we need to be helpful, and our goal at this point is to suggest avenues for understanding influences on our frameworks that are commonly important.

TRADITIONS DEFINED

What we will call *traditions* are established patterns of thinking, feeling, acting, and problem solving learned from our families and our culture. They are habits of thought and action that we use to structure our lives:

1. Shaping our perceptions
2. Guiding us in our interpretations of our experience
3. Selecting familiar behavioral responses
4. Determining how we feel, since the way we perceive, interpret, and act on our experience has far-reaching emotional consequences

Each of us employs such habits of thought, feeling, and action all the time, often unaware of the extent to which our self-authorship is influenced by distant voices, some of them echoes from several generations past. Like boundaries, traditions consist of beliefs and behaviors. The basis for traditions is the beliefs that underlie them, while what we observe is often their consequences (the behaviors they prescribe or prohibit, and their emotional impacts).

For the most part we benefit from traditions: they are an essential source of the structure we need to cope creatively with life. If we had to invent responses to every new situation from scratch, we would be immobilized. Also, many traditions are nurturing and supportive, prescribing and recognizing our capacities for generosity, celebration, and growth.

However, the point has been made that supports are also constraints, and it is often clinically useful to consider what traditions are scripting our responses to our lives in ways that cause pain or prohibit growth.

Traditions Illustrated

In the previous chapter, we discussed a dilemma that has affected three generations (at least) in the Doyle family:

1. As a young woman, John's mother falls in love with a man of whom her family disapproves. She capitulates to their racism and religious intolerance, and breaks off the engagement. She subsequently marries someone who is acceptable to her family, but whom she does not love. The narrative is a tragic one, John's belief being that she lived unhappily ever after.
2. A generation later, John shows a degree of independence by breaking his family's taboo against marrying across linguistic and religious lines. Nevertheless, he remains true to the traditions his family taught him in that he sacrifices his own needs to be recognized as an adult and for his family to be treated respectfully, rather than risk an escalating conflict with his parents. He does not take care of himself, or of his own family by clearly saying to his parents and uncles that they must stop treating his wife rudely and rejecting his daughters.
3. In the youngest generation, Maria has decided that she must sacrifice herself rather than ask her own parents to respect her healthy adolescent need for increased independence.

What Maria has inherited from her father and grandmother is a set of beliefs about loyalty, self-sacrifice, and conflict avoidance. These beliefs shape her perceptions and behaviors in predictable ways, so that her problem solving has a scripted quality to it—like her father, she prefers to sacrifice herself rather than to risk hurting others by asking for what she wants. It would not be a surprise, two decades hence, to visit her and find an unhappy person, inadvertently teaching her own children to stifle their needs rather than risk overt conflict.

SOURCES OF TRADITIONS

Culture, family, and the individual interact in the creation and transmission of traditions. The sources of tradition are therefore complex, but if we accept a degree of over simplification a Venn diagram (Figure 2.1) illustrates the possibilities. We all base our lives on themes for which we are the primary authors, on themes for which authorship is clearly shared with our families, and on themes that have been developed by us, our families, and our culture. Traditions that are embraced by the individual will be amplified if they are congruent with traditions promoted by the family and/or culture. Traditions can also become less powerful or muted under the influence of different ideas (from any source).

The traditions that influence our responses to life are absorbed from multiple sources: peers, churches, schools, television, movies, books, our neighborhoods—all these contribute to the themes we write into our stories. For many clinical social workers, a particularly important source of traditions is the family of origin. Over the generations, the family plays a critical role in interpreting, creating, and passing on traditions. It is sometimes described as a bridge between its members and the larger culture, but the family is not a simple conduit for transmitting influence. It is more like a bridge with a laboratory midway, in which information is examined, experimented with, and reinvented to some extent as it is passed on.

FIGURE 2.1. Sources of Traditions

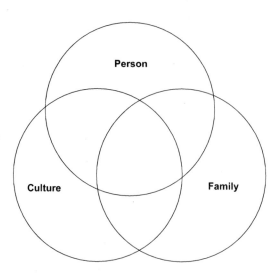

Similarly, as individuals within our families, each of us responds to the lessons we are taught with our own unique interpretations, drawing our own conclusions. John Doyle's reaction to his parents' generation and its intolerance was a healthily rebellious one; by marrying Anita he declared his unwillingness to follow a tradition that he had thought about and rejected.

Many of the rules a family commends to its members are cultural in origin—racism and religious intolerance were not attitudes that John Doyle's family invented unassisted. But the process of transmitting influence is not like programming, where instructions are accepted as written. Anita Doyle's family was undoubtedly also exposed to cultural ideas promoting distrust of religious and linguistic differences, but it did not evolve the same vitriolic and rigid stance that John ascribes to his extended family. Even in the most polarized, adversarial situations where religious or cultural differences have led to battle lines being drawn, families differ in the extent to which they buy into culturally prescribed animosities. The interaction between families and cultures is a creative one, and every family interprets cultural traditions differently to its members. As the family processes cultural traditions for its members, some are amplified and some are muted—and most if not all are altered to some extent.

There are indications that Anita learned to be diffident about asking for what she wants just as her husband is, though not out of a fear of conflict so much as out of guilt. She did not want to add to the burden of a family that had to stretch meager resources to provide for eleven children. Consider, though, how cultural traditions about gender are implicated as well, socializing women to be accommodating rather than making clear demands.

John's family is strongly patriarchal, and would amplify cultural sanctions against women being assertive. Anita therefore is dealing with multiple pressures. Her own inherited beliefs are reinforced by cultural prescriptions, doubly reinforced by her in-laws. John's family has always looked for reasons to reject her (and her daughters) and if she were clearer about her demands, she would give them ammunition to employ against her. Again, it would be easier to withstand that if John was clearer in his support, but he is too caught up in family traditions to help her effectively with this issue.

THE ADVANTAGES OF THE CONCEPT

Clinicians tend to be acutely aware of the importance of language. Inasmuch as all words are in a sense labels, it is hard to talk with our clients about their issues without labeling, but we are nervous about that, and for good reason. If we describe Maria Doyle as *depressed,* that is a label, and it can be useful. For a clinician, it suggests attention to a possible pattern that can include considerable emotional distress, harsh self-judgments, and a perception of oneself as unwanted and alone. It can encourage us to listen more carefully for problems with sleep, appetite, inadequate self-care, or even (in more serious situations such as Maria's) self-destructiveness.

Concurrent with the benefits of alerting us to patterns, however, labels can do harm. If the effect of labeling Maria as depressed is to suggest she is mentally ill or incompetent, numerous unhelpful side effects can result.

The concept of traditions has benefits for people, families, and therapists in that it gives us a way to talk about problems respectfully. Established patterns may be causing pain for a family and its members, but labeling them as traditions establishes a basis for discourse that is, first of all, less ominous and less blaming than labels that imply pathology or irresponsibility. We all rely on customary ways of doing things, and when the fit is poor between the traditions we have learned and our priorities in life, we are wrestling with something that is normal rather than exotic or shameful. Maria has learned to sacrifice her own needs to avoid conflict, and that tradition is not working for her or her family. This is not a symptom or an illness, but an unfortunate choice among options.

Identifying patterns that have been acquired over time as traditions also places them in a historical context (in addition to the present). This provides a flexibility of perspective and avenues for change that can be liberating. If Maria understands her struggle for space as involving rules and constraints that have been passed to her via her father and grandmother (among others), it is useful to add this perspective. In addition to experiencing the pattern as it affects her immediate family in the present, she can experience it as a tradition that did not originate with them, and with which she does not struggle alone. This perspective offers some psychological distance from the tradition, and a vantage point from which her freedom to choose new options may be clearer to her.

OUR RELATIONSHIP TO TRADITIONS

Byng-Hall (1995) uses the term *family scripts* in a way similar to (though by no means synonymous with) the idea of traditions, and makes a useful distinction that can be adapted to our discussion. Like Byng-Hall's scripts, it is useful to consider that some traditions are adopted in a *replicative* fashion, when we simply carry on following rules more or less as they were taught to us. An example would be an abused child who grows up to parent in the same way, responding violently to conflicts with his or her own children.

If we feel that some traditions were damaging to us and strive to develop a clear alternative, this is a *corrective* response to inherited traditions—an abused child who subsequently establishes a policy of nonviolence in relation to her or his own children is a familiar and reassuring example.

Finally, responding creatively to new problems, using fresh inputs gleaned from our own experience, we can *improvise,* and new traditions are born. An abused child grows up and marries someone whose experience has been more positive, and who has learned an effective and varied repertoire of skills for solving problems and resolving conflict. Together, they evolve parenting traditions that do not replicate the abuse and are not simply a reaction against it, but are something fresh and new.

Each of us employs all three of the strategies of replication, correction, and improvisation, and such a mix is certainly functional. We can make problems for ourselves, however, if we are locked into replicating painful traditions. Similarly, we can be so intent on correcting traditions that have been painful for us that our responses become rigid, and potentially useful options remain beyond our reach. Abused children who subsequently become parents who avoid any conflict whatsoever with their own children for fear of hurting them are an example of this—and helping them develop traditions for conflict resolution that are safe but more realistic will benefit not only them but future generations in their extended family.

Differentiation

For most of us, an important part of growing up involves developing and redeveloping boundaries that work for us in our relationships with our family of origin. We have discussed this in the previous chapter, with a special reference to the authorship of identity, arguing that the exercise of boundary creation and maintenance is vital to the process of developing a sense of self. When we develop boundaries vis-à-vis our families of origin, another important aspect of that task is establishing our relationship to its traditions. A similar point can be made about our relationship to our culture: with growth, we come to embrace some cultural traditions as valued parts of our identity, while we distance ourselves from others that seem less worthwhile.

Some clinical theorists give central importance to the need for us to establish our independence from the traditions we have grown up with. Bowen's concept of differentiation is a case in point—in part, it suggests that maturity in adulthood is achieved when we are no longer governed by inherited beliefs, especially their power to sway our emotions (Bowen, 1961; Kerr and Bowen, 1988). The less desirable possibility is fusion, which suggests that our beliefs, actions, and feelings are reactions to the dictates of our families of origin rather than our autonomous assessment of our own needs and priorities.

John Doyle's ability to claim the prerogatives of an adult are compromised by his lack of differentiation from some of his family's traditions, as we have noted. To the extent that he accepts certain ideas—that it would be disloyal to upset his mother by challenging her, for example—he remains cognitively and emotionally caught. Inasmuch as he is undifferentiated (or fused, or enmeshed) from his family of origin, he is unable to disentangle his needs and responsibilities (and emotional reactions) from theirs, and is consequently confused and ineffective in his responses to them. If he could relate to them in a more differentiated fashion, he would be clear about his own needs and responsibilities and could act on them effectively.

From the earliest days of family therapy (and psychodynamic therapies as well) the idea that differentiation is associated with maturity and health has been proposed. Virginia Satir (1983) suggested that differentiation was the sine qua non of self-esteem. Murray Bowen (1961) and others thought that a lack of differentiation is strikingly characteristic of families with schizophrenic members, and were tempted to believe (though this is not a popular hypothesis any more) that the relationship was a causal one.

The concept has also had its critics, primarily those who are concerned that emphasizing differentiation leads to equating maturity with distance in relationships. Bowen believed that differentiation from one's family of origin was linked to differentiation of another kind, which is the ability at an individual level to keep cognitive and emotional systems separate, so that emotions do not overwhelm one's ability to think and problem solve. Another concern therefore was that the concept could result in an overvaluing of thought and a devaluing of feelings. An extension of these concerns by feminist critics is that if the standard of maturity and health is someone who is relatively disengaged and cognitive, the consequence is to disadvantage women by imposing criteria for health that are male oriented. Distance and objectivity are more highly valued than connectedness and emotionality.

We would argue that differentiation is an important developmental achievement, but that it should be understood as clarity of boundaries (see Chapter 1) rather than as distance. Boundaries vis-à-vis one's family of origin that allow us to choose which traditions we replicate, which we modify, and which we replace are what we think of when we think of differentiation. As we argued in the previous chapter, when clarity of boundaries is achieved, our ability to distinguish our own thoughts and feelings from other peoples' and to ascribe responsibility appropriately is enhanced. Consequently, our choices of actions are more connected to our own needs and priorities. In this sense, we think Bowen's recognition that differentiation in relationships is linked to clarity in our thinking is useful, though we do not tend to see this as a matter of somehow freeing our thinking systems from our emotional systems. Indeed, a separation of those two modes of responding is unnecessary and probably ultimately impossible (Bruner, 1986). One can feel strongly and think clearly at the same time, given clarity of boundaries.

A Second Illustration of Traditions

To expand upon our discussion of traditions, we will introduce another client at this point. Mike Rothery saw Daniel Grey over a period of several months, with his wife, Rebecca. Both partners were in their late twenties. Daniel was a research psychologist in a mental health setting; Rebecca was a psychiatric nurse in the same clinic.

This couple presented with a crisis in their marriage. Rebecca was agitated and acknowledging some suicidal thoughts, convinced that Daniel was about to leave her. Daniel seemed numb and incapacitated, though he insisted that he had no desire to end their relationship.

The event triggering their crisis had been Thanksgiving dinner, which Daniel had offered to cook. Rebecca embraced this idea enthusiastically, and even told him about her grandmother's recipe for stuffing the turkey (the pièce de résistance being the addition of toasted pecans, properly seasoned). Daniel went all-out, buying flowers for the table and an excellent wine (a 1986 Meursault).

When the intimate feast was served, Rebecca noted to herself that there were no pecans in the turkey stuffing, and became cool and withdrawn. Daniel, uncomprehending, tried to keep the festive spirit alive for some time, but finally gave up, lapsing into a state of futile disappointment (and drinking more than his share of the Meursault). Over the next couple of days, they withdrew further, not speaking, Rebecca convincing herself that the relationship could not last and Daniel feeling hopeless, confused, and angry.

The meal was not just a meal, of course. Given their youth, and the flowers and the wine, it is reasonable to suggest that the second and more important agenda was seduction. Still, it is not immediately obvious why something as trivial as nuts in the stuffing could lead this intelligent couple to the brink of disaster. The answer to this riddle lies in the traditions that each brought to their relationship.

Although they had both inherited rules from their families of origin that contributed to their painful situation, we will conserve time and space by focusing primarily on Daniel. With respect to Rebecca, however, it is worth making a mental note of the fact that her maternal grandmother had been "dumped" with relatives by her parents (whom she never saw again) at the age of twelve. Her husband abandoned her when she was in her forties (having had one child, Rebecca's mother). Rebecca's mother married despite the grandmother's disapproval (she disapproved of most males), to a man whose memory she romanticized after he died in a car accident (when

Rebecca was twelve). The lesson is clear: even good men abandon you sooner or later.

When she married Daniel, Rebecca brought a number of traditions with her. Despite the tragedies they had endured, her family had stayed together and survived. Her mother, as a widowed single parent to Rebecca and three siblings, established a good career for herself as an accountant, and was able to provide her family a measure of comfort and security. Consequently, one set of traditions that Rebecca inherited had to do with persevering in the face of adversity, taking care of oneself and one's family. Another set of traditions, however, had to do with expecting abandonment—with not trusting that relationships will last, even very good ones.

But what about Daniel? Daniel's paternal grandparents (see Figure 2.2 for his genogram) came from farming origins, but relocated in a Midwestern city shortly after they were married. The grandfather established a furniture-building business that expanded into a factory employing dozens of people. After his early death, his wife took over management of the business, with the assistance of her sons. They were financially successful, but the business would not accommodate all four boys. Eventually Daniel's father, Jack, left home and joined the military.

After the marriage of her youngest son, the grandmother had what the family called a "nervous breakdown." Daniel never knew for certain what the diagnosis was, but suspected a severe chronic depression. In any event, her condition led to her being hospitalized, and she spent the rest of her life in institutions.

With Daniel's father gone and their mother incapacitated, the other two older brothers assumed management of the company. The youngest was depressed enough to require institutionalization himself on one occasion (he was taking antidepressant medications and had also been given electroconvulsive therapy). This uncle was employed in the family business, but Daniel's impression was that it was in a sheltered, secondary role.

Daniel's view of his father and uncles as a group was strongly negative. Although recognizing their intelligence and accomplishments, he gave more weight to their negative traits. He described an extreme level of machismo—they saw themselves as self-made men and pursued manly activities. They were disparaging of women and children,

FIGURE 2.2. Daniel's Genogram

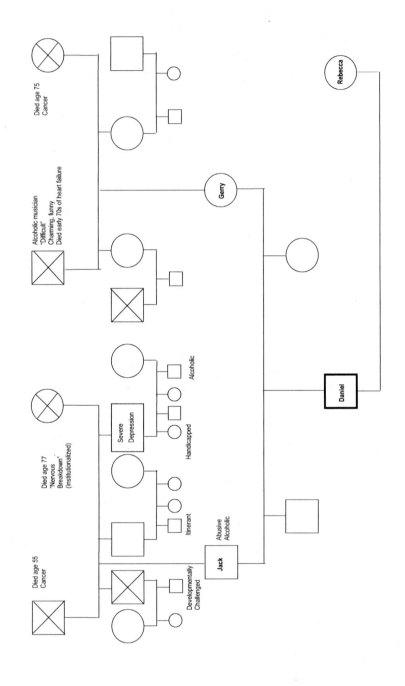

characterizing them as stupid and weak, and their main concern as parents was to "make men" out of their boys. Daniel recalled being given a pair of boxing gloves for Christmas, when he was ten. Boxing lessons with his father followed, during which Daniel inevitably found himself getting hurt, until, with his mother's support, he withdrew from the ring and put the gloves away.

Daniel's father, Jack, had a moderately successful military career. It is noted on the genogram[*] that he was both abusive and alcoholic. The abuse consisted of occasional physical harm and consistent, degrading verbal attacks. Daniel described incidents when, even as a rather large teenager, he was struck with sufficient force to send him reeling several feet across a room. However, he experienced more pain recalling episodes of what he called "terrorism," in which he was not hurt physically, but was subjugated by displays of unrestrained rage and threats of brutality, which left him feeling humiliated, frightened, and weak. Although he was not the sole target for abuse, he was the primary one: his father favored his older brother, and his mother (who protected him also to a degree, but not as effectively) protected his younger sister.

Jack's alcoholism did not emerge until after he retired from the military. Daniel remembered very little alcohol being consumed when he was young, but after retirement, his father began drinking on a daily basis, enough to make himself somewhat inebriated though he never developed a pattern of drinking to the point of illness or complete incapacitation.

Daniel's mother, Gerry, grew up with a father who was the kind of man Jack and his brothers despised—he was, in fact, offered to Daniel as a negative example of what he might become if he failed to achieve true manhood. This maternal grandfather was a professional musician, earning an adequate but unreliable living and always falling short of his aspirations. Longing for the status of the jazz greats of his day, he played piano at weddings and local clubs to audiences that simply wanted a musical background for their dancing and drinking. Frequently, he was invited to join in the drinking, and he did not often decline.

---

[*]For depth and detail regarding the construction and interpretation of genograms, see McGoldrick and Gerson (1985, 1989).

Daniel's knowledge of this grandfather came mainly from his mother, who felt the need to talk about him on occasion. He was, she said, "difficult" at the same time as he was charming, and witty, and sometimes provided his family with hilarious moments that were cherished in memory.

Gerry had two sisters. Both of these aunts were well regarded by Daniel (as were the aunts on his father's side). Daniel likewise saw his maternal grandmother as a solid, reliable, affectionate figure, though all of Gerry's family lived far enough away that he did not get to know them well.

Traditions and Daniel's Family of Origin

Though he never sought help for it, Daniel had experienced a significant clinical depression as an undergraduate at college. He was still living at home at the time, feeling increasingly trapped in a painful situation. He was psychologically distressed enough to experience quasi-psychotic events (hearing mocking voices when he was falling asleep) and perceptual distortions (he recalled times when the world literally seemed colorless and two-dimensional). One story he liked to tell about this period involved making his father a Father's Day present—an ornately framed embroidery of a quote from Shakespeare, whom he was studying in one of his college courses: "How sharper than a serpent's tooth it is / To have a thankless child" (*King Lear,* Act 1, Scene 4).

Ten years later, Daniel tells this story with a mixture of pride, amusement, and anxiety. What is striking about it is how it represents his struggle to come to grips with the traditions that have contributed to his pain, and does so at many levels. The initial choice of such a present was intuitive, in that Daniel did not consciously think through all its implications. He did, however, find the memory of the event emotionally engaging, and it is easy to see why considering his family history.

Traditions and the Self: Mastery and Growth

Traditions regarding mastery are present in all families, and it is a commonplace that they are important in the lives of our clients. A vital part of the identity we compose for ourselves has to do with success and failure, with our competence, our abilities, our chances of being a success in life—indeed, with what being a success means as far as we and our families are concerned.

When we communicate, we send messages at different levels, and they are often different from one another. At one level, Daniel's family of origin taught him to be an achiever in a stereotypically masculine fashion—the myth of the self-made man, pulling himself up by his bootstraps, may be banal to many people, but it was a powerful force in Daniel's early life. However, the genogram also suggests other traditions that are more ominous.

At the time when Daniel and Rebecca were being seen, Daniel's uncles had decided to sell the furniture factory. While the usual script for such a family would have been for the business to be passed to a son in the next generation, every male child had an impediment that prevented this from occurring. One of Daniel's male cousins was developmentally disadvantaged. Another "dropped out" as a teenager and lived an itinerant, nomadic life. A third had a physical handicap that, in the eyes of the family, would have made him incapable of managing the business properly. A fourth was severely alcoholic.

In fact, each generation in the genogram provides examples of people being incapacitated, the most common options being depression or alcoholism. Beside the myth of the self-made man, there is another tradition—the flawed child who grows up to be a failure and a disappointment.

When Daniel's father celebrated the Christmas season of peace and goodwill by buying him boxing gloves and initiating lessons, he was not really teaching him to be a stereotypically strong male. At a more important level, he was pursuing the usual abusive parent's goal of convincing his child that he was powerless and weak. By hurting and defeating Daniel while ostensibly instructing him in the manly arts, he was teaching him that his destiny was to fail and disappoint.

The tradition of being a failure in Daniel's family has important facets. Failures are weak and stupid, and they are not real men. When Daniel presented his father with the embroidery of the quote from *King Lear* for Father's Day, he hit on a symbolic gesture that is both sad and wonderful. He makes explicit his father's need for him to be a disappointment. He communicates the message intelligently and poetically, and in a medium (embroidery) certain to give his macho father pause.

The identity that Daniel has created for himself has naturally been influenced by the traditions identified. The story is not all negative, in that he values initiative, hard work, and humor. However, he has also come to view himself as weak and stupid, and is convinced that his ultimate fate is failure through alcoholism or emotional problems or both. This being the case, he does not trust his successes in life (his career and his marriage to Rebecca), and he does not think he can sustain them. Differentiation from his family of origin will mean, in effect, rewriting his story in important ways, recognizing his hardiness and competence, refusing to accept responsibility for his father's disappointment in him, and considering the option of a happy rather than a tragic ending.

Traditions and Relationships

When discussing traditions with our clients, it is always a matter of interest to consider their implications for their ability to sustain close, nurturing relationships. Some traditions support generosity, loyalty, and reciprocity, while others may discourage closeness, trust in others, or the expectation of inclusion and belonging (McClure Goulding and Goulding, 1979).

Mate Selection

When Daniel's mother and father married, they were not marrying each other as mature, differentiated people. Instead, their choice was heavily influenced by the traditions that affected them, and these traditions were complementary. Gerry was attracted to Jack because he presented as a strong man from a successful family, counter to her own father's unreliability. In Gerry, Jack saw someone to whom he could play the strong masculine hero.

It is a frequent irony in relationships that initial attractions become a focus for conflict later, and this was true for Daniel's parents: Jack came to treat Gerry's femininity with contempt, while she came to regard his excessive masculinity as coarse and his aggressiveness as bullying.

It is also not unusual for partners to engage in power struggles over whose family of origin their new family will replicate, and this is partly what Daniel's parents did. Put another way, this marriage became a battle of the sexes. Jack and their eldest son were on one side, Gerry and their daughter on the other. To a large extent (though not exclusively), Daniel was the battleground. For Jack, Daniel was the disappointment who proved what happened when Jack's attempts to raise him as a real man were thwarted by his overprotective wife. For Gerry, protecting Daniel was partly a wish to buffer him against abuse, partly a defense of her own family and its traditions and values.

If they were more differentiated people, a much wider set of choices would have been apparent to them. Jack might have decided that it was not in his interests to remain loyal to a rigid and narrow view of what an acceptable man is like. Not only could this have given him more flexibility respecting his own options as a person, but it would have freed him to relate in a more generous spirit to his father-in-law. Also, because part of the basis for his hostility toward women and children would be gone, his behavior as a husband and father would be less angry and destructive.

When his mother protected him, Daniel was denounced as a sissy; if she did not protect him, he was subjected to abuse in other forms. In developing his identity, he had to find a best solution to a difficult situation, which he did by distancing himself from his father as much as he could, giving up any hope of pleasing him but still hoping to please his mother. He endured Jack's scorn while growing up to be the kind of man he thought Gerry could approve of: studious, musical, and very nonassertive. As is often the case, however (we see the same phenomenon in John Doyle), Daniel could reject one set of traditions (the "real man") while remaining in the grip of the more subtle script: to be incompetent, a failure, and a disappointment.

Rebecca chose Daniel as her partner in part because he was somewhat atypical with respect to common masculine norms, and might therefore be exempt from her grandmother's blanket condemnation of the male sex. Also, Daniel's diffidence and anxiety to please made him someone unlikely to provoke Rebecca's fears of abandonment. For Daniel, Rebecca's many attractions included his sense that she would not disparage his lack of masculinity (in his own view, his weakness). Among the complex motives that guide the selection of intimate partners, the issue of security was therefore important for both Daniel and Rebecca. She was a safe person in relation to his fears about not being wanted because he was insufficiently masculine; he was a safe person in relation to her fears of abandonment.

*Traditions for Resolving Conflict
and Solving Problems*

The impact of traditions on our functioning is neither absolute nor constant. Rebecca and Daniel were capable of a good measure of intimacy much of the time. However, as is common, they found themselves least able to operate in a differentiated way when stress was high. Vulnerability to stress is a circular issue: our traditions play a part in determining what stresses will be hardest for us, and they often dictate responses that can make things worse rather than better.

When conflict entered into his relationship with Rebecca, it would be very easy for Daniel to respond as if he were in danger of attack, given his history of abuse. His most likely response under such circumstances would be to become immobilized and withdrawn, feeling like a failure. Rebecca, likewise, could be frightened by conflict if it aroused her fears of abandonment.

When Daniel reacts to Rebecca as if she is going to be coercive and attacking, or Rebecca reacts to Daniel as if he is inevitably going to leave her, each has ceased to relate to a real differentiated person so much as to traditions from the past. Their ability to encounter each other on the basis of their present needs and options is contaminated by history. Preoccupied with their fears, they have difficulty risking the vulnerability that comes with asking for what they want from each other; gripped by habits of thought, action, and feeling learned in the past, they have difficulty seeing options that are available to them in the present.

Traditions and Intimacy

Traditions as they affect our ability to establish intimate relationships are obviously important in our lives and the lives of our clients. A relationship is intimate when boundaries regarding expression of feeling and vulnerabilities are relatively open. Especially important is freedom to share vulnerabilities *safely* (L'Abate, 1990). Other elements contributing to intimacy include generosity, validation, and (in adults) reciprocity.

Sexuality as an aspect of intimacy is usually strongly affected by family traditions. Rebecca's grandmother did not like men, and Rebecca was quite certain that negative experiences with sex were a part of this. However, her mother had married happily, and romanticized her husband after his death. Rebecca's memories of her father and her parents' relationship were largely positive. She remembered them being physically affectionate, and this set of memories provided alternatives to her grandmother's perspective.

For Daniel, the situation was more complicated. He had created a masculine identity for himself that he saw as a rejection of his father's values (in Byng-Hall's [1995] terms, a *corrective* script), and his more sensitive, humorous, and gentle version of maleness worked well in his relationship with Rebecca. However, much as he disparaged his father's "macho bullshit" and the cultural image of the masculine hero represented in the cowboy movies and adventure comics of his youth, his failure to measure up to those ideals remained, for him, a badge of dishonor. Success as a research psychologist had not erased the humiliation of his defeat, at ten years of age, in a makeshift boxing ring.

When things were going well, he was a capable sexual partner. In the face of conflict, he could easily slip into his feelings of being inadequate as a man, destined to fail and to disappoint. This, of course, made it difficult for Rebecca to say "no" without seeming rejecting, or to be clear about what she wanted without him experiencing her as critical.

Another aspect of intimacy has to do with boundary maintenance: managing the rhythm of engagement and withdrawal that we discussed in the last chapter. This is commonly a problem for people who have experienced abuse, which teaches them to expect boundaries to be violated. At times of stress or conflict, Daniel is likely to find engagement difficult unless he remains clear that there is no danger of an assault (keeping his present differentiated from his past). Rebecca could help with this, finding ways to offer safety and support, but this requires differentiation on her part as well—clarity of the difference between Daniel's distancing and her historic fears of abandonment. Of course, moments of closeness can also be spoiled for Rebecca by her sense that they cannot last, and Daniel can be uncomfortable with distance if he interprets it as rejection for his having failed in some way.

REBECCA AND DANIEL'S CRISIS
REVISITED

The event precipitating Rebecca and Daniel's crisis, a lack of pecans in the turkey stuffing, appears trivial but is understandable in the light of their family history:

- Daniel offers to cook Thanksgiving dinner, and works hard at it. He is simultaneously trying to please—to be a good boy— and to be seductive. This is a frightening balancing act for him.
- At his request, Rebecca tells him how her grandmother (who disliked and distrusted men) would have cooked the meal.
- In a minor way, Daniel conforms to the tradition that requires him to be a disappointment when he leaves the pecans out of the turkey stuffing (the crisis, they acknowledged later, was a truly "nutty" situation).
- Daniel is not the only anxious one: Rebecca is nervous because everything is going so well. Her experience is that heroes can abandon you as readily as cads, which is even more painful.
- Daniel's small slipup is enough to suggest her grandmother was right, and to trigger fears of abandonment for her.
- When she begins to get upset, Daniel is quickly caught up in his own traditions and is incapable of helping her, withdrawing instead into his sense of inadequacy, rejection, and confusion. He drinks too much wine (now oblivious to what a good vintage it was) and even starts to experience himself as crazy.

This sequence has an inexorability that may be surprising. It is not hard from outside the relationship to see things they could easily have done to rescue the situation. Both intelligent and well intentioned, they nevertheless could not see or implement their options themselves. Instead, they found themselves moving in a direction that neither of them wanted and which could have been disastrous.

What we see in their difficulties is the power of past experience to shape present processes. A small problem occurs that another couple might resolve with ease. Rebecca and Daniel, who possess all the necessary skills to do likewise, nevertheless fail to manage it effectively. The problem-solving process that they could have employed is unavailable to them because the stressful event has hooked both of them into traditional responses from which they are still undifferentiated. As a consequence they are not free to explore what is happening, openly expressing their feelings about it and being clear about what they want from each other. They cannot solve a problem in the present to the extent that they are both caught in unresolved issues from the past.

Daniel cannot help Rebecca by exploring her withdrawal and helping her express what is wrong, because he is reacting to fears rooted in a history of abuse and denigration. Rebecca cannot understand this and allay his fears, because she is convinced she is about to be abandoned. Until one of them manages to refocus on the present issues and options, the possibilities for effective problem solving are slight.

We should note that such a small event triggering such a large crisis seemed (after the fact) strange to Daniel and Rebecca. At the point where they acquired at least that much distance from their problematic traditions, the crisis became an opportunity for growth as well.

We should also emphasize that though their example may be somewhat extreme, it is not particularly unusual in any formal sense. The experience of sometimes seeing our lives unfold in ways that we neither want nor feel able to control is common to all of us. Such is the importance of traditions in every person's life, embedded in their own unique mix of familial and cultural influences. Such also is the importance, for all of us, of respecting our need to determine how our traditions work for us, supporting creative coping with life—and how some work against us, closing off options for meeting our needs and relating generously to people close to us.

Chapter 3

Development of Individuals in Families: Themes and Variations

These are the soul's changes. I don't believe in ageing. I believe in forever altering one's aspect to the sun. Hence my optimism.

Virginia Woolf
A Writer's Diary

Twenty can't be expected to tolerate sixty in all things, and sixty gets bored stiff with twenty's eternal love affairs.

Emily Carr
Hundreds and Thousands

In the introduction and the first two chapters, we identified ideas that are broadly useful to families and their therapists. The necessity of frameworks as contexts for confronting life creatively is one such idea. A second is that understanding boundaries contributes much to our appreciation of how frameworks help us author our lives—including the basic themes that make up personal and family identity. Finally, we have suggested that the concept of traditions can deepen our respect for the familial and cultural context that shapes and informs our creative efforts at self-authorship.

Although every family is unique, there are also commonalities among them—shared themes. Such themes may be played differently by women compared to men, or by an African farmer compared to a New York advertising executive, or a villager in Saskatchewan. While each person is concerned with structure and boundaries, with creating identities, with establishing and redefining relationships to family and culture, each also works within variations on those themes that can be strikingly diverse.

Together with gender and culture, we have suggested that understanding development is important if we are to remain sensitive to how universal themes vary. The ways we use structure and the kind of relationships to family and society that suits us best are different when we are five versus fifty-five years old. Basic themes stay with us throughout life, but we experience them differently—there are some familiar tunes we never stop humming, but we do change their volume, introduce complexity, explore various emotional colorings, and invite different people to sing along.

THE ADVANTAGES
OF A DEVELOPMENTAL VIEW

Maria Doyle is a teenager who needs clearer boundaries and more space in relation to her parents. Her mother and father are anxious about this: If they give her more distance, will she still be all right? In this they are very normal. Few families with teenagers can claim they have not had to work through questions about how much personal space is desirable, and few parents will claim never to have worried about the ability of their teenager to handle increased freedom safely.

The advantage of a developmental view is that it helps us relate to families more respectfully and efficiently. Respect comes from viewing their problems as ineffective responses to common developmental tasks rather than as pathology. Efficiency results when a clinician can help the family focus on core issues more speedily, and with greater accuracy and depth.

It was his knowledge of how boundary issues commonly affect families with adolescents that permitted George to work efficiently with the Doyles to explore the key issues of space, loyalty, and self-sacrifice. Mike's knowledge of the common tasks facing new couples in relating to their extended families' traditions enabled him, with Rebecca and Daniel, to construct a useful understanding of the crisis in their marriage and why both were incapacitated in their efforts to respond sensibly to it.

Another advantage of the developmental view is that it brings attention to the *quality* of the person's narrative, as well as to the *content.* Personal narratives can be flat and impoverished or highly differentiated and rich in depth and detail. They can remain very concrete and immediate, or they can acquire scope and interest through the incorporation of abstractions, symbols, and metaphors. Such qualitative differences will, if we have good enough resources, develop over time: as children we tend toward very operational and concrete storytelling; as we grow our narratives may become more differentiated and abstract, more symbolically rich (Gardner, 1997). The family, educators, book publishers, and television producers all contribute to this development when they communicate in terms that match the child's narrative abilities and interests, at the same time as they encourage growth by presenting new, more differentiated possibilities.

A PERSPECTIVE ON DEVELOPMENT

Research and theory regarding our development as people has filled many volumes, and will continue to do so as work in this area progresses. Our goal is not to do justice to such a broad topic in one chapter so much as to address selected ideas that we feel have relevance to clinicians and their clients. Since the topic allows for a considerable diversity of viewpoints, we think it is important to state our own premises, which underlie the discussion that follows.

First, while we find it useful to talk about basic themes that are common to most people, we hope our respect for variations and difference is also clear. It is easy, in talking about development, to slip into suggesting that there is one proper or healthy pathway through life, when in fact there are many, and they can be radically different.

Another premise is that development occurs in response to multiple causes. Biological endowments play a critical role, as do experiences provided by the culture and the family. Biology dictates some fixed psychological (cognitive) developments (as Piaget's work has established), though these are scarcely independent of the effects of education and other social impacts. Dumb luck plays a role, with events outside our control (even awareness) shaping our needs and opportunities, as does our capacity for creativity and choice (an essential point for clinicians to stay aware of, if we are to help people change).

In keeping with the concepts we have relied on to this point, we believe development involves processes of assimilation and adaptation (cf. Rosen, 1988). New experiences and information are assimilated when they are taken into our frameworks and made part of how we understand and respond to the world. At the same time, our framework changes—we modify it to adapt to new needs and understandings.

Development also involves processes of differentiation. Differentiation implies increased complexity and clarity of boundaries, and it can be observed in many interrelated domains of our functioning and experience:

- Cognitively, we expand our awareness of our world, and organize that understanding in increasingly complex ways. A critical part of this domain has to do with our moral development inasmuch as we can think in more and more subtle and abstract terms about what we value and approve of in our own and others' behavior.
- We grow existentially or spiritually as well, constructing clearer and more sophisticated ideas about what we consider meaningful (Kegan, 1982) and what abstract goals and principles we want to honor.
- Emotional development is another area where differentiation occurs—a line of growth that leads from apparently straightforward responses like the rage of a frustrated child (or a regressed adult) to the complex emotional nuances we find in art, literature, or music.
- Another aspect of emotional development has to do with emotional control. The goal is not forms of control that rely on denial or repression of feelings, but the development of skills for managing emotions so that they do not cause us to become disorganized. Such skills include the ability to delay gratification, to channel feelings into goal-directed activities, to take care of ourselves effectively (e.g., through self-nurturing and self-soothing) when we are feeling anxious, depressed, angry, or alone.

- Behaviorally, we acquire more varied, complex, and effective sets of skills and competencies, better adapted to accomplishing our goals.
- We also become more differentiated in our relationships:

   1. Our understanding of ourselves and other people becomes more complex and our clarity respecting boundary issues is improved as we adapt more effectively, matching our needs to the resources our relationships provide.
   2. The development of reciprocity is critical to relationships; this implies learning to match the resources we have to offer with the needs of people who are important to us.
   3. Sexual development is, of course, a subtheme linking biological development to growth in relationships.

Another premise in our perspective on development emphasizes the fundamental drive to acquire a sense of mastery. From birth, we explore our world and work with it; we seem programmed to manipulate, build, and rearrange things. Our success at this, combined with our appreciation of our own growth along lines discussed previously, contributes to a general sense of mastery. Other terms that describe this include *competence, self-efficacy,* and *empowerment,* and the frequency with which these words appear in the clinical literature indicates how important the discovery and development of personal efficacy is seen to be.

A feeling of mastery combined with a well-differentiated (and secure) sense of self-in-relation to other people provides the foundation for a reliable sense of self-esteem. Self-esteem based on a differentiated view of ourselves and our world (recognizing reasonably complex sets of attributes that we value and coming to terms with attributes that do not please us) is reliable because it is sustainable. Someone whose self-esteem depends on an undifferentiated view of oneself and others is more vulnerable because that view can easily be undermined.

It is characteristic of development that it always entails boundary adjustments: "All transformations threaten previous attachments" (Garcia-Preto, 1989, p. 264). With growth, we can expect disruptions to the accustomed rhythm of distance and attachment. A flexible ability to engage in both behaviors is still needed, but the timing, complexity, and weight given different options has to change, as do the people involved.

In any stage transition, problems tend to be replicated. A parent such as John Doyle for whom leaving home was highly anxiety provoking is more likely to make the same step difficult for Maria and her sister, unless he finds ways to resolve the issue for himself.

Traditions can impede but also support growth. When traditions are formalized, they become family and cultural rituals. These persist in most cultures because they serve important purposes: "Ritual and rites of passage around engagements, marriage, birth, and death can give people an opportunity to work out previous unfinished business . . . particularly . . . where the person is motivated for an ongoing venture or engagement with the extended family" (McCullough and Rutenberg, 1989, p. 306).

THE NEW COUPLE

In every culture and apparently throughout history, the role of family in determining how we organize ourselves and anchor our lives is indisputable—the idea has a core social and emotional meaning for people, though agreement about what the family definitively *is* escapes us. However we define its membership, the family begins with people getting together, making commitments, and establishing mutual obligations. This is true of other social organizations, of course, but families are a special case. Often "family" as a concept expresses a sense of connection extending across generations. Although it may fail in this aim, in most societies the hope is also that the family will offer people bonds which are more durable than any other—we expect family obligations to last even as friendships die and colleagues drift away to better jobs or warmer climates.

Most (probably all) cultures also recognize that one frequent purpose of the family is to lay the groundwork for new families to emerge. Bonds of affection and obligation must change to endure, and each family faces the ongoing task of adapting its boundaries to the demands of growth. Old obligations shift to create room so new ones can develop; children distance themselves from their parents so that they can create familial commitments of their own. If they have children they will repeat the process with them a couple of decades later.

An examination of individual development usually starts with infancy and ends with old age, but family development is cyclical and lacks a clear beginning (or end). We have elected to begin our own discussion with the point at which a couple declares its commitment to be familial in nature. For many people and in many cultures a marriage ceremony is a public, formal recognition of this significant step. For all of us, the move toward adult commitments of this sort raises important boundary issues and will be affected by our cultural and familial traditions.

Boundaries and Forming Intimate Relationships

When people commit to a long-term, intimate adult relationship, boundary issues must be worked out on two fronts. One is their relationship to each other as partners; the other is their relationships to various people and systems beyond themselves, such as friends, colleagues, and families of origin.

Example: Erica and Colin

Erica and Colin have recently begun cohabiting. Neither has moved in with a partner before, though Colin was engaged to marry someone else three years earlier. Erica has found their relationship to be increasingly prone to angry times, with Colin becoming withdrawn and accusing her of not meeting his needs. For her part, Erica is frustrated by the sense that her efforts to respond to his needs will never be enough. Indeed, she claims that the harder she tries, the more accusatory he becomes, and she is considering terminating their relationship. They have requested counseling first, agreeing that if that does not help they will go their separate ways.

Early in their second session (with Mike), Colin makes it clear that he is dissatisfied with the therapy as well as his relationship with Erica.

Colin: I'm not sure there's any point talking about this. . . . I just feel unsupported. It's like I explained last time, but it's no different. I'm trying to look at the positives, but I have to say I don't see things getting better . . .

Mike: There's a change you're hoping for, and it's not happening . . .?

Colin: We've talked about all this . . . you know . . . lots—sometimes for hours. I just don't think this relationship is very loving. It just doesn't feel terrific—there are days when I don't even feel like coming home from work. It's too bad . . . this is not what I wanted . . . but, maybe . . .

Erica [looking agitated]: We spend time together. We went to a movie on Sunday. We went out with Larry and Jane on Friday. . . . I don't think you've looked so miserable—you laugh a lot, and looked OK. When we talk I think we listen all right, most of the time . . .

Colin [wistfully]: It's not just doing things . . . you know . . . or how much time we sort of put in. That's all fine. It's how I *feel* that I'm trying to explain. I feel unsupported, and that kind of . . . well . . . I'm sad about it, that's all. Too bad. C'est la vie.

Erica: Well [long pause] . . . I don't want you to feel like this either—OK? I just don't know [another long pause] . . . I'm just having a problem thinking what . . . [gives up, looking tearful and resentful].

Mike [to Erica]: Are you struggling to figure out what Colin wants from you?

Erica [tearful and angry]: Yeah! I just need to know . . . I want to know what the f_____ I'm supposed to do.

Mike: So you maybe want Colin to be clearer about what he wants . . . what would help him feel better . . . ?

Erica [looking depressed, a bit sarcastically]: That would be real nice.

Mike [to Colin]: Can you help us understand more clearly what you want—what change you have been looking for?

Colin: Like I keep saying—I want to feel supported. I want to feel loved.

This short sample of dialogue captures the "stuck" flavor of a situation that is unhappy and becoming entrenched. Already, Colin's sense of grievance has a scripted quality, in that it seems he will end up feeling unloved and dissatisfied no matter what happens. Without being prematurely too certain, we can hypothesize that his personal narrative is a story that ends with him feeling badly and holding other people responsible for his suffering. If the hypothesis is valid, and this is indeed an unfortunate and painful theme in his story, the traditions to which both he and Erica are bound are implicated. We will return to this shortly, after considering the boundary issues that this couple illustrates.

"A basic dilemma in coupling is the confusion of intimacy with fusion" (McGoldrick, 1989, p. 212). Put another way, a major issue for most couples is to reconcile what sometimes is experienced as a contradiction: differentiation and intimacy. Clarity of boundaries actually enhances development of intimacy, but this is a complicated lesson to learn and not everybody understands it.

Fusion or lack of boundary clarity between Colin and Erica is evident in his pressure on her to read his mind. It is striking that Colin is holding Erica (and Mike) responsible for meeting his needs by resisting being clear about what he wants. When Colin says, in effect, "I am feeling unsupported and unloved, and that is your fault," he is saying, "I am going to try to hold you responsible for my bad feelings." The outcome is likely to be unhappy: Erica tries to make him feel better and fails, in which case they both end up angry and disappointed. Erica may well feel blackmailed, in that she is being made to pay for her partner's unhappiness.

Lack of clarity of boundaries (or differentiation) in relationships is commonly expressed in the expectation that partners should read each other's minds. For some, the failure of a partner to intuitively understand the other's feelings, wants, and experiences is taken as a lack of caring or closeness, and triggers fear and anger. Other signs of "fusion" or unclear boundaries lie in the fixed expectation that others should take responsibility for our thoughts, values, feelings, actions—feeling something on our behalf, making up our minds for us, deciding for us what we should do.

Colin and Erica would be in a much clearer and more workable situation if Colin were to say something such as: "I am unhappy and don't really know why, but I'd like to use our time in counseling to understand it better and figure out what to do about it" or "I have been feeling unsupported and unappreciated, and it would help if you would take time to help me sort out my feelings." Clarity of boundaries comes partly with clear requests.

It is important for couples and their therapists to recognize that we may resist establishing clear boundaries because it feels risky to us. One part of the dilemma, as we have indicated, is that we may confuse clarity with distance, and fear a loss of closeness if our relationships become more differentiated. Another issue is that when we clarify boundaries by clarifying what we want from one another, we may feel that we are giving up power. If Colin asked Erica for what he wants in concrete terms, he would be more vulnerable, because she would be empowered to say "yes" or "no," or "how about this instead?"

Colin exerts power if he can hold Erica to ransom for his unhappy feelings, though this is self-defeating because it blocks opportunities for closeness. If he chooses instead to be clear, that clarity also has a price, which is heightened responsibility and shared power (reciprocity). Vulnerability is one cost of intimacy.

Later in their therapy, Colin remembered how, as a teenager, he received counseling because he was depressed, and his parents were concerned about his mood and failing grades at school. When his counselor asked him what he thought he needed to be happier, his response was something like: "How am I supposed to be happy when we all have to die?" The counselor could not offer him or his friends and family immortality, and Colin confessed to experiencing this exchange as a strange kind of victory.

There is an unintentional inauthenticity about requests that are impossible to fulfill, since there is a hidden agenda—the narrative being written involves continued disappointment rather than an honest effort to get one's needs met. Authentic requests ask for responses that can reasonably be provided, and are invitations to discuss and negotiate. Rigid, unconditional demands that are unlikely to be met (or will not resolve the issue if they are met) are indicators of a continued boundary problem—a narrative that entails maintaining unclear boundaries around responsibility for one's needs and feelings.

BOUNDARIES WITH THE COUPLE'S EXTENDED FAMILY AND OTHER SYSTEMS

When people declare themselves to be a couple through cohabitation or marriage, they acquire revised identities—their partnership becomes a new aspect of their lives to which others need to accommodate: "Marriage . . . requires that the couple negotiate new relationships as a twosome with many other subsystems: parents, siblings, grandparents, and nieces and nephews, as well as with friends" (McGoldrick, 1989, p. 224).

Although "letting go" is emphasized as a critical task for extended families at this time, boundary renegotiation is more complicated than simply accepting greater distance. Relinquishing closeness in some areas usually coincides with increased involvement in others, and an openness to including new members. "It places no small stress on a family to open itself to an outsider who is now an official member of its inner-circle" (McGoldrick, 1989, pp. 209-210).

Especially with younger couples, it is true that marriage may be an effort at boundary setting in relation to a family of origin. Mate selection can be a rebellious rejection of family controls and values, or it can be a simple effort to achieve distance (McCullough and Rutenberg, 1989, p. 296). A new partner may be cast in the role of rescuer, saving his or her loved one from a painful situation. Partners may see themselves as coconspirators, working to keep old sources of unhappiness at bay while they create a healthier life for themselves. Sometimes, this means fairly drastic distancing from families of origin, or even a more general social isolation, if the couple subscribes to an "us against the world" stance. More commonly, relations with extended family will evolve into "some contact, some closeness, some conflict, and the avoidance of certain issues" (McGoldrick, 1989, p. 226).

The general goal for new couples is to develop or maintain the attachments that will assure them the validation and other supports they need to succeed. Clear boundaries will free them to invest in each other; less clear boundaries may result in continued involvement with ongoing problems in the family of origin. Sometimes old problems are re-created by the new couple, with new players being assigned old roles.

Lack of boundary clarity can also be maintained by the couple as a way of avoiding dealing with their own conflicts, commonly through triangulation with members of the extended family. Anita Doyle does not confront her husband John with demands that he protect their marriage and family by being clearer with his family when their behavior is damaging. Instead, she avoids this conflict by joining him in focusing on his extended family: "In-laws are easy scapegoats for family tensions. . . . It may be easier for a daughter-in-law to hate her mother-in-law for 'intrusiveness' than to confront her husband directly for not committing himself fully to the marriage and defining a boundary in relation to outsiders" (McGoldrick, 1989, p. 228).

The parents have their own issues, and this can mirror (to an extent) issues they see enacted with their children. "Marriage of a child will set in motion a whole host of reflections, feelings and strong emotions, depending on the state of their own marriage" (McCullough and Rutenberg, 1989, p. 297). The issue again is clarity of boundaries: whose marriage is being experienced and where do issues belong?

With respect to friends, a new couple also has boundary work to do. They may be influenced by traditions that suggest that their formal commitment means that all their former friends must now relate to them as a couple. Some couples are comfortable with each person individually maintaining independent friendships, though these may be restricted with regard to the friend's gender. Other couples attempt openness even to the extent of extracurricular sexual involvements; some cultures offer traditional sanctions for this, though such permissions are almost always extended to men while stricter boundaries are prescribed for women.

A Caveat

It is important to be careful in assessing boundary issues with couples, since opportunities to pathologize are frequent. Bowen (1978), for example, maintains that it is unhealthy for partners to look to each other to repair their self-esteem. McGoldrick (1989) concurs, arguing that fusion is apparent in people who turn to their intimate relationships to achieve a sense of completeness or, again, to bolster self-esteem. These positions address real potential problems, but they also suggest an absolute standard of health and criteria for declaring a relationship healthy that is idealistic and culturally biased (and bench-marks according to which a great many intimate relationships could be judged dysfunctional).

If someone's motivation to enter a committed partnership is partly a fear of loneliness or a sense of "incompleteness," that is not *necessarily* an unhealthy thing. We all use our intimate relationships in myriad ways, which vary among couples, families, and cultures. Most people use relationships for validation and support for self-esteem, even for security of identity and a sense of continuity. For most, intimate relationships are partly a buffer against fears of aloneness or other existential anxieties, and some ambivalence about distance and closeness is part of most people's experience. Professionals do not need to declare such aspects of relationships unhealthy as long as certain practical criteria are *adequately* (as opposed to *absolutely*) met. Among others, these criteria include the ability of partners to (1) take responsibility for understanding their situation, (2) determining what they want, (3) making clear and reasonable requests of each other, (4) remaining flexible about how their needs are met, and (5) remaining open to each other's right to say "no" (or "How about this alternative?"). More generally, can they develop commitments to each other that are supportive of growth instead of constraining, with each taking responsibility for his or her part in relationship struggles?

Traditions

In the previous chapter, we defined traditions as habits of thought and action that we use to shape our lives. These habits are most open to change during transitions such as the formation of a new partnership.

The time when young adults forge new familial commitments is recognized as highly significant in most cultures, often through elaborate ceremonies invoking the weight of religious institutions, the extended family, and the community at large. The importance of the event has had to do with its role in renewing and perpetuating the family and society—a new generation assuming adult roles and the responsibility of creating its own eventual replacement. This remains widely true, though changes in developed Western societies are emerging:

- The tendency to delay marriage has increased, especially for women. We are also seeing the weakening of a tradition whereby marriage is the point at which a young woman leaves the protection of her family of origin, transferring dependency to her husband.
- Second marriages for one or both partners are much more common, which may give the transition less weight and finality.

- The association of marriage with permission to become sexually active is changing rapidly in adaptation to new social realities.
- The automatic assumption that a main purpose in getting married is to have children is less often valid.
- More options exist: a pattern of cohabiting before marriage is increasingly common and accepted. Ways of formalizing same-sex unions are still more contentious, but pressures in this direction are clearer and the case is at least more openly argued than it could have been a generation ago. Voluntarily childless couples are more common, and dual-career couples are now the norm in some social sectors.

Despite these changes, the transition to "couplehood" remains an important one, and our society and families continue to look for ways to recognize and support it. If a couple cohabits and subsequently marries, they are likely to have to address some issues twice, at the same time as new adaptations are required. Our society (and families) still has complex ideas regarding the roles of wife and husband, and the expectations associated with each (McGoldrick, 1989).

With the decision to commit to a new intimate relationship, we must adapt our traditions to those of our new partner, and this is not a small undertaking:

> Marriage requires that two people renegotiate together a myriad of issues they have previously defined individually, or that were defined by their families of origin, such as when and how to eat, sleep, talk, have sex, fight, work, and relax. The couple must decide about vacations, and how to use space, time, and money. There are also the decisions about which family traditions and rituals to retain and which ones the partners will develop for themselves. (McGoldrick, 1989, pp. 209-210)

As we suggested in the previous chapter, the couple may replicate some traditions from their families of origin, correct against others that they consider undesirable, and improvise where they feel free to be inventive. Unfortunately, we do not always replicate traditions that are in our best interests. Returning to Colin and Erica, for example, it is reasonable to consider whether Colin is inclined to let Erica meet his needs, or if he is following a tradition of exercising control by being depressed. Does the fact that Erica is "hooked" mean that she was raised to accept traditions regarding women as responsible for family members' emotional well-being?

Intimate relationships go through stages that often include a honeymoon period in which the partners idealize each other and their union. Subsequent disillusionment is common when romance gives way to reality and partners confront things about each other that are less than wonderful. Hopefully, this is a healthy step, leading to reaffirmation of commitment in the context of a more realistic (more differentiated) perspective. This is not a one-time task, but a process that is repeated for different themes as a relationship matures. There are two risks: abandoning the relationship in favor of a new romance (and, later, another and another), or a retreat into rigid disengagement.

Traditions are important to this process, with both the culture and the family of origin playing a role. Some cultures emphasize the romance of courtship and marriage, but provide few supports for dealing with disillusionment and reconciliation. Some families model dealing with disappointment and disillusionment through denial, blaming, withdrawal, defensive anger, drinking, having affairs, triangulating children or parents into the conflict, overworking, or acquiring expensive possessions (to suggest only a few possibilities). Others model realistic comfort with such relationship issues and a willingness to explore and problem solve in relation to them.

Frequently, traditions that serve us well at some times and in some contexts may, on other occasions, be problematic. Rebecca, featured in the example at the end of the previous chapter, used her family's tradition of romanticizing one's partner to mute her grandmother's scripting to distrust all men. This served her well in that it freed her to marry Daniel. The same tradition, of course, contributed to problems later—when Daniel disappointed her in what could have been a minor matter, she became too fearful to tell him what she was experiencing and how he could help.

A common tradition affecting marriage and conflict management is make war, not love, with conflict serving as "a chief mechanism by which the family deals with anxiety and 'undifferentiation'" (Bowen,

1966, cited in McCullough and Rutenberg 1989, p. 291). Unable to clearly negotiate needs for intimacy, partners use conflict in an effort to deal with anxieties over distance and closeness; fighting may be painful, but it feels safer than the vulnerability that comes with being close.

BEARING AND CARING
FOR CHILDREN

Transitions from one stage of family development to another involve realignment of boundaries (patterns of attachment and distance change) and adjustments in role (peoples' expectations of one another also change). For couples who decide to have children, this step is the beginning of a radical shift in roles, as well as a stretching of the family boundaries that will continue for many years. In addition to adding children, the family's involvements will increase with their children's friendships and relations to a range of social systems such as the schools, pediatric health care, sports organizations, music teachers, fast-food vendors, and so on.

Not all the developmental action is driven by the children during this period, either, though their effects on the family are huge. Adults' lives also change significantly as they move from young adulthood toward middle age: partners may come and go, careers unfold, and relations to aging parents often require significant adjustments. Traditions about closeness and distance, nurturance and control, divisions of domestic labor, mastery, conflict resolution, obligations to the community, values, reciprocity, and more are all critical elements of the family framework as the tasks of child rearing are undertaken.

Violence by partners against women often begins during pregnancy. This can be understood as rage over the requirement to begin establishing new boundaries, making room for another person whose demands for care and intimacy eclipse one's own. For a man who is extremely vulnerable regarding attachments (Goldner et al., 1990), this is a powerful threat of loss of intimacy and control. Similarly, it is not uncommon for child abuse to begin when the child enters toddlerhood, and begins experimenting with personal boundary setting through insistent declarations of independence (mixed with continued, unrelenting demands for caretaking).

Thus, traditions and boundary issues need careful attention for families at this stage—the opportunities for developing new strengths and maturity are clear, as are the risks of establishing patterns with ominous implications for everyone concerned.

Boundaries: The Young Child's Needs

As we discussed in Chapter 1, boundary issues in early childhood are of fundamental importance. Learning to form and maintain secure attachments and developing confidence about moving out to explore the world of other people and things—these contribute much to our later happiness and success. Indeed, we have argued that the early experience of managing boundaries reasonably, competently, and safely is crucial to the authorship of identity.

Ideally, the goal of the family is to provide children with richness and diversity (open boundaries) and, at the same time, the protection and support that comes with a clear structure (clarity of boundaries). When these conditions are adequately met, the child will develop a secure sense of self. With this solid base, she or he can also learn to accommodate to other people.

Reaching out from a secure base, we gradually acquire "the ability to decenter . . . to assume another's perspective, especially when that alternative perspective is different from one's own" (Rosen, 1988, p. 323). This is not a matter of substituting one perspective for another so much as developing a more differentiated capacity to manage multiple perspectives.

Having a "secure base" (Bowlby, 1988) provides a context within which a rich identity can be composed. Being supported in venturing forth from this base, reaching out to other people and exploring the world provides a basis for developing a capacity for empathy, reciprocity, and mastery—all significant for future success in the areas of love and work, and for the development of socially viable values. It follows that one important attribute of the parents is to be attuned. Attunement implies an awareness of and responsiveness to the child's needs for attachment and space, and readiness to adaptively grow.

In brief, what we hope for on behalf of young children is that they will have good enough opportunities to develop:

- The beginnings of a differentiated and secure sense of self
- The beginnings of a clear, differentiated sense of other people
- The foundations for a differentiated view of the world—its possibilities and constraints
- A sense of comfort with their needs and a beginning appreciation of their ability to meet them adequately
- A beginning understanding of reciprocity, which involves the belief that they have something to offer others and the capacity for generosity in the give and take of important relationships

Parents who have themselves been unable to create lives incorporating these qualities will be less able to support their children in discovering them, so a lack of clarity can be passed on from one generation to another (though each has fresh opportunities for innovation as well).

Boundaries: The Parents and Systems Beyond the Family

Beyond the developmental needs of the individual child, parenthood raises boundary issues for the new parents (and for the family as a whole) that are also far reaching. When there are two parents, an important task is to find ways to maintain intimacy as a couple in what has now become a three-person household. Distance to protect the couple's autonomy while they work out arrangements that are best for them is obviously vital, but new or heightened dependency in some areas is common as well. For single parents, the task of maintaining supportive relationships with other adults can be doubly difficult.

Children present a high level of demand, and the joys of parenthood are normally mixed with the feeling that one's personal resources are severely stretched, and one's flexibility in coping with often unpredictable demands is challenged daily. The ability of new parents to respond effectively is enhanced if they are properly supported and protected by the systems with which they are engaged: their extended families, their networks of friends, their employers, and social services (health, education, recreation etc.).

The daunting challenges facing new parents individually and as partners include (among many others):

- Physical demands: the physical care of children requires considerable time and energy, despite sleep deprivation, fatigue, and exposure to pediatric infections.
- Psychological demands: chronic high stress levels, especially learning to cope with the extensiveness of young children's dependencies, set a difficult context within which numerous other adjustments have to be made.
- Having to find ways to protect their intimacy as a couple while incorporating new intimate relationships with the child(ren).
- Renegotiating responsibilities for the myriad tasks associated with running a family.
- Reorganizing and redefining every relationship they have— friends, parents, siblings, etc.—while introducing a new person into these multiple systems.

Although it is important to consider the effects of parenthood on couples (in two-parent families), we also need to recognize that even in highly egalitarian relationships the experience of parenthood is different for men and women. Because of this, it presents special opportunities for growth as well as risks to the relationship.

For the woman, the biological impact of pregnancy and birth continue for several months, and is very significant (Bradt, 1989, p. 242). Hormonal changes and lowered immunity to infectious disease are added to fatigue and sleep deprivation as a context within which drastic relationship adjustments have to be made, new work arrangements negotiated, opportunities for intimacy and support created, and a host of new tasks learned. Especially since women are often strongly socialized to the view that the emotional needs of the family (including their partner) continue to be their primary responsibility, the incidence of postpartum depression should not surprise us (15 percent of new mothers experience full depression, 50 percent some degree of a less debilitating "postpartum blues").

The number and diversity of tasks that must be mastered, together with social and familial traditions, exert a tremendous pressure toward differentiated roles for women and men. Obviously, some differentiation is inevitable during pregnancy, but the pressures extend well beyond what is biologically dictated. Hopefully, the couple will make this transition without the burden of accommodating to new demands falling primarily to the woman, and differentiation with respect to roles will not contribute to a significant loss of mutuality and understanding.

The arrival of children also requires yet another revision of relationships to the extended family. Not uncommonly, they are called on for instrumental assistance in various forms (parent relief, for example), for emotional support, and for advice regarding the many decisions that child rearing demands. The relationship of grandparents to new grandchildren also needs to be worked out, with different needs to be accommodated regarding the level and nature of involvement.

The extended family is faced with a balancing act. It is often called on to find ways to be supportive, while remaining sensitive to the couple's need for distance, for room to maintain their continued independence as a family and to develop their own traditions.

Major adjustments are also often required in relationships to friends, especially when a first child is born. Friends who do not themselves have children may well not understand the new constraints and demands that the parents are coping with. Some friends may have difficulty accepting the decreased availability of new parents, who cannot provide the same levels of involvement as in the past. Others respond very well, of course, with interest and support.

Validation regarding their competence to fulfill a difficult new role is important to young parents, as is emotional support, information, and instrumental help. Friends may be as active as extended family members in meeting such needs; with friends who have children themselves, there is often a very significant exchange of information, goods such as toys and clothing, and services such as transportation and babysitting.

Finally, parenting brings with it involvement with numerous formal social systems that serve children: health services, schools, and recreational organizations—even, in less happy situations, child welfare. With these systems, working relationships are required, and can easily involve emotionally charged issues (the first week of day care is seldom easy for parents or children, for example, and children's inherent vulnerability can make health problems especially worrisome).

Traditions

In our culture, many ritualized traditions celebrate events up to and surrounding the birth of a child, and support may fall off afterward (unless partners and extended families respond well). This loss of social support at a critical time can work with biological and other factors to increase vulnerability to postpartum depression for some women.

As we have noted, people need to rework several aspects of their relationships with partners, extended family, and others when they have children. For couples, values such as egalitarianism, mutual support, and balancing work with home responsibilities are put to a severe test (Bradt, 1989). Since parenting is such a basic human endeavor, it is no surprise that strong cultural and familial traditions are there to support (or complicate) the transition.

As always, in relating to traditions about child rearing, the parents have choices about replicating or correcting the traditions they themselves were raised with, or of inventing something new. Couples have two extended families and their traditions to contend with, and often a degree of cultural difference as well. This expands the choice of what traditions to replicate or modify, but also presents opportunities for conflict. Daniel, whom we introduced in the last chapter, experienced his own parents' marriage as a battle between two contrasting family traditions: his father's family's cult of masculinity and his mother's defense of her family's gentler orientation.

Accommodations among different traditions may be required with respect to a number of potentially emotionally charged issues:

- Goals and approaches for providing nurture and structure; managing issues such as discipline, chores, expectations regarding manners, permissiveness, and generosity (with time, affection, and material things).
- Priorities in socialization and interests, such as sports, music, religious instruction, reading, free time, and television.
- Other aspects of parenting style—managing play, feeding schedules, and bedtimes are examples.
- The allocation of roles such as the disciplinarian, the nurturer, the emotional supporter. Who interrupts work to parent? Who

negotiates with grandparents to define their relationship to the grandchildren? Who manages relations with the schools and other necessary services? Who hires the baby-sitter? Who suffers through the birthday parties?

- Continued recognition of partners as individuals and as a couple, distinct from the parent role.

For many new parents, relations with their own parents and between their own parents and their children are a very significant issue: "The grandparenting function has wide variations. . . . For many families this role is steeped in tradition" (McCullough and Rutenberg, 1989, p. 297). For parents with limited resources (single, socially isolated, or economically deprived parents), dependency on grandparents for instrumental help and other supports may be strong, and can cast the grandparents in a coparenting role. In other situations, the grandparenting role may be more restricted. Some families develop a role that emphasizes nurturing; in others the grandparents feel free to act as disciplinarians.

With respect to extended family members generally, some tacitly understand the need for sensitive supports at this time, while others may become caught up in their own traditions and be unable to respond effectively. They may resurrect loyalty issues, and even be angry about the arrival of the child in hidden ways, experiencing him or her as an intruder. The child may be seen as a source of anxiety (needing their intervention to protect him or her against the neglect or incompetence of the new parents). The event may bring in-law difficulties to the forefront: criticism of the young mother for continuing her career instead of devoting herself totally to her family would be an example.

CARING FOR ADOLESCENTS

Progress from early childhood through late adolescence involves a continuance of basic developmental themes as well as dramatic changes for the growing person and the family. If the tasks discussed in the previous stage involved providing for high levels of dependency and external structure, the tasks associated with parenting an adolescent require a significant change in direction. The demand to offer more distance or space, and to allow the teenager's growing capacity for self-responsibility to replace parental authority in managing behavior is increasing: "The adaptations in family structure and organization required to handle the tasks of adolescence are so basic that the family itself is transformed from a unit that protects and nurtures young children to one that is a preparation center for the adolescent's entrance into the world of adult responsibilities and commitments" (Garcia-Preto, 1989, p. 255).

However, the issues being addressed in this stage of development are far from entirely new. They are, as we have said, variations on themes. The themes, as in childhood, have to do with boundary management, autonomy, and identity. Still, declarations of independence by a two-year-old are a very different matter than when the protagonist is seventeen, is larger than his or her parents, and has a driver's license and a colorful vocabulary.

As with other stages, development is occurring for all the family's generations and issues have a way of interacting with each other. At the same time as the teenager's hormone levels escalate, grandparents may well be in physical decline, and the "middle generation" family members have to reorient their lives and relationships. This often entails a reduced preoccupation with child rearing and a renewed focus on themselves and the priorities that will provide them with direction and satisfaction as the children become autonomous.

The Teenager's Boundary Needs

Authorship of identity is never a nonissue, but it is an especially strong developmental imperative during adolescence. A new physical body has to be recognized and valued, and new cognitive abilities contribute to the identification of the self with more abstract values, ideals, models, and possibilities. There are personal styles to be experimented with, career options to consider, talents to discover, and styles of relating to explore. There is steady growth toward full physical stature, sexual maturity, a license to drive, and legal access to adult pleasures such as alcohol, tobacco, and questionable movies. All this means that the quest for identity and independence is more complex and fraught with risk and possibilities.

Maria Doyle's reaction to boundary issues in her family is dramatic, but the issues themselves are not at all unusual: she needs more space and new traditions to discover her own competence and self-authority, and her family is having difficulty recognizing and responding effectively to that need. As with other adolescents, Maria's need is not simply for more distance. She needs space, but she needs it within the security of reliable attachments.

Writing about toddlers and their foundational efforts to establish a degree of independence, Mahler (Mahler, Pine, and Bergman, 1975) describes what she calls a "rapprochement" crisis, in which the child, having experimented with independence, becomes anxious and clingy. As Kegan (1982) emphasizes, depression or anxiety in adolescence can be an expression of the same ambivalence: we want to grow toward independence, but are also frightened by the prospect. When such fears are strong enough, the young adult may be driven to abdicate the responsibilities of adulthood for the security of continued dependence. It is for this reason that adolescents and young adults are the favored recruitment targets for cults and other organizations that are willing to take them on as dependents, promising to love them without expecting them to ever grow up.

As in caring for young children, the parents of adolescents such as Maria Doyle must find a balance. Over time, this balance involves increasing flexibility and the ability to accommodate new directions and priorities in the young person. At the same time, enough structure to keep the young person feeling attached, stable, and safe is equally necessary. Although we are perhaps more familiar clinically with families that have responded to the young person's need for space by becoming too rigidly restrictive, the difficulties faced by young people from families where adequate structures are missing are no less serious.

The literature concerning adolescent development commonly stresses growth toward independence and autonomy:

> As a result of sexual maturation, moves toward solidifying an identity and establishing autonomy from the family (which are really lifelong developmental processes) are accelerated during adolescence. . . . To establish autonomy they need to become gradually more responsible for their own decision making and yet feel the security of parental guidance. (Garcia-Preto, 1989, p. 257)

There has been considerable confusion about the idea of autonomy in the clinical literature over the years. If the goal of independence is taken to imply a state of functioning that requires radically diminished inputs from others in the form of help, advice, information, and validation, then we risk placing unrealistic expectations on young people and ourselves. Dependency in the form of needing such supports from others is simply part of the human condition throughout life.

However, important changes in maturity occur between early adolescence and young adulthood, and these do have to do with increased independence. Partly, our capacities and our networks become more complex; partly, we develop the clear boundaries we need to cultivate our own competence and responsibility.

What this means, first, is increased responsibility for independent decision making. Although remaining dependent on others for information, ideas, and support, adolescents are increasingly perceived as the primary authors of their actions. They move to the stage where they can drive cars without another person beside them, helping them assess traffic and road conditions, reminding them about all the rules of the road, and consulting as they make all the choices that the task of driving requires. Similarly, they become the center for choice regarding relationships, career, recreational activities, self-care, and many other lifestyle matters.

Increased responsibility accompanies an increase in personal accountability, or responsibility for the outcomes of our actions. Even under the law, the extent to which we are accountable as thirteen-year-olds is limited, while a twenty-three-year-old faces the same rules and consequences for breaking them as any other adult. The formal position of the law expresses a much broader social and familial shift with steadily increasing levels of accountability being assigned.

Although we are never independent in the sense of not needing other people, during the period leading into young adulthood it is common for our dependencies to become more widely distributed. In early adolescence, we are relatively strongly dependent on our families of origin (or surrogates) to meet physical, cognitive, and emotional needs. By young adulthood, we have many other supports relevant to such needs: intimates from beyond the family, mentors, peers, and colleagues play a much greater role—without necessarily replacing the family, they do supplement it and reduce its centrality.

A final important sense in which we become more independent has to do with reciprocity: although other people are still meeting our needs, we see ourselves and are seen by others as able (and obligated) to give generously in return. These quids pro quo define our relationships as equitable and adult, while without them we remain more childlike in our dependencies.

Increased responsibility, accountability, reciprocity, and a network of supports outside the family are impressive developmental achievements requiring parental sensitivity to the adolescent's readiness for growth. Combining independence with accountability is not a simple matter of "letting go" but a subtler balancing of permissions, supports, and expectations. A capacity for reciprocity is rooted partly in self-esteem, a product of reliable nurturing, but it also requires modeling commitments to others and respect for their needs and rights. Building a network of personal resources extending well beyond the family requires permission, but also encouragement and guidance. And all these changes require patience on the part of adults with false starts and unsteady progress. We do not achieve maturity with a single step off the edge of the nest and the discovery that the air will support us. Our physical and social world is too complex for that.

Boundaries: The Parents' Needs

As young people become more emancipated from their parents, the parents become emancipated from them (Garcia-Preto, 1989). Loss of the parent role can represent a challenge to the parents' self-esteem, but can also be an opportunity to renew relationships between partners or with other adults.

Sometimes the departure of young adults means parents can no longer avoid issues that were kept buried while the stresses of parenting served as an alternative focus—discomfort with the increased absence of children can be rooted in a fear of having to confront marital problems. Partners who originally married to solve boundary issues will often have problems letting go of their children, if they have not developed the skills and understanding required for effective boundary negotiation.

Often, rediscovering new intimacy and shared interests is a challenge, especially with teenagers still living in the house. Despite their emancipation, they continue to take up room—and teenagers who are very jealous of their own boundaries may have less appreciation for the same needs in other members of their household. Conflicts in families with adolescents very frequently have to do with parents feeling that their right to personal space is difficult to protect as the stream of visiting friends swells and the volume on the stereo system edges up.

The demands posed by boundary negotiations with adolescents are difficult enough to overwhelm some families. We commented earlier that the challenge to boundaries posed by the toddler's experiments with independence might explain why child abuse begins at that stage in some families. In other families, abuse emerges (or reemerges) with adolescence, and vulnerability to sexual abuse is greater as children (especially girls) move toward sexual maturity and the proper protection of clear boundaries is not present. In addition to abuse, the risk of extreme emotional rejection and its consequences can be strong at this stage:

> Parents who are overwhelmed by the tasks of adolescence may give up all responsibility and call outside authorities to take control. Frustrated and feeling hopeless about changing . . . the expulsion of adolescents . . . may lead to a permanent family rift . . . [and] the casualty rate due to other-inflicted or self-inflicted violence . . . is high. Vulnerability to exploitation is also high. (Garcia-Preto, 1989, p. 265)

Traditions

There are tremendous differences between cultures and families regarding how adolescence is understood and dealt with, and the narratives recommended to young women are highly dissimilar from those young men are persuaded to adopt. The ages that define the stage, and the desirable outcomes attached to it by the community are so variable that some commentators conclude that adolescence is purely a social construction. If so, it is nevertheless true that most if not all cultures have traditions that recognize a shift from childhood dependency to sexual maturity and responsible adulthood.

An important aspect of traditions is that it is natural for adolescents to challenge them. One of the tasks facing families and society generally is to accommodate the young person's questioning of established values and behavioral norms, without conflict escalating to damaging levels (Erickson, 1968). Families and cultures respond differently to adolescent rebelliousness: when the response is an abdication of authority the consequences can be chaotic, while overly harsh and rigid efforts at containment can easily become abusive.

Sexuality, of course, is the focus for a host of powerful and sometimes convoluted traditions, and these are very influential in shaping responses to adolescence. Adolescents' beliefs about their sexuality are written into their developing identity, so their perspective on sex and sexuality cannot help but shape their view of themselves: "The physical and sexual changes that take place have a dramatic effect on how adolescents describe and evaluate themselves, and radically alter how they are perceived by others. Coping with this upsurge [in sexuality] . . . is a major task for all family members" (Garcia-Preto, 1989, p. 258).

It is a rare society or family that does not have some ambivalence about sexuality, especially in young people, but general attitudes can range from relative comfort and openness to a rigid, fearful repression of this aspect of our nature.

Traditions will tend to dictate the quantity and quality of information about sexuality that is shared with adolescents: How are their biological changes received (denial, celebration, or embarrassment)? How are the potential risks and benefits of sexual activity discussed, if at all? More important, what are the prevailing attitudes and myths regarding women's and men's sexuality? What traditions are present regarding homosexuality, and how do these impact the identity and attitudes of the young person? What relationship values (respect, equality, nurturing, and reciprocity, for example) are implied in the traditions that are most strongly communicated?

Boundary issues are so critical in adolescence that the family at this time may function as a laboratory in which lifelong traditions for boundary maintenance are learned. We noted earlier that some families have traditions that involve using conflict to establish boundaries. These may be brought into play as the family grapples with the need to redefine boundaries in response to adolescent development—and for some families sexuality is especially likely to evoke this kind of prob-

set

lem, being an emotionally loaded issue that demands good boundary maintenance.

Sexuality is not the only highly charged boundary issue for families at this stage. Also important are social and familial traditions for coping with loss, which becomes an issue when the adolescent contemplates leaving home. Some cultures and families (John Doyle's is an example) adhere to traditional beliefs that independence is dangerous or disloyal. They may "tend to become overprotective, and parents may try to exert control by reinforcing excessive childlike behavior" (Garcia-Preto, 1989, p. 265). Other situations may be made easier by traditions that acknowledge loss as a predictable aspect of life and a manageable if difficult aspect of most transitions.

Finally, adolescents can be strongly impacted by social and familial traditions regarding commitments to areas of mastery. Societies develop educational systems and traditions of apprenticeship and mentoring that are designed to help the young discover and develop the talents that will eventually become adult occupations. The more complex a society, the more difficult this is, since there are more avenues to consider and the skill requirements for many may be relatively high. The more specialized the interest pursued the longer the preparation is likely to be, and the more difficult it may be to find effective adult mentors or teachers.

The issue is not simply preparation for the employment market, but the more general development of mastery—a sense of competence and efficacy that affects identity and performance in many roles. As Erickson (1968) and others emphasize, the adolescent's enthusiastic commitments to sports, computers, cars, or rock 'n' roll is often experimental (or at least temporary), but it is nevertheless very important. "Roles may be tried on, prized briefly, and then discarded or clung to in an attempt to anchor a sense of self. While some of these roles are consistent with family values, they frequently challenge, if not assault, the mores of the family" (Garcia-Preto, 1989, p. 261).

Experimentation with areas of mastery can be a creative opportunity to learn about options and to enrich one's sense of self. It is also a chance to come to terms with social and familial traditions: to replicate, correct, or innovate in relation to them. As with sexuality, it is now widely recognized that young women and men are treated very differently in our scripting regarding mastery—arguably in ways that disadvantage both genders, and clearly in ways that are more restrictive for women. For both men and women, however, the most difficult outcome respecting this issue is familial scripting to be *globally* incompetent, as we know from clinical work with clients whose belief is that they are somehow fundamentally flawed and are convinced they will fail in any adult role they attempt.

LAUNCHING THE YOUNG ADULT

When and how one leaves the nest varies widely from person to person, between men and women, from family to family, and across cultures. But, in one form or another, we all face choices about relinquishing the comfort and control (or confusion and conflict) of our family of origin, freeing ourselves socially and emotionally to form independent adult relationships, families of our own (perhaps), and to find our own means of support and livelihood.

The process of emancipation from the family of origin in young adulthood is in some ways a distinct phase of development, though it is also partly just an extension and consolidation of developments that have been occurring throughout adolescence. "The existence of positive relationships with grown children represents the culmination of a long process of gradually 'letting go,' starting in childhood, gaining momentum in adolescence and leading to some kind of physical separation of the young adult through college or work" (McCullough and Rutenberg, 1989, pp. 293-294).

Some writers define the stage in terms of physical departure: "The period of time when the individual has physically, if not emotionally, left his or her family of origin, but has not yet established a family of procreation" (Aylmer, 1989, p. 191). The problem with this kind of definition is that so many exceptions spring easily to mind:

- A farming family simply builds an extension on its home to accommodate a young adult who is about to marry. She or he does not physically leave home (not to any distance, in any event).

- A highly spiritual young person enters a religious order and takes vows of celibacy, thereby choosing a career path that involves physically leaving home but never establishing "a family of procreation."
- A gay young adult establishes an independent household, career, and committed sexual relationships, but no family of procreation.
- A young woman becomes pregnant without marrying and elects to stay with her parents while raising her child, establishing a new family of procreation without physically leaving home.
- A young person with a debilitating chronic health problem cannot realistically leave home to live independently, but still needs changes to her relationship with her parents that recognize her maturing into adulthood.

Different life paths are chosen for social and economic reasons, and variations are common due to history and culture. Undoubtedly, diverse paths each offer special problems and challenges, but few preclude continued growth toward maturity. The task is not to achieve physical distance, to marry and have children. These are worthy goals, but they are just indicators of more basic processes:

- Reworking relationships to family of origin toward more equality and reciprocity, and diminished authority and control
- Commitments in the areas of love and work that share priority with and often supersede commitments to parents and extended family; long-term commitments to people and organizations separate from the family, and with which other members of the family may have little (if any) connection
- A life narrative for which authorship is perceived and felt to belong to the individual more than to parents and other authority figures—and which is increasingly focused on a cast of characters selected by the person in addition to those inherited through family membership

The shift is from dependency (in childhood) to ultimate reconnection from a more autonomous, equal position. This implies a transfer of responsibilities: parents relinquish power and control, and offspring give up dependency for reciprocity. The goal is not distance in the sense of rigidly restricted attachments, but a reorganization in which dependencies are redistributed and expectations or obligations are renegotiated. Often this is accomplished through a process that includes a period of relative distance as a prelude to establishing new types of attachments, but this is not necessarily the case for all relationships.

Boundaries and the Young Adult

Levinson (1978), writing about men, suggests on the basis of his research that young adults are driven by two needs: one to explore and grow, the other to maintain a sense of personal continuity, stability, and structure. Aylmer (1989) sees evidence that similar basic motives are important to women as well: "Thus both autonomy and attachment are functional adult goals, in love and work, for both men and women" (p. 192). As we have repeatedly suggested, these themes are about boundary maintenance, and are crucial throughout life, with variations that characterize different stages.

A boundary issue affecting young adults (and which, as we noted earlier, is likely to affect committed intimate relationships) has to do with distinguishing fusion from intimacy. According to some (Kegan, 1982) the first entails using relationships to create a sense of self, the second more of a sharing of self. In our terms, young adults are consolidating their capacity for reciprocity in relationships. We may never really stop using our relationships for self-definition and validation; what changes is the extent to which this is (over time) an equal exchange.

A very similar concern is sometimes expressed in terms of *enmeshment* and *cutoff,* both considered symptoms of unresolved issues in relation to the family of origin. Rigid attachments and rigid distancing can obviously be problematic because they restrict the options available to the people concerned. However, strong distancing or cutoff in a toxic relationship can be a good thing (it is sometimes a sound option for people who have been severely abused by their families). Also, periods of enmeshment are normal for young people (falling in love involves a period of strong attachment and little tolerance for distance). The question is whether rigidity is generalized across relationships and over time, or if a broader view of the person's life shows evidence of flexibility managing the rhythm of contact and withdrawal.

As with adolescents, young adults normally experience some ambivalence about growth to adult independence and responsibility. Having to set one's own goals and boundaries can be anxiety provoking, and progress does not take place in tidy steps. Sometimes efforts to separate are highly conflicted and confused, and one witnesses what has been termed "pseudolaunching"—which can involve various unhealthy flight responses into addictions, or a precipitous marriage, or some other variation on running away. There may also be a pattern of continued rigid dependence on the family for support, which becomes a problem if the young adult's personal competence and responsibility remain underdeveloped as a result.

Boundaries: The Young Adult's Parents

As with other transitions that we tend to think of as defined by milestones in the lives of the younger generation, significant changes also affect other family members with equal force.

Parents have an opportunity to renegotiate their relationship to their children. The same issues of loss that begin to emerge in adolescence continue and may be heightened with a young adult's departure, and as the familiar parenting functions of caretaking and control lose importance. On the other hand, a more equal, reciprocal relationship may be a welcome change for many families.

Continuing a shift begun in adolescence, parents increasingly refocus on their lives beyond the parent role; in two-parent families this means a new emphasis on the marriage (which changes somewhat in its function for the partners). Some couples achieve greater intimacy; others adopt a greater distance from each other (less intimacy, but also less conflict). In still others, long-buried conflicts may be less easily contained:

> By this time the marriage has endured many shifts; from the more romantic idealistic, and/or sexual emphasis, through the more prosaic, child-rearing, teammate era. These previous sequences might have culminated in a relationship that is seasoned, stable and more satisfactory than at any other time. It might also be more conflictual, more tenuous, and more alien-

ated. In the absence of children, the conjugal bond, whatever its nature, will gain prominence. By the same token, more reliance on it will make existing strains more obvious. (McCullough and Rutenberg,1989, pp. 289-290)

Young adults who are accustomed to feeling responsible for their parents' happiness have difficulties to confront at this stage. The task is to leave responsibility for their parents' lives with the parents. This can mean less responsibility for relieving tensions between the parents, and also letting go of some of the resentments and disillusionments that have colored the parent-child relationship to this point.

When sufficiently clear boundaries have developed, the family will be able to adequately meet key new demands for flexibility presented by the young adult's growth: "(1) an ability to tolerate separation and independence while remaining connected; (2) a tolerance for differentness and ambiguity in career identity of adult children; and (3) the acceptance of a range of intense emotional attachments and life styles outside the immediate family" (Aylmer, 1989, p. 195).

Career development is a critical part of entry to adult status for many young adults. As we noted in our discussion of adolescence, this can involve some experimentation and vacillation, which may cause anxiety for the parents. If there is sufficient clarity of boundaries, they will be able to find ways to be supportive without attempting to reassert inappropriate controls. John Doyle's experience illustrates less happy possibilities: his leaving home for university stimulated efforts at control via strong emotional pressures (the price of freedom being guilt in his case).

Traditions

Throughout late adolescence and young adulthood, rethinking the traditions with which we have grown up is a critical task. The young person and the family are required to renegotiate their relationships, as we have discussed. Part of this renegotiation involves the young person challenging the family's traditions, and deciding which to continue to use, which to reject, and which to modify. This is a test for the family's flexibility: can it maintain solid commitments at the same time as its values and traditions are being subject to scrutiny? If rejection of cherished beliefs and ways of dealing with life occurs, are the conflicts that this triggers managed adequately, or do they threaten alienation between the generations? "Success is probably determined more by the degree, quality, tone, and completeness with which original family relationships . . . are renegotiated than any other factor" (Aylmer, 1989, p. 191).

Fundamental change often implies loss and families that handle change well also have traditions for dealing with loss. Because the relationship changes that occur during the transition to young adulthood are fundamental, and require the family to give up an established set of dependencies and degree of control, it has been popular to describe this transition as painful—the "empty nest syndrome" has been widely discussed. However, many families find much to enjoy in the changes that take place, and couples find the freedom to rework their marriage enables them to make it richer and more gratifying. Always, at every stage, transitions provide opportunities to grow as well as to suffer: Do our traditions help us adapt creatively, or keep us stuck in patterns that are not going to work well in a new reality?

John Doyle's extended family treated the move to adulthood as a betrayal, and John's willingness to exercise choice by rejecting traditions rooted in bigotry were greeted with an ongoing effort to punish him (and his family) for his disloyalty. Daniel and Rebecca were strongly affected by Daniel's belief that he would ultimately fail in his bid to reject his father's abusiveness and sexism, by falling into substance abuse and/or mental illness. Both examples clearly illustrate the difficulties that can emerge when familial traditions impede rather than support adaptive change.

Every family has different traditions regarding how much autonomy is considered desirable, and how it is to be negotiated. In some, choices of friends and intimates, and initiation into the world of work or higher education are handled autonomously by the young person, with the parents accepting a supportive role. In others, the parents will assume an ongoing prerogative to attempt to direct the choices the young adult makes in these important domains. This, of course, involves significant cultural differences and strongly different experiences for women versus men.

There is a wide range of traditions regarding how autonomy is achieved. In some families, the approach is simply to acknowledge the changes that are occurring and to openly discuss how to manage them, coupled with applause for the young person's successes and growth. In others, autonomy may be achieved only through rebellion and whatever conflict that triggers. Others have traditions whereby autonomy is achieved through physical and/or social distancing, and a degree of emotional cutoff. Again, there are strong variations on such themes due to culture, and the script for men is often very different than for women.

The autonomy of the young adult is strongly evident in two domains: (1) career, and (2) adult commitments to intimate relationships outside the family. Love and work are central to our satisfaction with life, and every family and culture has traditions that will affect the young person's choices at this critical juncture. Traditions shape our decisions about whom to commit to: how important are physical appearance, wealth and social status, intelligence, particular values and tastes, for example? With respect to work, the culture and family will have influenced the young adult's beliefs about the importance of achievements, material success, the kinds of work that are (or are not) worthwhile—generally, what does one have to do to be a success in life?

ATTACHMENT AND DISENGAGEMENT
IN LATER LIFE

In the developmental stages we have discussed so far, we have not ignored the extended family, but we have focused largely on what transpires for children and their parents. At the same time as young adults are establishing an independent life, perhaps marrying and venturing into parenthood themselves, their grandparents are frequently adapting to old age. The final stage of growth for us to consider concerns the grandparents' generation. This transition also involves the middle generation, which, while they are accommodating increased independence in their children, may be working out new relationships to aging parents. The new arrangements may be characterized by a reversal of dependency whereby the elders now look increasingly to their adult children for care.

As with any stage, adaptations to aging require a capacity for change: "The successful functioning of families in later life requires a flexibility in structure, roles, and responses to new developmental needs and challenges" (Walsh, 1989, p. 326). As with other stages, the adjustments the family makes to the needs of aging members are affected by what it has learned in earlier transitions: "Each family's response to later-life challenges evolves from earlier family patterns developed for stability and integration" (Walsh, 1989, p. 312).

The Older Person's Boundary Needs

With the launching of young adults, the family begins a process of contraction, with a loss of members and a loss of roles. When children leave, the role of parent is diminished; with retirement the occupational role is lost and an important network of colleagues may also shrink significantly.

Reverting from being a family with children to being a single person or couple living alone again can entail feelings of loss, as can the attenuation of valued roles. However, for many people the changes have a positive aspect: less stress and responsibility can be welcome, and couples at this stage often report increasing satisfaction from their marriage. A chance to focus more inwardly as individuals or couples can be associated with isolation, but it can also contribute to the development of interests and capacities that could not be explored in earlier, busier times.

Physical changes interact with social and familial transitions, and progress from middle to old age entails diminishing strength and vitality. Actual incapacitation is by no means inevitable, but some loss of physical abilities is to be expected if one lives long enough, as is the diminution of cognitive abilities to some degree.

Family members growing up and leaving, loss of role, and loss of physical and mental abilities at some point combine with a loss of friends and partners through death. Unfortunately, it is sometimes surrounding such potentially emotionally painful issues that people distance themselves, perhaps because of a sense of futility, perhaps fearing the intimacy that shared grief promotes.

To the extent that aging is accompanied by increased dependency, boundaries change so that extended family members, neighbors, friends, and service providers may accept responsibility for tasks and needs that were managed unassisted in the past. Comfort with this new reality may not come easily, though it is likely to be more acceptable if it is managed sensitively by the caretakers. Basically, the elderly person exercises the skills that have been necessary in the past for boundary maintenance: engaging others to get needs met (continuing to maintain reciprocity as much as possible), and maintaining autonomy when appropriate. Adjusting to increased dependence without losing one's sense of competence depends on the continuing ability to balance attachment and distance.

For someone who has been heavily invested in a career, a sudden change to retirement can be very difficult. At best, there is a need to rework boundaries within the home (for people with partners), and with extended family and other social systems.

The loss of a partner can be one of the more difficult transitions to be faced with advancing age: grief is often accompanied by a degree of withdrawal, though emotional support is normally required as well. As grieving is worked through, learning to live alone can also take time and support. Later, one may see "shifts to new activities and interest in others. A realignment of relationships in the family system also occurs with this transition" (Walsh, 1989, p. 316; see also Walsh, 1999).

A final common set of boundary issues occurs in relation to the grandparent role. Families and cultures have varying expectations of grandparents, and the type of involvement expected can demand a subtle balance between being available and respecting the younger nuclear family's autonomy: "Overinvolved grandparents can be drawn into marital conflicts, particularly regarding parenting issues.... While most ... may be relieved not to have primary caretaking demands, the expectation to be a resource and yet not an interference can be as burdensome.... The discomfort ... leads some elders to cut off from their families" (Walsh, 1989, p. 318).

The Middle Generation's Boundary Needs and Tasks

For the middle generation, seeing their parents get older may be a stimulus to attend to relationships with them, resolving unfinished business while there is still time to do so. Topics previously avoided may be broached, old barriers set aside, and new connections established. Even very rigid boundaries, maintained out of a felt need for safety, may be opened somewhat as a previously powerful parent becomes less threatening.

Managing increasing dependency on the part of aging parents is an issue that can require sensitivity. Adult children may not always stay clear about the importance of older parents maintaining responsibility for their lives and relationships. Interference with living arrangements, lifestyle choices, even friends or new partners can be an unwelcome intrusion for someone who is accustomed to self-sufficiency.

The requirement is therefore that the middle generation makes appropriate judgments about the elder's level of need. Withholding necessary supports is one risk, while overgeneralizing dependency can be another. This occurs with the assumption that diminishing competence in one area implies incompetence in others as well, with the consequence that the elderly person feels infantilized. This risk is heightened when a partner dies: adult children accustomed to seeing their parents as a couple may think that the death of one leaves the other incapacitated (an especially tempting idea if physical abilities are in decline). A fresh appraisal of the surviving parent and her or his competencies as an individual is required.

Chronic illness, when it occurs, is a strong invitation to become more involved, offering increased levels of help and support. Clarity in such cases involves caregivers making decisions about how they will weigh this new responsibility against their other commitments and their own needs. Also, part of coming to terms with increased dependency for the elder may include understanding the limits to the demands it is reasonable to place on any one relationship.

As a parent ages, the level of demand he or she poses may increase to the point where it is necessary for caretakers in the middle generation to say "no" to pulls to give more and more. If institutionalization has to be considered as an option, guilt can contribute to a blurring of boundaries: "Feelings of guilt and abandonment can make the decision for institutionalization highly stressful for families, and particularly for adult daughters, on whom the caretaking responsibility is typically concentrated" (Walsh, 1989, pp. 322-323; see also Walsh, 1999).

In general, feelings of guilt and the recognition that very real losses are occurring can make maintaining clarity of boundaries especially difficult. Losses and grief can pose confusing boundary issues, with some people distancing themselves at a point where their support is needed, while others become rigidly attached as a way of avoiding feelings of loss, failing to respect the elder's ability to work through loss and carry on.

Traditions

Every culture has traditions that shape how members relate to their elders, and families subscribe to influential beliefs about being old. Together, culture and the family create models of aging, which affect how elders are regarded by themselves and others:

- There are beliefs about age and vitality. In some cultures and families, the prevailing model for being an elder may involve continued physical vigor and energy. In others, the expectation that weakness and incapacitation accompany age will be stronger.
- Some cultures and families prescribe respect for elders, ascribing a heightened wisdom to people who have lived a long time and have a perspective on life that comes with extended experience. In other cases, the elderly might be stereotyped as mental has-beens, out of date, and with little to contribute relevant to the needs of the generations that are busy taking care of business.
- Some cultures and families may have clear roles that elders can assume and out of which they continue to make a contribution to social and familial life. Others regard the elderly as redundant at best, and an economic liability at worst.
- Some cultures and families provide a model for elders as fulfilled and capable of actualization, while others may see old age as just a period of futility—the loss of possibilities and an end to life.
- When old age is accompanied by frailty, it becomes evident that cultures and families vary regarding their prescriptions about sickness, dependency, filial obligations, and community responsibility for assuring ongoing support.
- Finally, cultural and family traditions shape the grandparent role in myriad ways. Grandparents may be stern authority figures, enforcing high standards of behavior. In other families, the expectation may be that they are free to be permissive and generous in ways that the parents are not, even acting as a kindly refuge from parental controls and conflicts. Freud must have had the latter case in mind when he suggested that children and their grandparents are strongly tied to each other because they have a common enemy.

FURTHER VARIATIONS

We have commented frequently enough on gender and culture as sources of variation on the family life cycle that their importance for maintaining a differentiated view of "normal" development should be established. Other avenues that people and their families follow are identified here as possibilities to which clinicians need to be sensitive. Opportunities for innovation are unlimited, so no list of different developmental pathways can be complete. Our point really is that although patterns and themes are useful to contemplate, they are always capable of variation. The point is easy enough to make with examples that are familiar to most of us, each of which has been the focus for entire volumes (see Carter and McGoldrick, 1999, for more detail on some of these issues).

Poverty

The creativity with which people adapt to life's demands is obviously heavily influenced by the resources available to them. The impacts of social and economic deprivation are considerable at every stage of development.

Young couples, for example, who lack the resources to establish a separate household may unwillingly have to live with one of their extended families, in which case the boundary issues we discussed in reference to this stage will have a special quality and significance. If they do have separate but insufficient accommodation, this can have important effects as they establish their life together.

Couples with young children are often part of an informal economy with significant benefits. Middle-class families with growing children normally exchange an impressive amount of clothing, toys, information, baby-sitting, and transportation. By comparison, an impoverished single mother, perhaps socially isolated, may lack access to a tremendous range of concrete, instrumental, and emotional supports from which her more fortunate counterparts benefit (often without full awareness).

With age, an increase in need for supports and services is common, and a lack of social and economic resources affects the ability to have such needs met. When aging and poverty coexist (a more frequent occurrence for women than for men) opportunities for continued health, comfort, and engagement are reduced.

Professions such as social work, which are accustomed to working with socially and economically disadvantaged clients, are also accustomed to giving due weight to resource issues. Successful adaptation to developmental challenges presupposes the availability of adequate supports: when these are not present, a clinical focus on boundaries and traditions may be less important, for a time, than advocacy and resource development (see Chapter 7 for an extended discussion of this issue).

Trauma

A history that includes severe trauma has well-documented effects on individuals as well as serious (albeit less well understood) impacts on family development. Referring to the couple introduced in Chapter 2, it is clear that Daniel's ability to establish and maintain boundaries that provide for intimacy as well as safety is deeply affected by the physical and emotional abuse he suffered as a child. For victims of sexual abuse, achieving a comfortable sexual identity in adolescence and young adulthood is more complicated and difficult than for teens who have been more fortunate.

We are slowly learning how the impact of trauma affects not only the victim but also subsequent generations of her or his family. The increased tendency for children who experience violence as they grow up to become violent parents and partners themselves is quite widely recognized. The subtler development of traditions in response to such issues as the effect of sexual abuse on the victim in relation to the victim's own children is important and less well-studied.

Losses of parents in middle age and losses of partners and friends are predictable traumas, and there are cultural and familial traditions designed to assist in ameliorating their impacts. Traumas that are not predictable (e.g., crime, assaults, accidents) or which tend to be hidden from public attention (family violence, for example) are not associated with the same formal traditions, and may evoke less support from others. Family and cultural traditions involving denial and victim blaming can make matters far worse for a traumatized person than they would otherwise be.

A degree of rigidity regarding boundaries (keeping distance or hanging on) is an understandable strategy that victims adopt to protect themselves. Clinicians are learning to be especially sensitive to a possible history of abuse when serious boundary issues are present, and to respect the safety needs that motivate the behavior. Although some therapists see any instances of emotional cutoff between family members as antithetical to growth, a more cautious (and supportive) view is that maintaining distance from an assaultive person is often a very intelligent response, even if that person is a close family member. The ability to establish flexibility and safety in alternative relationships is often a more appropriate clinical issue than pressure toward reconciliation with a perpetrator.

Sexual Orientation

Sexual orientation is another potential difference that can have far-reaching effects on each stage of development. For adolescents, authoring a comfortable sexual identity while coping with a society (and often a family) that stigmatizes one's orientation can be enormously difficult.

Cultural and familial traditions regarding homosexuality can be dangerously harsh, and the boundaries that gay and lesbian people require to feel safe and supported may consequently seem rigid. In part, the development of gay communities offering independence from heterosexual society responds to the need for a safe place in which to develop and maintain sexual identity. In young adulthood, the common task of claiming the distance needed to establish an independent lifestyle while maintaining nurturing ties to the family of origin may be very difficult. In some cases it will prove impossible. For families that do weather the transition, accommodating long-term sexual commitments by a lesbian or gay offspring is seldom uncomplicated; to the extent that they ascribe to homophobic beliefs and values the adaptations they must make during adolescence and young adulthood will be all the more challenging.

Divorce and Remarriage

In contemporary Western societies, the frequency with which marriages end in divorce has increased radically in the past generation. People tend not to remain single, however, so families in which one or both partners have been previously married are more and more common.

In remarriage, the boundary issues tend to be somewhat different than with younger couples. With younger couples, as we have indicated, marriage can be a bid for independence, while it can be experienced as a loss of independence for older individuals accustomed to managing their own lives unimpeded by the needs and priorities of another person (McGoldrick, 1989, p. 212). The boundary issues to be sorted out may include relationships to ex-partners, stepparenting relationships, and relationships between sibling groups that are not biologically related and have a limited history with one another.

Expectations regarding attachment and distance between stepparents and stepchildren are often confused and can be the source of considerable tension in a blended family. Partners may enter a remarriage with commitments to traditions from their family of origin, complicated by traditions developed in a previous marriage (perhaps supported by their children out of loyalty to their first family).

The developmental stage at which remarriage takes place makes a real difference; arguably, families with adolescent children have the most difficult adjustment to make, since the dual tasks of learning to be independent while forging a new familial relationship with a relative stranger has inherent contradictions.

Our culture provides our families and us with a rich set of traditions to facilitate marriage, while the transitions associated with divorce and remarriage are less well supported. Although it has been the subject of considerable speculation and some research, it is still not clear what the effects of increased divorce and remarriage will be on the next generation. Having lived with a previously unknown frequency of family dissolution and reformation, the current cohorts of young adults and adolescents have a new understanding of "family," and it will be of considerable interest to see what traditions evolve in response to this relatively unfamiliar, less stable family model.

Chronic Conditions

When family members have a chronic condition that affects their physical or mental functioning, the family's response to developmental issues will be influenced by this fact of life. Chronic conditions can include congenital physical health issues, mental illnesses, and addictions.

The impact of chronic conditions varies. One issue is the severity of the condition: a propensity to migraine can be crippling, but if it is responsive to medical intervention, it will have less impact than congenital deafness. A vulnerability to moderate depressions, similarly, may be more manageable and less of an issue than a schizophrenic condition. Though serious, addictions to tobacco tend to be less disruptive to family development than addictions to alcohol or other substances.

The strengths, resources, and traditions that a family has to support it will also make it more or less resilient in its response to chronic conditions in one or more members. While one family may weather the stresses of raising a chronically physically ill member competently and with no apparent loss of emotional commitment, another, with fewer resources to call on, may find the stresses unmanageable.

Clinical social workers have not always been helpful in their work with such families. One reason is that the adjustments families make in response to a chronic condition have been seen as abnormal and dysfunctional. The classic example has been the belief that the response of families to a schizophrenic member may include acceptance of a relatively high degree of dependency, and a heightened responsiveness to emotional issues. This has frequently been characterized as a kind of fusion and attributed as a cause of the condition rather than an understandable, often positive effort to respond supportively to it. The consequence was that families felt blamed for a member's pain rather than supported in finding ways of meeting their responsibilities to provide love and support under challenging circumstances.

Similar confusion persists in the minds of clinicians regarding issues such as addictions. Families that have an alcoholic member will adapt to that set of behaviors in various ways: attempts to help the addicted person, attempts to keep the addiction secret, even unwitting support for substance abuse are examples. However, recognizing that familial responses to a problem may fail to solve it (or may even, in time, exacerbate it) is different from assuming that family structure and dynamics are a primary cause of the condition and require its continuance.

When a chronic condition affects a family member, the developmental stages will occur with that condition as part of their context. Growing toward independence is an issue for schizophrenic young persons, for example, but this developmental goal has to be understood somewhat differently if their condition compromises their ability to become economically self-sufficient. A physically disabled adolescent, deprived of full mobility or perceptual abilities, will face extra challenges (very often including discrimination) in the quest for recognition as a competent adult. Academically disadvantaged young people will benefit if their families can define success in unconventional ways, permitting them to develop a sense of mastery based on criteria that make sense for them.

THE THERAPIST'S DEVELOPMENTAL ISSUES

We conclude our consideration of developmental issues with a brief acknowledgment of therapists as participants in the same processes they must help their clients with. Therapists' personal experience with developmental themes and their variations will inevitably affect (positively or negatively) the way they work with clients.

As a useful speculation, consider Maria Doyle's situation fifteen years hence if she decides to become a family therapist. Imagine further that she finds herself working with a family with a depressed teenager exhibiting substance-abuse problems. Her own experiences as a teenager potentially could have significant effects.

If she has resolved her own issues with her family of origin well, and has been fortunate enough to receive good training and supervision, she may be especially insightful and effective in her response to her clients, helping them focus on core issues accurately and efficiently.

She may also experience difficulty keeping the boundaries clear between herself and the family members. She could identify with the daughter and be tempted to collude with her against her parents, following an impulse to rescue her from a smothering family. She could respond strongly to the parents' fears, and collude with them in an effort to prevent the daughter's self-destructiveness by becoming increasingly controlling.

The advantages of having experienced the kinds of difficulties our clients present are a matter of some debate. Traditionally, clinicians with psychoanalytic backgrounds insisted that analysis during training was essential preparation for clinical work; without it, therapists' histories would inevitably distort their relationships with their clients. It is also argued that personal experience with parenting or marriage is a prerequisite for work with people experiencing problems in those areas, and similar arguments are made for employing former addicts to work with substance abusers, or former victims of violence to work with assault victims.

It seems clear that training and experience can equip us to work effectively with problems other than those we have experienced (George did not have to have been a suicidal teenager to help Maria Doyle). It is also true that a personal history with a problem can work for or against us as therapists. There is an argument here for a professional helper to develop disciplined self-awareness. Through training, supervision, personal therapy, and simple self-reflection, it is important that clinicians should be sensitive to how their own histories may affect their work with a given family.

Awareness at this level is helpful in all cases, but it is especially important if we are working with a client and find ourselves getting stuck, feeling frustrated or angry (or unusually emotionally reactive in other ways), getting drawn into power struggles, or simply working too hard. In such cases, perhaps with the help of a consultant, it is useful to consider what connections (if any) may exist between the client's experience and one's own: what was the therapist's own life like during the developmental stages that present a problem to family members? How were issues resolved, and how have they continued to exert an influence? What boundary issues and cultural and familial traditions are shaping our responses to the family and its concerns?

Since client problems are variations on universal themes, the issues we confront professionally will almost always have a degree of personal relevance. The development and maintenance of clear boundaries between us and our clients requires disciplined self-awareness, and it is the best guarantee that we will use ourselves and our skills for our clients' benefit. Given that none of us works effectively with all people and problems, time for self-reflection along these lines can often prevent us from being ineffectual (or even harmful) in responding to issues which are closest to our own experience.

PART II:
FACILITATING CHANGE

Chapter 4

Understanding Change

It is our nature to restlessly take things apart, put them together, rearrange the world, recreate ourselves. If we sometimes yearn for a quiet life, this is usually when we are tired or fearful, or our imaginations have failed and we see no future that seems worth the effort.

Constance Nissen-Weber
Essays and Aphorisms

THEORIES OF EXPLANATION AND THEORIES OF CHANGE

Maria, the troubled teenager whose family we discussed in earlier chapters, is suicidal. We can understand why, having examined her situation. Complex family traditions have resulted in her feeling futile about ever finding the space she needs to grow.

Daniel, whom we introduced in Chapter 2, is also depressed and has a tendency to drink too much wine. Again, this is something we can explain. He is acting out an abused child's narrative about powerlessness, and family traditions in which his destiny is to be a disappointing failure through emotional illness and/or alcoholism.

Often clients will show a deep interest in exploring issues of this sort, developing a richer understanding of their stories and how they came to be written. However, the initial energy and curiosity can be a prelude to disillusionment: "So," our client says at some point, "now I understand. But what do I *do* about it?"

The question can be disconcerting, but it is also instructive. What our client is recognizing is that the theory we use for *understanding* is not the same as our theory of *change*. The frameworks that help us explain situations are important, but we need additional knowledge about how we can make things better. Useful as it is to explore the themes that we have written into our lives, this is not the same as knowing how to change the story we have written and our role in it.

RELATIONSHIP AS A PRECONDITION FOR CHANGE

The most important generalization about change we would suggest is that changes are normally (probably always) made in the context of relationships with other people. Our relationship to ourselves develops in interaction with others. The reasons why we want to change, our motives, often have to do with the relationships we value. The goals we set for ourselves frequently have to do with others and our wishes in relation to them. The behaviors we adopt as we discover new options are likely to have been modeled or suggested to us by another influential person. When change is maintained successfully, it is usually because there are people in our lives who support it.

Clearly, some relationships are destructive and impede change, supporting the continuation of unhappy patterns. Others, though, can help us come to terms with ourselves and our circumstances in ways that are permanently enriching. One teacher of the many dozens we encounter as students seems to have a special, enduring effect on our thinking, for example. People who create good lives for themselves despite brutal abuse in childhood invariably credit this accomplishment to the fact that someone was there to help them through—another parent, a relative, a neighbor, or a therapist. The strengths they drew on were in them, but special relationships set a context within which they could discover, trust, and use those strengths creatively.

Our next challenge is to understand what it is about some relationships that makes them powerful contexts for growth. Fortunately, this problem has attracted the interest of some powerful and creative thinkers in the past several decades, and their insights into the question are compelling.

The Helping Relationship: A Historical Note

The ability to develop relationships that support change is not restricted to professional helpers, but can be found anywhere. In fact, "natural helpers" in the local church, bar, locker room, or beauty salon have been the subject of academic inquiry for many years. Professional helpers, however, learn how to use such skills systematically and at a high level of competence. By doing so we increase the frequency with which our relationships with our clients are a context that will support the changes they need to make.

Our present understanding of the relationship conditions that support change is the result of many decades of practical and theoretical work. In social work, Mary Richmond (who called her work "friendly visiting" at first, and later "social casework") conducted the first systematic inquiry into the relationship conditions that are necessary for promoting change:

> Friendly visiting means intimate . . . knowledge of and sympathy with a . . . family's joys, sorrows, opinions, feelings. . . . The visitor that has this is unlikely to blunder . . . [while] without it he is almost certain . . . to blunder seriously. (Richmond, 1899, p. 180, cited in Rothery and Tutty, in press)

In the intervening decades, many terms (some still current) were advanced to describe the essence of helpful relationships, such as *empathy, rapport, emotional bridging, engagement* and the *therapeutic alliance* (Biestek, 1957; Coady, 1999; Rothery and Tutty, in press; Smalley, 1967).

Such developments in social work were paralleled (and influenced) by important work in neighboring disciplines. Otto Rank, for example, had been an orthodox psychoanalyst until he was expelled from the movement for propounding ideas that deviated too much from accepted Freudian doctrines. The revolutionary beliefs that had led to his estrangement from mainstream psychoanalysis were embraced and developed by clinical social workers (of the "functionalist" school) and have been influential in the subsequent development of clinical theory. These included the notion that therapeutic change is accomplished mainly through the provision of a special nurturing relationship. A second important heresy committed by Rank was to replace the strong determinism of Freud's thinking with a theory that celebrated the human capacity for creativity and choice (Menaker, 1982).

In clinical psychology, Carl Rogers initiated a program of research and theory building that has resulted in an enormous body of knowledge about how we relate to facilitate change. Interestingly, Rogers' work is an elaboration of Rank's, which Rogers came to know about through his early collaboration with clinical social workers:

> Social workers trained . . . where Otto Rank had been lecturing . . . were telling him that "relationship therapy"—not "interpretive therapy"—was [Rank's new] emphasis. . . . Rogers invited Otto Rank to Rochester to conduct a . . . seminar on his new . . . therapy. (Kramer, 1995, pp. 58-59)

Carl Rogers spent the rest of his long and productive career expanding on the implications of making relationship central to clinical work. A simplified version of the basic thesis he developed over that time is that "people are naturally inclined toward growth, and given the right conditions they will come to know themselves more fully, heal old wounds, and develop greater authenticity and congruence. They will become more knowledgeable and honest, first in relation to themselves, and then in relation to others" (Rothery and Tutty, in press).

The "right conditions" that facilitate such growth are relationships characterized by congruence, acceptance, and empathy. *Congruence* is interpersonal honesty and directness (Rogers, 1961, p. 61; see also Rogers, 1980, p. 115). Rogers' second core condition is *acceptance,* or "unconditional positive regard." Although we may be troubled by some aspects of how clients think, feel, or behave, we are able to maintain a spirit of generosity and respect toward them as people.

The third and most important characteristic of helping relationships is *empathy:*

> [Empathy] means that the therapist senses accurately the feelings and personal meanings that the client is experiencing and communicates this understanding to the client. When functioning best, the therapist is so much inside the private world of the other that he or she can clarify not only the meanings of which the client is aware but even those just below the level of awareness. This kind of sensitive, active listening is exceedingly rare in our lives, . . . yet [it] is one of the most potent forces for change that I know. (Rogers, 1980, p. 116)

Rothery and Tutty (in press) identify three important implications in this discussion by Rogers of his key concept:

> First, there is a role for intelligence, insight, training and experience: the social worker should grasp accurately and sensitively the emotional content and meanings implied in what the client is saying.
>
> Second, empathy as Rogers defines it is not simply understanding feelings: he is inclined to emphasize emotions, but also returns constantly to words like "experiencing" and "meaning." Thus, the point of empathic understanding is to communicate awareness of both the emotional and narrative aspects of what the client presents. Perhaps the word "experiencing" is attractive because it addresses both feelings about events and the meanings attributed to them—aspects that are always so interdependent that the wisdom of separating them is questionable.
>
> A third point is that empathy implies a strong psychological attunement by the worker to the experience of the client, but not a loss of boundaries. The therapist "can grasp the moment-to-moment experiencing which occurs in the inner world of the client as the client sees it and feels it, *without losing the separateness of his own identity.*" (Rogers, 1961, pp. 62-63, italics added)

BOUNDARIES AND THE HELPING RELATIONSHIP

Although the rhythm of contact and distance that characterizes boundaries is an ongoing aspect of helping relationships, there is no prescription for determining what is optimal, and this varies across clients and over time. The balance one seeks, however, is sufficient involvement that the client feels supported (when that will be helpful) and motivated to work. Distance is useful for establishing the limits of the relationship (the amount of time and support it is legitimate to expect from us), and for encouraging clients to exercise their own competence and responsibility.

While empathy is sometimes discussed in terms that imply a kind of boundary dissolution, we never fully share our clients' understandings and feelings, no matter how sensitively attuned we may be. A deep *under-*

standing of others' stories or frames of reference is empathy, while imagining we can fully *experience* what they are going through is identification (Rogers, 1959)—a rather different and less useful interpersonal operation.

When boundaries are clear, our clients benefit from our ability to listen carefully to their stories, conversing usefully about what they tell us, and correcting perceptions when they tell us we have not quite got it right. What evolves is a shared, coconstructed understanding of important aspects of the client's narrative. When this task is performed competently, clients will feel emotionally supported knowing that someone else has taken the trouble to appreciate their situation and experience. This combined with the knowledge that we are receiving what they tell us with acceptance and compassion is basic to good clinical work; it provides a context in which fear of change is contained and the creative exploration of options is encouraged.

This aspect of our work is more complicated with families than with individuals. A family therapist, always encouraging systems where people can experience both understanding and safety, must think on two tracks, simultaneously considering his or her own interactions with family members and their interactions with one another. The goal is to help the family members establish ways of relating in which boundaries are clear and protected at the same time as they offer one another support. A further goal is that the family improves its ability to act as an emotional support system with a shared narrative that facilitates growth in its individual members. These general goals, involving systematic attention to boundaries and narrative meanings, require considerable skill and sensitivity on the part of the clinician, who must take responsibility for managing the change process for a time (without attempting to control the people involved).

Boundaries and Safety

Otto Rank observed that for all of us intimacy is simultaneously attractive and threatening. The experience of being understood is not an unmixed pleasure, and it is not a pleasure at all unless it comes in a safe relationship. For very good reasons we control the extent to which we are open to others until we know it is safe to do otherwise. A client's reluctance to being as open with us as we might wish is often not "resistance" in a negative sense so much as a healthy exercise in self-care.

A major reason why clinicians consistently clarify and protect boundaries is that empathy may otherwise be experienced as unsafe. For example, Daniel did not always welcome being well understood. For him, as for other clients who have experienced childhood abuse, a therapist's perceptiveness is power, and power may be used to inflict pain or humiliation. With anyone prone to such fears, it is important to watch for times when they feel vulnerable in relation to us, which is often when therapy is going well and new insights have been achieved.

Maria Doyle has a somewhat different concern, which is that her exploration of her need for independence might be hurtful to her parents. In her case, it is important to carefully establish that she can negotiate openly for her legitimate needs to be met without damaging her parents.

Room to See: Boundaries and the "Observing Ego"

Another important contribution of boundaries to the helping alliance is that when we distance ourselves from the client's narrative (emotionally and psychologically), we can see it from a fresh perspective, identifying themes and options that have been unrecognized to that point. This can be important modeling for some clients; when we use distance from their narratives to advantage in this way, we are also demonstrating something useful they can do for themselves.

When psychodynamically oriented therapists speak of an "observing ego" they suggest that it is important for us to self-reflect, like authors reading our own work (even observing ourselves in the process of writing). The psychological capacity to take the position of a reader and author (as opposed to a character helplessly enmeshed in a story that has gone to press and cannot be changed) is very freeing. The distance helps us confront painful themes more comfortably, and makes the creative discovery of options more possible.

TRADITIONS AND THE HELPING RELATIONSHIP

The ability to establish understanding in the helping relationship is much enhanced by considering traditions. As we listen to clients' stories and develop an appreciation of how they came to be written, we recognize and discuss essential themes. When George articulates the difficult theme of Maria's need for space to grow, Maria and her family feel understood in a new way. When Mike highlights Daniel's narrative in which he is destined to be a failure and a disappointment, Daniel and Rebecca respond with numerous insights into how this affects his life and their relationship.

A time-honored principle of clinical social work practice, "starting where the client is," is in large measure a matter of being attuned to clients' assumptions, needs, priorities, and values, and finding ways to validate these. "Going where the client isn't" is much less often discussed, but is an equally important principle. When aspects of clients' traditions are contributing to their problems, it may be empathic to validate those enough to show that they are understood, but not in ways that are likely to perpetuate problems. A violent partner, for example, will not benefit if we provide support for the misogynistic traditions he has been raised in and adheres to. There may be much in his traditional worldview that we can recognize and support, but patriarchal assumptions and attitudes hostile to women will not be among them. Similarly, Mike might well join with Daniel over traditions his mother inculcated emphasizing good-humored forbearance, but not those that support using alcohol for respite from depression.

Knowledge of traditions also helps us as therapists to maintain the self-awareness we need to be effective. We are always influenced by our own traditions when we respond to clients' issues, and it is always useful to reflect on how this is affecting our ability to form a helping alliance. For example, empathic understanding of clients' narratives can be difficult when our own traditions are either highly dissimilar *or* similar to those the client struggles with.

If George grew up in a family that easily allowed teenagers to individuate, he might become impatient with Anita and John Doyle denying Maria enough space. With training and experience he would learn to see and understand such issues better, but he would not be as naturally sensitive to them. Conversely, if his family's traditions made the struggle for independence difficult, his responses will be different. If through his training and growth he has successfully resolved the issue for himself, he may be especially attuned to the themes in which Maria and her family are enmeshed. If he is less clear in himself about these concerns as they have affected him, there are less positive possibilities.

He may be drawn in by an impulse to rescue Maria, seeing her parents as oppressors, or he may become angry with Maria, seeing her as inappropriately passive and emotionally dishonest.

Culture also plays an obvious role. If George was raised with Northern European traditions valuing privacy and distance in relationships, he might easily misread Anita's reactions, shaped by her Latino culture, which favor a more intense and open emotional involvement in the lives of her daughters. Distance between the traditions we have inherited versus those of our clients can be helpful if it allows us to be helpfully removed from their narratives—the "observing ego" idea alluded to previously—though we may be slower to understand them with sensitivity and depth than is desirable. Alternatively, a high congruence of our traditions with our clients' can help us be more effectively attuned to their issues and needs, but can make it more difficult for us to step back when it would be useful to do so.

Traditions About Change: Common Themes

Each of has been exposed to traditions about change, through our training as well as our families and culture. Common themes respecting change are useful to consider, as an opportunity to examine the assumptions that support and constrain us in our practice. Also, since clients come to us with beliefs about change of their own, it is helpful to be aware of when their assumptions are (or are not) congruent with ours.

As with all traditions, our culture and families provide us with the ideas and experiences on the basis of which we develop themes having to do with change: Are we in charge of our lives, or is our story largely predestined? Do we know we have the ability to make a difference, or do we consider that this resides in more capable and powerful people? When we experience a failure or setback, is this an event to be dealt with or symbolic proof of our unhappy lot in life?

Narratives of Hope and Defeat

Martin Seligman (1989) is widely respected for his contribution to our understanding of depression in recent decades. His research and scholarship are sophisticated, though his basic conclusions are surprisingly simple. "When a patient walks through your door for the first time, there is a word in his or her heart. Is it 'no?' Is it 'yes?' Can you detect it? Can you measure it? Can you change it?" (p. 6).

In short, people are pessimists or optimists. Some of us live narratives inspired by hope, some by defeat. This has fundamental consequences:

> The word in your heart, "no" or "yes," is a powerful determinant of depression, achievement, and health. . . . People we love reject us, our stocks go down, we give bad speeches, we write bad books, our patients drop us, and the like. . . . Those of you who chronically believe that those bad events are your fault, that they are going to last forever, and will undermine everything you do, seem to be at greater risk for depression, poor achievement, and ill health. (Seligman, 1989, p. 25)

When we listen carefully to our clients, from the first moments of the first contact we hear evidence—in their words and in myriad nonverbal cues—of narratives of hope or defeat. Not everyone believes that change is possible, or that they are capable of bringing it about, or that it will be worth the effort if they do somehow make it happen. Not surprisingly, this basic stance is considered a primary variable determining if intervention can succeed or not (Frank and Frank, 1991). If we can find a way to help our clients develop hope, this is often a crucial accomplishment.

Narratives About Preconditions for Change

Other themes that clinical social workers and their clients entertain have to do with preconditions that must be satisfied for meaningful change to occur. There are sharp differences of opinion on this topic between professionals, and even between helper and client.

Insight and Understanding

Some hugely influential clinicians base their beliefs about change on the motto "The truth shall set you free." For example, no one has done more than Freud to shape modern beliefs about how we create pain in our lives and how we heal. He maintained that understanding precedes meaningful change, and a great many people agree with him on this point. A corollary to this idea is that change occurring without the foundation of insight will be temporary and weak in its emotional benefits. Further, it is feared that such superficial behavioral changes may leave the client vulnerable to recurrence of difficulties or to new problems rooted in the old underlying confusions and conflicts (symptom substitution).

Clients as well as therapists may be drawn to this position. Perhaps not surprisingly given his career in psychology, Daniel was highly motivated to understand why he tended to drink too much. He accepted as axiomatic that understanding his motives and their origins would enable him to behave more sensibly.

If Daniel were a behavioral psychologist, he might favor a very different view about change. Symptom substitution, he could argue, is an unsubstantiated myth. There are no underlying emotional causes for problem behaviors, he might say; behaviors are the problem rather than a symptomatic expression of something deeper, and changing them is a full and sufficient resolution. He might focus on learning and enacting specific strategies for drinking less rather than digging for causes of his addiction in emotional conflicts originating in his childhood.

If strategic family therapists influenced him, Daniel might see his drinking as both a symptom and a cause, as part of a pattern in his network of relationships that has become self-reinforcing. Change to both the drinking behavior and relationship dynamics would be potentially helpful, and neither requires insight into supposed deeper issues. In fact, he might say, insight and understanding often follow change rather than preceding it.

The Locus of Change

Another important theme in our thinking has to do with where we believe the power to bring about change resides. One common narrative features the powerful healer, whose expertise is the key that will unlock the door to new possibilities. Clinicians attracted to this belief will tend to relate to their clients from an "expert" role, which can easily become directive. Clients who believe similarly may tend to disempower themselves, counting on the clinician to produce a strategy that will make things better.

This narrative about helping is influential and has a long history. It is probably natural when we are in pain to hope that someone else can simply make our troubles go away, without our having to take responsibility for them. In earlier centuries, when healers were primarily religious figures, they were often attributed unusual powers in the form of spiritual gifts or a special relationship with a divinity. In our present culture, clinicians are more often secular, but we are still accustomed to assuming professionals have abilities that surpass our own, deriving from advanced training and a specialized knowledge base. Modern medicine is perhaps the clearest example of a discipline in which this kind of expertise is assumed.

Another pervasive narrative is that the solution to our problems is for someone else to change. Maria Doyle may feel that she has no options for making her life better other than waiting for her parents to act differently toward her. Her father, John, may think his relationship to his family of origin is essentially outside his control, and that improving matters will require his mother to make the next move.

Alternatively, our culture is also fond of narratives that emphasize our ability to take responsibility for our lives, exercising our capacity for choice and self-determination in the face of whatever challenges confront us. Clinicians who strongly endorse this belief will tend to see their role as a facilitative and empowering one, in which their goal is to help clients discover their own creative ability to develop new options.

It is arguable, with support from outcome research, that each of these positions is valid to some extent. Qualified professional helpers do have a knowledge base that their clients do not possess. Through our training, we have learned ways of understanding problems and approaches to resolving them that will not be part of our clients' frameworks. This is why our clients come to us, and why we are paid for our time with them.

It is also true that solving problems may involve other people changing. When clients suggest that someone else could contribute to their happiness by behaving differently, they are not necessarily being irresponsible. They might simply be acknowledging a reality that any abused child or oppressed employee will attest to, which is that we are social beings and other people strongly affect the quality of our lives. It is legitimate for Maria Doyle to ask her parents to treat her differently, and her enjoyment of life will increase if they do so.

We are all embedded in families and other social networks, and our well-being is influenced by what important other people do in relation to us. Nevertheless, our well-being is also strongly affected by our sense of personal efficacy (Bandura, 1977). Maria will benefit most if solutions to her problems are found which help her discover that she can declare her need for space and negotiate with her family to meet that need. For many clinicians, helping clients claim their right and responsibility for authorship of their own narratives is the primary goal of intervention. The basis for any meaningful change is recognition of our ability to choose, based on our own needs, values, and priorities (Goulding and McClure Goulding, 1978).

There is no need for dogmatic positions about where the locus for change resides. Resources that will support change can come from a number of places—from within us as well as from our networks of relationships, and from various professional helpers. For clinicians, creative practice implies a flexible choice of focus and interventions, and effective work is often multifaceted. This said, we are persuaded that treatment is most effective when clients are full participants in discovering new options for themselves and feel more personally powerful as a result.

CHANGE AND THE BOUNDARY DYNAMIC

In Chapter 1, we described a boundary dynamic, suggesting that boundary issues are rooted in cognitive explanations (stories), with an associated emotional experience, approach to problem solving, and behavioral expression. Among clinicians there are distinct differences as to which of these is thought to be the best locus for change. Currently, there is very strong interest in cognitive models, which consider changing beliefs or narratives to be most effective. Other clinical theorists feel that encouraging awareness, expression, and integration of feelings is critical. Some emphasize helping clients modify their problem-solving approach, and still others focus on more discrete behaviors.

For example, if Daniel decides his wine consumption is a problem he wants to solve, one focus for change could be the narratives that require him to be a disappointment and a failure, replacing them with alternative stories highlighting his toughness and accomplishments. One also could work with him to find alternative ways of assuaging depressed feelings that he treats by drinking, as well as building awareness of exceptions—his experience of aspects of his life that please him. We could address how when a problem arises in relation to Rebecca, he may become immobilized, and contrast that with experiences using more effective problem-solving strategies. Finally, we could work directly with the drinking behaviors, looking for and highlighting examples of when he has utilized other self-soothing strategies to cope with depression or stress, controlling his alcohol consumption.

Although he is clearly the person responsible for how much wine he consumes, there are many ways in which Daniel's narrative, feelings, problem solving, and behaviors express what is going on between Rebecca and him. They co-construct important events, and they could work together to change them. If Rebecca experiences Daniel's depression as abandonment, for example, she may become highly distressed herself. If her boundaries are such that she remains clear that his depressed feelings are not her problem, however, she is much freer to create responses that respect her own needs and are appropriately supportive to him in his struggle.   at a time

Inevitably, an effective intervention focused on one area or level will have an impact on other parts of the system, since they are all interrelated. What if John Doyle changes his relationship to his mother, deciding he will no longer accept her mistreatment of him and his family? Making this change at a narrative level could affect his feelings, with the result that he would feel less stuck and angry. Behaviorally, he could then begin making clear demands instead of building increasingly rigid boundaries.

In one interview described in Chapter 1, John becomes aware of and expresses painful feelings regarding his mother's history. This is a change from avoiding to acknowledging his feelings. With the decision to be open about his emotional distress, he is also freer to consider the narrative that has been its source. Dealing more clearly with his story and feelings about it, he is better able to think about problem-solving and behavioral options.

Looking at the same issues with an interest in John and Anita as a couple, we would note that Anita has accommodated to John's problem-solving strategy. She could be very helpful to him by expecting him to be more assertive in protecting his family from mistreatment by his mother and uncles.

With a history of abuse, Daniel felt, even as an adult, small and powerless in relation to his father. Interestingly, he was also unable to describe his father's physical appearance in any detail, and claimed that this was because he literally avoided looking at him. A task that he agreed to was to spend time at a visit with his family studying his father and to bring a written description to one of his sessions. He discovered through this that the father who had terrorized him as a child was aging, and was now the physically weaker of the two of them.

This behavioral experiment had a powerful impact because it was well chosen. Daniel was keeping alive a narrative in which his father was an overwhelming figure, and continued to harbor the expectation that so simple an act of assertion as looking would have painful and humiliating results. It did not, and his story began to shift as a consequence—narrative change often follows experiments with new behaviors. Effective behavioral experiments succeed because they induce cognitive dissonance, so we search for new narratives that match our modified behavior (and affect).

Emotionally, Daniel's fearfulness in relation to his father began to subside, and his feelings of powerlessness were ameliorated. Then, when conflicts with Rebecca arose he was less quick to lapse into hopelessness and withdrawal, and more able to problem solve successfully.

SUMMARY: GENERALIZATIONS ABOUT CHANGE

We can draw a number of lessons from the discussion of change to this point that we regard as safe generalizations. Earlier we devoted considerable attention to one critical point—that change always takes place in the context of relationships—and can now offer others.

First, it is useful for the clinician to intervene flexibly, looking for changes that can simultaneously impact multiple systems. Preferences about intervening at different levels, emphasizing narrative, emotions, problem solving, or behaviors have much to do with the clinician's style and training. Hopefully, they will be selected mainly in response to client preferences and needs. As with most issues, we see little reason for dogmatically valuing one focus over the others.

Second, real change takes place with a change in behavior. This can happen quickly or slowly, and it can be temporary or lasting. However, changes in behavior and the exploration of new problem-solving options have a deeper and more permanent impact to the extent that they allow clients to alter their narrative about themselves in some significant way.

Third, the ability to maintain changes depends on one's emotional comfort with them. Change almost always has emotional consequences, and whether it will endure depends on whether clients find those consequences positive, or at least manageable. When the affective expression of an issue is explored, this is frequently the benefit: the client discovers that the feelings associated with an issue are manageable, and need not block the discovery of new solutions. When John Doyle confronts his deep distress over his mother's unhappiness, he faces a painful reality, but learns in the process that it is something he can cope with in ways other than denial. He is then freer to consider creative options.

Fourth, the narrative fit and emotional consequences associated with change are typically a social as well as personal issue. Family or friends may offer emotional supports in the form of encouragement and understanding, and can also be helpful by actively developing narrative meanings supportive of change. In unhappier situations, negative feelings about change are shared by a number of family or social network members, and this results in pressure to give up.

We all have experience with such issues. For example, in a class or workshop, we learn about the importance of assertiveness. We proceed to experiment in selected areas of life with more assertive options. This may or may not last, depending on the issues we have identified: Is there an accompanying narrative change whereby we change our story to accommodate our new assertiveness? Are the emotional consequences of our experiment positive for us, or, if not, can we tolerate them? What is the impact of the change on those who are close to us—is assertiveness as a problem-solving strategy likely to be accepted and supported by them? The answers to these questions each have weight in determining if we will continue with our new behaviors, or feel tempted to revert to older, more familiar ways of being.

Another generalization is that a change in behavior may mean the acquisition of entirely new skills, but more often suggests using familiar behaviors in new ways, in new contexts, or in the service of new objectives. The latter situation is desirable; change is easier when clients know that what they are going to experiment with is the application of established competencies to new purposes. When this condition is met (and they are clear that the reasons for trying something different are rooted in their own needs), they will approach change with more energy and confidence than if it seems like a leap into the unknown.

EXAMPLE:
IDEAS ABOUT CHANGE IN ACTION

Noting that he feels triangulated in that John and Anita are talking to him—frequently at the same time—about Maria, George decides to invite them to give Maria more space by arranging their seating differently. John had been sitting with an empty chair between himself and Maria and Anita, who were sitting together.

George [to Anita]: Could I ask you to do something? Could I ask you to sit next to your husband?

Anita: Certainly.

George [to Maria]: And where would you like to sit? Do you want to stay there or do you want to move over? Where would you feel more comfortable?

George now invites Maria to take another step to clarify her personal boundary. She is invited to make a choice involving space and independence.

Maria: I'll move over. [She moves one chair over, leaving an empty chair between her and Anita.]

George: Okay. So even physically it is helpful to have a little more space for you. One thing that I wanted to do is find a way to get you out from between your parents so that you would physically be a little more independent. [To parents] Does this feel okay for you?

It is often useful to clarify even relatively straightforward moves, and to indicate how they can be taken at different levels.

Anita, John: Yes!

George [to John]: Now, you were saying that in the last week it has been 100 percent better.

John: Well, maybe I'm reading it wrong, but I have the feeling . . .

George: I am interested in knowing from your point of view what you saw that made you feel that it was better.

John: I had a feeling that she looked happier, that . . .

George: And what were people doing different in the past week?

George is interested in helping John identify solutions that can be repeated. This is more effectively accomplished by clarifying the behavioral aspects of changes that have occurred.

John: What was I doing differently? I was trying hard not to encroach on her territory, and give her some breathing room.

George: What were you doing to make that happen?

John: Ah, just kind of leaving her in peace, I guess. Just not, maybe not acting like a police station [laughs].

George: Did you stop asking her questions?

John: That's right, that's right. And I felt before where I would feel rejection sometimes I'd come over to just stand beside her or something like that. I would give her a little bit more room, but then when it did happen that we'd come near each other then I felt that she responded.

George: So by giving her more room she was free to be more loving . . .

John: That's right.

George: She didn't feel so smothered.

John: That's right!

George: What else did you do besides not asking as many questions?

John: Ah, one thing I did is that she tends to feel as if we were the perfect parents, in a sense. Academically perfect and socially perfect.

George: She told you that?

John: Yes. And that her cousins are perfect. I have done my best to point out to her that her cousins have their warts and that her dad has his warts.

George: Is this new for you to share this with her?

The discourse about space has opened up significant territory, with John's laughter indicating he is feeling more hopeful. George checking to see if a behavior is new is another attempt to highlight solutions that family members can continue to use.

John now refocuses the conversation on his own struggle for independence—the family tradition we addressed in detail in the previous section.

John: I thought I had done it in the past, but maybe I haven't. Maybe it is true. When I was a kid growing up I was always the perfect kid . . .

George: You worked very hard to please your family.

John: Yes, I guess I did.

George: That must have been even more difficult for you when you finally wanted your own life. You must have felt tremendous loyalty conflicts when you wanted your own life . . .

John [interrupting]: Oh, extremely! Extremely—I was . . .

John's readiness to acknowledge his struggle provides George with an opportunity to highlight how they have a shared issue in their fight for independence. The fact that neither Maria nor her parents have connected their current difficulties to family traditions is not at all unusual.

George [interrupting]: Can I just . . . [turning to Maria] Did you know that? Did you know that this fight you are going through your father went through before you?

Maria: I saw the arguments, the fight, but I didn't think it was like mine.

George: You didn't know that it was like yours. See, he was fighting to please his parents and also to be his own person. This sounds as if that's like your fight. Part of you would like to please your parents—in fact, part of you wanted to protect them and it is only lately that you decided you need more space. Does that fit?

Maria [nods affirmatively].

George: I am curious to know, is your perception the same as your dad's? Has he been asking fewer questions in the last little while?

Maria [nods affirmatively].

George: Has that made a difference in the way you feel?

Maria: A little bit.

George: Has he done other things to give you more space?

Maria: No. That's about it.

George: Have you done things to encourage him?

Maria [interrupts]: To give more space?

George: To give you more space. Besides telling him you didn't want to be interrogated?

Maria: No.

George: OK . . . [turns to John] Now, is there anything you can think of that you did to create more space?

George asked this question in order to encourage exploration of further steps that can be taken toward more space and independence for Maria. Instead, it elicits worrying memories, and triggers old response patterns involving protection and triangulation.

John [talking softly and very emotionally]: Other than leaving her alone? Like for a while she went through a period where we go downstairs and she is sleeping in bed late and she would still be in a fetal position and that kind of stuff, and I guess maybe I did kind of hover over her like a . . .

Anita [interrupting]: But we were worried—that's why. We were very concerned at this time because we thought there was suicidal tendency. We would check on her. We would want to be near her often just in case.

George moves quickly to interrupt this pattern and highlight the exception discussed earlier. He also checks whether Maria still feels suicidal; when she indicates that she does not he again defines the problem in transactional terms (rather than as something wrong with her personally). He further refocuses the conversation on the changes the family has made, crediting Maria for the progress she has made.

George: You see, that is what impresses me so much. In the past week not only have you [looking at John] done things different, but [turning to Maria] you have done things different. Now, it sounds like you felt very sad in the past and you even considered suicide. Do you still feel that way?

Maria [shakes head negatively].

George: So right now you don't feel suicidal?

Maria [shakes head negatively].

George: And you've been different with your parents. The more you allow the sadness to overpower you the more they hover over you, and the more they hover over you, the more you feel sad. Now you have told them you want more space, they are giving you more space, you start taking more control of these feelings that were so powerful. Does that make sense?

Maria [nods affirmatively].

George [to Anita]: What have you done differently in the last week?

Anita: I have tried to be more aware of what she would want us to do.

George: So you have tried to tune in more to her feelings, rather than have her tune in to yours. How did you come up with that idea?

Anita: We were worried for her so the first reaction we had was the problem is not with her, the problem is with us and what we are doing wrong.

George does not want John and Anita to blame themselves, either, so he moves once again to connect the present problem to family traditions.

George: Are you realizing now that it was kind of a vicious cycle?

Anita: That's right.

George: That these are patterns from the past—were you aware that the patterns from John's family of origin and your family of origin were all part of this?

Anita: No, I wasn't. So for me this suicidal tendency was a cry for help, so we thought, well, we better do something. Because the worst that could happen . . . we love her dearly and if something happened to her that is something we could not live with. So this is our second chance type of thing so we thought we have to kind of look at how we are doing things and see what we can do differently.

George: Does this help, to put the pieces together?

Anita and John: Yes it does.

George: Because you can only do what you were taught and you live the way you were taught to live.

Anita: That's right.

Finally, George highlights, again, how Maria and John are engaged in the same struggle, and recognizes Maria's success. He also uses the opportunity to raise the question of what it would take for John to negotiate a more independent relationship with his mother.

George: And so your daughter fits into this whole pattern, but [turns to Maria] now you have broken some of the molds. Your father, at his age . . . I don't know [turns to John] . . . Have you ever told your mother you want more space? And you are forty?

John: Yes.

George [to Maria]: And you are thirteen. So you already, at your age, are starting to share with your parents . . .

FINAL NOTE:
TECHNIQUE AND CREATIVITY

George begins his work with the Doyles with a sound professional framework that includes much knowledge at a high level of abstraction, such as the ideas presented in the first section of this book. As he and the family develop a shared understanding of the situation, George's thinking becomes more concrete. A general knowledge of boundary issues, traditions, and development recedes and a more direct, detailed appreciation of Maria's needs for space to grow begins to take its place. At the same time, George's abstract ideas about how change occurs become more specific as he begins bringing them into his thinking about the Doyles. General principles are translated into particular options, deliberately chosen and modified to fit with this unique family's experience.

The process of drawing on our abstract understandings in order to generate specific interventions always poses creative demands on clinicians and their clients, because common ideas and principles require adapting to fit each unique situation. This fact impacts us as educators as well as in our clinical roles. As educators, we are aware of how we may occasionally be obliged to disappoint our students. Sometimes they want us to tell them exactly what they can do, and we can only demonstrate how one takes general ideas and principles and makes them more specific and concrete with reference to each client system. Ultimately, this understanding is operationalized in an intervention designed to achieve a goal, and this is always creative, as Figure 4.1 illustrates.

FIGURE 4.1. The Creative Interface Between Frameworks and Situations

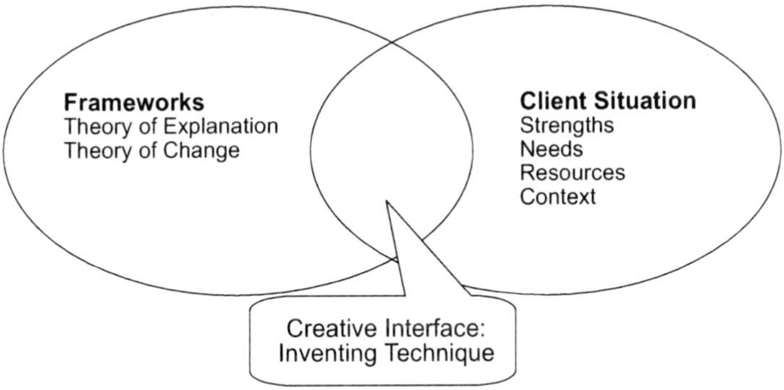

Like educators in the classroom, supervisors also sometimes have the unpleasant duty to disillusion beginning clinicians, presenting them with the limits of what we have to offer. We can teach the means for understanding situations and the principles that guide efforts to change. We can help with the development of the skills required to facilitate exploration and a rich understanding of client narratives, feelings, problem-solving strategies, and behavioral predispositions. But the important action that occurs at the interface where technique is enacted presents limits that must be respected—what happens there is the product of the creative interplay between the client and clinician, and can never be completely prescribed (or predicted).

Chapter 5

Setting Goals,
Discovering Solutions

*Ours is a world where people don't know what they want and
are willing to go through hell to get it.*

> Don Marquis
> *Archy and Mehitabel*

*It is a mistake to look too far ahead. Only one link in the chain of
destiny can be handled at a time.*

> Winston Churchill
> *The Hinge of Fate*

Above all, try something.

> Franklin D. Roosevelt
> *The Essential Franklin D. Roosevelt*

Determining goals and discovering solutions to problems are the basis for all planned change. Setting goals is a matter of declaring what
we want. Finding solutions means determining what we have to do to
attain what we want.

Like many aspects of the helping enterprise, this seems simple
enough: clients decide where they would like to be and together we figure out how they can get there. As usual, however, there are subtleties
and complexities behind this apparently straightforward formula.

DEFINING PROBLEMS
AND DISCOVERING SOLUTIONS

There is a platitude to the effect that if a problem is well defined it is 90 percent solved, and it has more than a grain of truth. The key is the term "well defined."

Problems are situations that require a solution. An inevitable circumstance is not a problem in this sense, since there is nothing to be done about it. Clients who tell us their problem is death (we have heard this from teenagers on occasion) are not really describing a problem so much as a fact of life. If they tell us they are worrying obsessively about death, or seem immobilized by grief over a loss, they are then describing circumstances about which one can imagine doing something useful, and meaningful problem solving can begin.

It is not terribly uncommon for clients to present us with situations that have no solution. "My problem," says one of Mike's clients, "is that I'm getting old." However gifted he may be as a clinical social worker, there is nothing Mike can suggest that will arrest the aging process. In the sense of the definition just offered, the situation of which the client complains is an inevitability, not a workable problem. The first task is to work with the client to understand the situation differently, finding some aspect of it about which something useful can be done.

From the outset, then, problem definition is a search for solutions: "Since clients frequently have difficulty stating a goal, therapists need to construct problems in such a way that a goal or vision of the future emerges" (de Shazer, 1985, p. 93). Our initial interest is in understanding what has brought the client to us, and to understand it *in a way that contains the potential for useful change.* Mike needs to explore with his client in what ways getting old is a problem, and that exploration will be helpful to the extent that it results in an understanding that implies eventual action. Getting old per se is not a workable problem. The prospect of a *lonely* old age is, because something can be done about it. The desire to make lifestyle changes that will increase chances of staying healthy can also lead to problem solving.

If Maria Doyle were to say to George something like "My problem is that I'm depressed," she would be presenting him with a very difficult definition of her situation. Until it is possible to imagine the direction that helpful changes might take, a working problem definition is not really in hand. When the problem is understood as Maria feeling trapped because her parents are not giving her enough space, then we are much further ahead, because we can easily imagine things that people can do differently that will improve matters. In another family, a perceived lack of love might be the opposite problem— someone might want increased involvement and support rather than more space. Again, the way problems are defined influences the possibility of doing something about them.

Looked at this way, all effective problem-solving therapies are necessarily solution focused. The solution-focused agenda to bypass a "problem-saturated" discourse about clients' circumstances emphasizes how important it is to avoid becoming mired, with our clients, in an exploration of their pain and unhappiness with no promise of relief. Problem exploration in the absence of solutions can, in fact, be an act of cruelty, confirming a client's sense of hopelessness and defeat.

Generally speaking, the definition of problems (and the search for solutions) is a matter of helping clients explore these areas (cf. Goulding, 1990; Tutty, 1999):

- What would you like to change?
- What would you like to stop doing/what would you like to do more of/or begin to do?
- How will we know when you have achieved your goals— when our work is completed?
- How is this concern a problem?
- What have you tried that has not worked?
- What have you done that has been useful?
- What are you doing differently when the problem is not present?
- How are other people in your life likely to react as you make these changes?

What Requires Change?

The process of developing explicit contracts or agreements to pursue certain goals is an opportunity to facilitate exploration of solutions that are meaningful and achievable. For a solution to be *meaningful,* it must be perceived by the client as relevant to her or his needs, as something that will make a difference that he or she will value.

Achievability implies that in pressing the question "What exactly are we working together toward?" we are inviting discourse about what the client wants in terms of what it is realistic to hope for. If the Doyles' unspoken goal in talking to George is that Maria should be ceaselessly happy in a family that is an impregnable fortress of peace and harmony, they will inevitably become discouraged. If they agree that they will be sufficiently changed when they learn to give her the right amount of space, so she feels supported without being smothered, they will have identified goals that are within their reach and about which they can feel hopeful. If their wish list is expanded to include a changed relationship to John's extended family, requiring it to be more respectful toward Anita and their daughters, we are still contemplating goals that are meaningful and achievable.

Achievability is present when goals are concrete and modest in scope and the steps to achieving them are clear. Not uncommonly it is a bit of struggle to reduce goals and expectations to achievable proportions, in part due to traditions that both we and our clients have been influenced by. An important example is narratives valuing radical rather than incremental change.

In many cultures, people grow up absorbing narratives about magical transformation. Potions make ordinary weaklings all-powerful, or change the social outcast into someone irresistible, coping bravely with sexual opportunities that would exhaust the average person (even the average teenager). Spiritual advances are often described as epiphanies sparking radical change (being "born again") rather than developmental processes requiring time and work.

Clinical social workers and other helpers also are drawn to stories about therapists with extraordinary insight and powers of intervention. Abusive bullies emerge from a single session reborn as sensitive and caring nurturers. One brilliant paradoxical prescription changes a constricted, depressed professor into a charming, fun-filled husband with a penchant for dancing.

For all their attractions, such stories often have deleterious effects. Pete Hamill (1995), for example, believes his addiction to alcohol partly originated with fascinating tales, absorbed in childhood, about magically powerful elixirs. Many clinicians will admit to having felt inadequate because their clients normally progress in small steps instead of finding instant relief through powerful interventions or insights.

Change is normally a process taking time, characterized by backward steps and unfruitful efforts along with halting progress toward goals (Prochaska, 1995). Breakthroughs do happen, but narratives suggesting that change should be a dramatic event may be misleading and disillusioning to both client and helper. Time can be wasted holding out for miracles instead of getting on with small, ordinary, incremental changes that will simply make things better.

It is part of most clinical workers' training to come to grips with our limitations, learning to value small, perhaps incomplete changes when more profound transformations are not achievable. With experience and good supervision, we relinquish rescue fantasies in which we help people achieve enlightenment and happiness for more realistic hopes of facilitating good enough improvements in the limited areas where change is required.

When clients come to us with grand goals in mind, an early task may be to help them cope with the disillusionment attending the news that what we can honestly offer, while substantial, is less than what they want. Whatever disappointment this engenders is often eventually mixed with relief, however, since we can then negotiate or co-construct goals that are both meaningful and attainable. Small steps that fit for the client create less stress and tension, and can be used to develop hope and a record of successes (where grand goals are often ultimately self-defeating).

A final quality of goals that supports hope is clarity, and this can also require considerable attention. Sometimes people ask for professional help knowing only that they are troubled and want relief, but have difficulty articulating their needs more precisely than that. This is normal enough, since we are all unclear about what we want at times, and help specifying our needs is a necessary prelude to finding ways of meeting them. Vague goals become increasingly achievable as we work to be more specific. If my stated goal is to be happy, I will feel more hopeful about achieving it when I stipulate more concretely what it means for me—a more gratifying job, for example, or improvements in my intimate relationships, or lifestyle changes that will make me healthier.

What Does the Client Want?

Defining meaningful and achievable goals usually begins with some exploration of what it is in clients' lives that troubles them. A consequence is that sometimes the first ideas by clients respecting what they want are negatively stated; understandably, they would like to be relieved of whatever pain drove them to seek help. John and Anita Doyle would like not to have to worry about Maria's self-destructiveness. Rebecca and Daniel would like not to be embroiled in conflicts that leave them confused and frightened.

A useful early exploration is often an invitation to find more positive ways of conceiving the change that is desired. When we ask the "miracle question" (O'Hanlon and Weiner-Davis, 1989) we hope it will stimulate thinking about what clients' lives will be like when their work is completed. Hopefully, this will be stated not just in terms of an absence of pain, but also in terms of what they will be doing differently that will make their lives more gratifying in a positive sense. If Daniel's goal is to quit depressing himself by overusing alcohol, that is certainly sensible. However, he will benefit from thinking about what else he is going to do—what pleasures will replace the one he relinquishes. If John and Anita give Maria more space by ceasing to anxiously interrogate her, will this be a loss of involvement for them or will it be replaced with a different, more relaxed kind of engagement?

In exploring the difficulties that led our clients to seek help, we are also interested in exceptions (times when the presenting concern is not present). If Daniel is willing to recall times when he dealt with stress in his life without reaching for the corkscrew, he will engage in talking about his successes and competence as well as his problems, which is powerfully hope-inducing when it works well. The more John and Anita can recognize times that they support Maria without smothering her, the more they will see change as achievable and themselves as capable of achieving it. Similarly, when Maria can talk about the times she has claimed space for herself (without provoking disaster), she will be emboldened to do more of that in the future.

What Is the Motivation to Change?

Another purpose of the kind of exploration discussed above has to do with client motivation. If the process goes well, we and our clients will identify goals that are, as we have said, both meaningful and achievable. The idea that goals should be meaningful implies that they are somehow relevant to the client's own needs.

Teenagers who are referred for help often perceive the situation as one in which they are being pressured to change to please other people: their parents, their teachers, or the police, for example. Their willingness to engage wholeheartedly in a plan to change is undermined if they cannot be helped to identify how doing so will be rewarding for them as well.

Parents charged with child mistreatment, partners guilty of domestic assaults, and people with substance abuse problems are very frequently in the same situation. The demand that they change is perceived as a demand to satisfy the child welfare authorities, or their abused partners, or an employer—but not themselves. Clearly, the chances of successful work are enhanced to the extent that we can help them see a payoff in changing for themselves as well as others.

It is very common that the reasons clients give for changing are to please other people. There is nothing wrong with this, except that positive outcomes are more likely if they are positive for the client as well as for others in his or her life. If part of Daniel's desire to curtail his drinking is based on the perception that this would be pleasing to Rebecca, that is supportable. However, full recognition about how he personally will benefit in terms of his own needs and experience will make the change more attractive and meaningful to him.

A related aspect of motivation to change has to do with a more general stance or attitude toward the process. The way we construe our motives for changing and the feelings with which we anticipate something new in our lives are powerful determinants of success, and the clinician's goal is often to discover and nurture a particular basic perspective on change—what it means and how it feels. Remembering Seligman's work, cited in Chapter 4, do we approach change with a "no" or a "yes" in our hearts? Do we edge into the unknown feeling supported and curious, or with a sense of reluctance, helplessness, or dread?

While it is true that change can be demanding and unsettling, it is also rewarding, which is why we actively seek out new and stimulating experiences. The Doyles, experimenting with new ways of relating as a family, may find the prospect of change daunting, but they are also embarking on a course about which they can be excited and curious. At the same time that Daniel might be anxious about bypassing the wine shop on his way home from work, he may be genuinely interested in the new possibilities and self-understandings that will emerge for him if he does so.

We can understand something about contexts for change if we reflect on our own experience, as children and parents. We seldom, as children, easily accommodate to demands when they are made coercively. Threatened with punishment or criticism, we might comply in the short term out of fear or guilt. However, this is frequently a temporary behavioral change rather than the development of a narrative that will produce lasting benefits.

When we approach our children with respect for their competence, recognizing that problems are a part of life, not a sign of personal failure, we launch a quite different process. When we discuss issues and solutions in the context of their needs as well as our own, they are likely to be interested at a much more useful level. When our dialogue about options is an invitation to think creatively, driven by curiosity, the motivation to try something new is deeper than if solutions, however valid or well-intended, are prescribed with force and authority.

The same principles apply in clinical work, and some of the more refreshing recent writing in the area is an exploration of such themes. We easily become preoccupied with what is wrong in our clients' lives, despite good evidence that we (and they) need to know what their strengths and resources are. When we look at change as a painful, difficult necessity we will look at it gloomily, without the ease and energy that we experience when we are being curious about what creative options are available to us.

Past Attempts: Unsuccessful and Successful

One avenue that can be fruitfully explored in most cases is past attempts on the part of clients to resolve their own difficulties. There are two experiences of interest. First, times when clients have been partially or temporarily successful deserve attention because they are valuable "exceptions"—examples that they have demonstrated the competencies they need to make more lasting changes. Solution-focused therapists (building on earlier work by the Palo Alto Mental Health Research group) have placed a valuable emphasis on this concept (Watzlawick, Weakland, and Fisch, 1974; de Shazer, 1985, 1988; O'Hanlon and

Weiner-Davis, 1989), emphasizing its importance for pushing clients and their social workers to learn from times when problems have been successfully circumvented (or even simply experienced differently). Such experiences are a source of hope, and valuable ideas about where solutions can be found and built upon.

The second type of noteworthy experience is repeated use of unsuccessful strategies for problem solving. The Doyles' efforts to resolve their problems with Maria by repeatedly intruding into her life are an example of the latter. *why is this a problem?*

As one of our more enigmatic colleagues liked to say, "The problem isn't the problem; the problem is that the problem's a problem." The point (deciphered) is a good one: if we are steadfast in believing our clients have the creativity and competence required to manage their issues more effectively, the question of why they have not already done so becomes interesting. Nothing is wrong in their family that the Doyles, intelligent and well intended as they are, could not analyze and fix on their own. Why is their problem a problem? What constrains them from drawing on their considerable resources to avert potential disaster? How is it that Rebecca and Daniel, also bright and committed people, find themselves defeated by trivialities?

This line of questioning commonly brings problematic traditions to light (the sort of narrative we discussed earlier). When people are committed to problem-solving strategies that do not work, it is usually the case that those strategies have been prescribed for them by their families and cultures—the Doyles' efforts to resolve conflict through passive compliance is an example, and Daniel's temptation to treat his depression with alcohol is another. Problem solving, then, is very often a matter of relinquishing some strategies and reinforcing other, more successful options.

Anticipation of Support from Others

In Chapter 4, we indicated that a major component in contexts that facilitate creative change is support from family and other influential networks. Consider the extreme example (Mike's client) of a young woman determined to rid herself of the habit of using illegal narcotics. She was part of an urban network of friends who were also users, and their response to her quitting was instructive. Initial efforts to undermine her resolve were relatively gentle (systematic invitations to party, and frequent voicing of the opinion that she could not possibly maintain the change). However, the longer she persisted, the more efforts to force her back to her old behaviors escalated, to the point that she was receiving threatening telephone calls. Knowing whom she was dealing with, she took the calls seriously enough to conclude that she would have to divorce herself from this former network entirely, and change communities. She was able to implement this plan largely because she had alternative support from her parents and siblings, who remained committed to helping her straighten out, even though they had been threatened as well.

This is an extreme example of what clients very often confront. Many people will recognize that in making healthy changes (quitting smoking, for example) the support they receive from friends and families is equivocal, and subtle invitations to fail are a variable to be contended with. Part of planning with our clients is therefore to explore the familial and social reactions that changing might stimulate. Identifying potential supports and deciding to access them, working to create or strengthen support from important others, and developing options for dealing with negative reactions to change can all be extremely helpful.

TRADITIONS AND THE SEARCH
FOR SOLUTIONS

"When your son is thirty, what kind of relationship do you think you will have with him?" an abusive father is asked. Reluctantly, he acknowledges that if his son is sensible, he will learn to maintain a safe, healthy distance, just as he did with his own father. "Is this what you want, or would you chose something else if you could figure out how?" we ask. Then, if the conversation proceeds as we hope, we begin to explore alternative goals and the changes that will achieve them. Reauthorship of narratives often starts by contemplating the ending, and asking if this is really what is desired. When meaningful, feasible alternatives are identified, the task of reworking the plot, in small, achievable steps, can follow.

The traditions that shape our growth provide us with various narrative themes about change and problem solving. We have already alluded to this: one social worker or client might be convinced that insight is a necessary concomitant of lasting change; another might disparage "navel gazing" as a waste of time, preferring a get-on-with-it behavioral approach. Achieving agreement with our clients as to what fits for them and their situation is an important ingredient in an effective helping alliance.

As usual, the issue of traditions and problem solving can be both good and bad news. A primary task facing us as clinical social workers is to identify and amplify the nurturing and empowering aspects of our clients' traditions. The Doyles inherited, via Anita's family, a tradition of accepting and even valuing difference. They were able to utilize this to counteract the more prejudiced beliefs prescribed by John's extended family. Objectionable narratives aside, we can see in John examples of how he has learned positive lessons from his family as well. He is loyal, hardworking, and accomplished, and (faltering though his attempts are) demonstrates a real desire to protect his family. These are admirable traditions, and it is a good practice to take note of them, deliberately recognizing their virtues and utility.

On the other hand, traditions are often present that impede creative change. It is equally important for the clinician to be sensitive to these, ready to help the client understand and challenge them. However, even when this is our focus we can remember that often both positive and negative lessons are present in the same experience. While we are exploring the sources of our clients' troubles, we have the opportunity to discuss with them how they have learned to take care of themselves. When Daniel's father gave him boxing lessons, using the opportunity to inflict pain (see Chapter 2), three noteworthy themes were established. First, there was the ostensible scripting regarding what pursuits define manliness (which Daniel rejected). Second, a more insidious (less explicit) theme revolved around Daniel's weakness, failure, and vulnerability (which he was less able to counteract). Third, when his mother supported him in putting a stop to his ordeal, he learned something important about protection and nurturing, and about the fact that he had options in life. Though his story was not happy, consider what it might have been if his mother had aligned with his father in denouncing him as a disappointing failure. In working with Daniel, it was important to challenge the tradition that required him to fail; but equally necessary was recognition of the sources of strength that sustained him through difficult times.

Narratives About Personal Power and Vulnerability

When John Doyle expresses the belief that he cannot insist on his mother treating him like an autonomous adult, he is signaling the presence of a type of narrative clients often struggle against. Supporting his inaction is the belief that if he were to be more assertive, her anger would be too destructive to bear in some unclear way. Although we can respect this as his belief, we would be unhelpful to him if we were to concur with him as to its literal truth. In fact, it is almost certain that he can find ways of confronting her that, while difficult, will not be catastrophic. In John's view, the dangers associated with solving his problem are great, and his options look untenable next to the risks. As long as he is convinced of this, he is unlikely to entertain change. If he is challenged to recognize that he has exaggerated the force of his mother's displeasure (based on his experience when he was much younger) and, consequently, dismissed perfectly viable options, he may then feel empowered to respond more creatively.

When our clients or we are stuck, a narrative akin to John's is very commonly contributing to our impasse. Echoes of the powerlessness we experience as children have stayed with us, and fuel beliefs exaggerating the costs of changing and minimizing our power to implement options. Since experience with bad habits is common to everyone, perhaps reflecting on the process of modifying them will help make the point.

The example could be any change: such as weight reduction, implementing an exercise program, stopping smoking, improving study habits, or unplugging the television set. In the frequent cases where such change poses difficulties, the narrative issues will be formally similar to those encountered by Daniel when he decided to stop drinking wine. His first reaction was that such a change would be too difficult: (1) the loss of pleasure would be too much to bear; (2) friends and colleagues with whom he socialized would notice the change and would conclude he was an alcoholic, which would be too embarrassing; (3) he had no options for enjoying himself that were nearly as satisfying; (4) many special moments in his history with Rebecca were associated with wine, and he was afraid their relationship might prove empty if they were restricted to sharing a pot of herbal tea instead; (5) he personally lacked the willpower required to make the change.

Daniel is entertaining a narrative that leads to one conclusion: if we accept his premises it would be unreasonable to think he can change. Smokers who know their practice is life threatening will acknowledge activating similar arguments as they struggle with a decision to stop. So too will anyone who has had to wrestle with a weight problem. Quitting smoking or saying no to chocolate can admittedly be difficult, even painful. However, if we as social workers support clients in exaggerating the costs of changing (and minimizing the resources they bring to the task), we are supporting a self-defeating narrative. If we acknowledge difficulties while insisting that they are manageable, we are better positioned to help our clients plan effectively to carry changes through to a successful conclusion.

Clients who have suffered a traumatic history may be struggling against narratives in which their opportunities for self-worth seem negligible and even their right to exist may seem a tenuous thing. Such beliefs can be vitally important because, in a sense, they have the power to govern everything else. If children learn, under painful and powerful circumstances, to believe that their most basic rights can (and will) be abrogated at the whim of more powerful people, what are they to make of a social worker who wants them to take better care of themselves? At some level, they may feel they are being asked to do the impossible by someone who cannot appreciate how powerless reason and good intentions are.

Supporting the ability of clients to step back from their narrative, to achieve a psychological distance from it through "externalization" (White and Epston, 1990) or strengthening of the "observing ego" can be very important for such clients. A primary early goal is to discern what is necessary to support such distancing from painful and frightening experiences, so that they can be rendered less powerful, and the client's ability to think more freely about options is enhanced. Allowing oneself to wish for something different is often the result of achieving such distance from troubling past experiences. As Daniel comes to regard his history of abuse and his identity as a disappointing failure as a narrative that he can, as an adult, step back from and reconstruct, he is much better able to identify attractive alternatives. Without taking this step, he is less able to think about what he wants because doing so is seen as just a painful exercise in futility.

Permission to Make Demands

All of us have incorporated, into our narratives, rules about making demands. Quite powerful cultural influences can be seen in these—in some societies making direct requests is considered rudely aggressive, and a high degree of circumspection is valued. In others, directness is seen as a virtue, while more oblique requests trigger frustration. In many, the rules are different for women, who are expected to be more oriented to the needs of others than of themselves, and for children, from whom demands are seen as inappropriate breaches of etiquette. For men, identifying needs (especially needs for nurturing) can be extremely difficult in the face of male socialization that applauds toughness but is contemptuous of vulnerability.

Sensitivity to such issues requires us to be attuned to the discomfort we may be stimulating for our clients when we ask them to clarify their needs. People who have been raised to abhor selfishness in themselves and others can become highly anxious when confronted with such a question; some may feel diminished as people by the fact that they need something from someone else (especially a professional helper). The exercise can be frightening, and helping clients develop comfort with declaring their needs is often an important part of our early work.

Undesirable Goals Implicit in Clients' Narratives

At the same time as we think about how traditions may support or impede goal setting, we also can think about how narratives that clients have incorporated into their life plans contain goals of which the client may or may not be aware. For example, while he would not have expressed it as something desirable, there is a sense in which Daniel's narrative has a pernicious goal: for him to be a failure and a disappointment. Clinically, this is worth exploring with him. Sometimes, it is a shock for a client with a tragic story to acknowledge where it is leading, and that recognition provides motivation to change. Another clinical consideration is that regardless of how painful such implicit goals are, it is not always a simple matter for the client to give them up. In Daniel's case, the difficulty was the strength of his conviction that his fate was inexorable and that it was futile to think he could change it.

Maria Doyle's unspoken pernicious goal was to protect her parents by sacrificing her independence—and it was as important for her parents to hear that as it was for Maria to articulate it. For Maria, reworking that aspect of her narrative was difficult because of her belief that her self-sacrifice was necessary to her parents' happiness. In her view, to give that goal up would be to cause them pain, and this (in the traditions of her extended family) would be an unforgivable act of disloyalty.

Other narratives (John Doyle comes to mind) have a quality of being stuck, because there is no clear future or goal beyond maintaining an unhappy status quo. The client appears immobilized, and has trouble recognizing any clear path forward out of an impasse that can, without help, become a lifelong trap.

INTEGRATING DIFFERENT AGENDAS

Clinical social work and related fields have a history of inadvertently disrespecting clients in relation to goal setting. For example, to the extent that helpers relied on expert interpretation as a key to therapeutic change, it was common to assume that they were best equipped by virtue of training and experience to determine what change was required. A structural family therapist, schooled in the belief that young peoples' problems normally signal dysfunction in the parents' relationship, might automatically assume that John and Anita need to resolve marital conflicts if Maria is to be happier. A psychodynamic therapist might believe that Maria's depression expresses a crippling emotional conflict over her emerging sexuality, and prescribe treatment to help her become more comfortable about herself and her sexual needs. A therapist trained in the human potential movement's framework might consider that barriers to intimacy between Maria and her parents are the source of their pain, and assume that greater openness about how they feel toward one another will restore them to health.

Theory and clinical experience support such goals, which make sense (given certain assumptions) and have been appropriate with other clients. But none is necessarily going to be meaningful to Maria and her parents. If we are so theoretically committed that we do not hear them when they try to suggest we are on the wrong track, we are showing disrespect toward them as capable people. If they are strong enough to reject what we are doing to them, they may terminate their work with us while Maria is still at risk. If they accommodate to our viewpoint despite their misgivings, the result will be a degree of dis-empowerment and frustration.

It is critical that goals are co-constructed by our clients and us. This will not be the case unless clients feel they have been partners in defining those goals, and see them as congruent with their needs. This said, we seldom are able to simply ask clients what they want and leave it at that. A man in a highly patriarchal family tells Mike that his marriage will be happy if only his wife can be persuaded to become more expert at cooking the meals he likes and ironing his socks properly—and his wife, who is very depressed, agrees. Mike will obviously do the couple a disservice if he simply accepts this goal and intervenes by helping them find and enroll her in a cookery course.

Though it was not the case, suppose that John and Anita believed their family would be restored to happiness if Maria were persuaded to become a more compliant child, following her parents' advice more assiduously. While George agreed with the ultimate goal of helping them create a family in which Maria no longer feels suicidally depressed, he would not agree with the imagined prescription for achieving that. In fact, his training and experience would tell him that he would contribute to a worsening of Maria's situation if he followed her parents' lead at this point. Some time spent in negotiating a mutually acceptable common ground would be required.

So it is critical that our clients' perception of their needs and priorities must be heard and respected, and we should always be alert to the danger of promoting inappropriate goals based on our training and prior experience. We remain, nevertheless, active partners in determining what the goals of intervention are to be. Goals are, as noted, co-constructed, a product of open discourse and negotiation between our clients and us. What is critical is that we bring an attitude of openness and respect to this negotiation process.

GOALS AND STAGES
IN THE PROCESS OF CHANGE

The work of Prochaska (1995) has garnered attention for research into the process of change, which has led to the identification of six stages clients typically go through when they solve problems in living. Originally, the clients studied were involved in changing specific habits (e.g., smoking cessation), but the work is currently being applied in understanding how people resolve more complex issues, such as extricating themselves from abusive relationships.

The kinds of goals that can be developed with clients differ with the stage of change they have reached. The first possibility is *precontemplation,* in which there is little recognition that a problem exists: "It isn't that they can't see the solution, they can't see the problem" (G. K. Chesterton, cited in Prochaska, 1995, p. 409). Typically, such clients are seen because someone else is concerned about them, or someone else is affected by their issues (a child of an alcoholic parent who is in denial is a common example). In cases such as this, the goal is a matter of inviting the clients to explore the issues that are of concern to others, and to consider ways in which those concerns have personal relevance for them. For example, a client may not be willing to discuss drinking as an issue, but may well agree to spend time looking at his child's unhappiness and ways of ameliorating it.

Obviously, there are significant limits to what will be accomplished unless some way can be found to support clients in acknowledging the problems they face. If movement in this direction eludes us, then in a sense we do not have a client—there is no therapeutic contract and no viable helping alliance.

A second stage in Prochaska's model is *contemplation,* in which the client is aware of a problem and may be thinking in terms of an eventual need to do something about it, but has made no clear commitment to any substantive action. At this point, clients can benefit from considerable attention to the sometimes-difficult question: "What do you want?" Commitment to change need not be assumed, and may be premature where an agreement to simply assess, with the client, the relative merits of changing or not changing will be more acceptable and productive.

The third stage, *preparation,* denotes an intention to change and some experience with tentative actions and incompletely successful attempts. Goal setting at this stage involves exploration of past attempts and exceptions to the problem, and utilization of such information to explore options. The need to consider the familial and social context in which changes will be enacted also becomes important at this stage.

The fourth stage, *action,* is one in which new behaviors, changes to the environment, and new perspectives are adopted (Prochaska, 1995, p. 410). Goal setting in this case is a matter of identifying and reinforcing successes, clarifying what works, and supporting a continuation of those options. With many clients, ongoing monitoring of familial and social effects is important. Also, there is often crucial work to be done helping clients integrate, cognitively, the meaning of changes that they have experimented with behaviorally. The goal in this case is to expand the impact of change across levels, in the belief that when changes in behavior have positive narrative impacts and emotional consequences they are likely to be much more enduring.

The last point regarding the action stage introduces the fifth step, *maintenance.* The therapeutic goal at this point is continued exploration of the benefits and meaning of changes that have been achieved, and options for managing any negative side effects. Also of continued importance are steps to assure ongoing social and familial support for new ways of being, since these will be important in helping the client maintain the changes.

The last of Prochaska's stages, *termination,* occurs when there is confidence that previous problem situations or behaviors are resolved to a satisfactory degree. Goal setting and planning for termination are normally a matter of solidifying options for maintaining the changes made, and, sometimes, discussing what steps will be taken if more help is required in the future.

Of course, no assumption can be made that progress through stages of change is a straightforward matter, with clients being helped to move systematically from stage one through to termination. First, clients present for service at different points, and some are reluctant to acknowledge problems while others are already engaged in taking significant actions. Another complication is that the same person may be at different stages in relation to different important issues—Daniel could, in principle, be highly motivated to take action to improve his marriage but unready to see his drinking as something needing attention. Finally, the process of change is a matter of cycling through the various stages a number of times, in relation to different aspects of problems or the implementation of different solutions.

Chapter 6

Clarifying Boundaries: Boundaries As a Framework for Therapy

*Only in solitude do we find ourselves; and in finding ourselves, we
find in ourselves all our brothers in solitude.*

Miguel de Unanimo
Three Exemplary Novels

A fourteen-year-old boy's return home is dramatic, with doors
slamming and the house shaking from the force of his tread as he
makes his way upstairs to his room. His father feels challenged by
this—it is not what he was anticipating, and he is a parent who places a
high premium on maturity and emotional control. He goes to his son's
room and asks him what is wrong, but the tone of the question is critical and his son, who is already feeling miserable (and somewhat embarrassed by his behavior), picks up on his father's disapproval. He
responds with defensive anger, and the conversation deteriorates from
there, ending in a recriminatory impasse that neither really wanted.

The father is ineffective in this situation because the boundary
defining his relationship to his son is (at least for the moment) un- *true!*
clear. To some extent, he feels that his son's turmoil is a challenge to *Dad*
his authority. In some sense, he feels as though his son's loss of control threatens his own.

Suppose the boundaries were different, with the father understanding clearly that his son's explosive feelings were something he could
be concerned about without wishing to control them or taking re-

165

sponsibility for them. He would then be able to ask what is the matter more respectfully. If his son responded with resentment he would be unlikely to take that as a personal affront, and would remain more able to offer his support and willingness to talk. He might even be able to let his son know that temper tantrums in a fourteen-year-old are not the preferred option for dealing with stress, once the problem is known to him and there has been some opportunity to defuse it. Teaching and direction offered from a position of independence are much more likely to be effective than when they are complicated by struggles for space and power. The consequences for the boy will be to feel understood, respected, and safe—in contrast to the angry alienation of the first scenario.

Every person we meet, professionally or otherwise, has a unique story to tell, and each tells that story from a particular position or perspective—the boy and the father in our brief example will each view their problem quite differently. The sequencing of the story as each person tells it, nonverbal communications, and other process variables give the clinical social worker additional information about its meaning for everyone involved.

When a family is telling its story, members may become emotionally aroused (often intensely so). If the discourse is about conflict, each will want the social worker to join him or her, accepting that person's position and rejecting the perspective of other family members. The father in our example will want us to commiserate about how his son's unreasonable behavior burdens him, and his son will be watching carefully how we align ourselves: will the adults in the room gang up on him, or is the social worker a potential ally, ready to appreciate how he has been mistreated and misunderstood?

For a new or poorly prepared clinician, this situation can be overwhelming, because it involves strong feelings and demands to go in different, mutually exclusive directions. Without a good frame of reference, workers can easily be overwhelmed, losing their focus and their ability to help the family envision goals. The *amount* of information is in itself a challenge; within minutes there is a flood of data that the social worker needs to organize and prioritize. In addition to simple quantity, the data we confront in a family interview can be demanding because of their emotional intensity. Feelings about their conflicts and problems are often very strong for family members, and they will communicate their urgency to the clinician verbally and nonverbally. If family members themselves are overwhelmed, this results in a sense of hopelessness and the threat of disorganization. If the clinical social worker joins them in feeling the same way, the result is to reinforce their sense of powerlessness, and that is obviously not helpful. A constant goal is to inculcate and support a sense of optimism in the family, which is difficult to do without a framework we can use to make sense of a large amount of emotionally laden information, and to maintain a sense of direction in relation to it.

The concept of boundary, presented at length in Chapter 1, provides a basis for such a framework. For purposes of assessment and intervention, we suggest viewing a family's* boundaries through four lenses, focusing in turn on the *generational boundary,* the *parent/ marital boundary,* and the *personal boundary,* which includes a subset, the *social worker/client system boundary.* We hope to demonstrate that this practical application of theory about boundaries adds life and sharpness to our frameworks, helping us to respond more efficiently to inherently confusing circumstances.

The metaphor of *lenses* is a popular one, and is useful in this case because we want to emphasize that these are different ways of looking at the same phenomena. It is not a matter of saying that the examples that follow belong in one category or another, but that when we employ different lenses, different important aspects of the family's experience are brought into focus.

A final general point is that we would be remiss if we did not emphasize that there are other lenses in addition to the four we are highlighting, especially *gender, development,* and *culture.* These issues have been dealt with exhaustively by other authors, which may at least partly excuse us for not giving them the attention they merit here.

CLARIFYING BOUNDARIES:
A NEW EXAMPLE

To illustrate the points made in this chapter we would like to introduce a new example. This is a family that was seen by George: a

---

*As a convenience, we will focus this discussion on nuclear families with children. It will not be difficult for the reader to extrapolate the discussion to other types of family, since variations on the theme are common to all.

single mother, her two children, and a gentleman friend that the mother had been dating for a little less than a year.

The mother, Connie, made contact first by telephone, relating to George that her son, nine-year-old Matt, was demonstrating behavior problems at school. Connie indicated that she thought the problems were quite serious, but that Matt's father (Mathew senior), her estranged husband, was less worried about them.

George asked if Connie would feel comfortable inviting Matt's father to the first interview. She said she would try, but came instead with her boyfriend, Phil, a statement about how she wants to view this new relationship. Also present in the interview is Connie's daughter, Crystal, who is seven.

THE GENERATIONAL BOUNDARY

In work with families (and also work with individuals or couples with extended family issues) the generational boundary is a frequent focus for assessment and intervention. The clarity of the boundary that regulates attachment and distance between Connie and her ex-husband and their children (or, perhaps, Connie and Phil vis-à-vis Connie's children) will have an ongoing impact on their well-being. It is vitally important because our relationships to our parents and our children matter deeply to us, and the quality of the boundaries defining the "generation gap" (in either direction) determines how effectively needs for affection, support, structure, and room to grow are managed.

Before we return to our example, some generalizations about generational boundaries in families are in order. First, when the generational boundary is clear, young people have more free energy to devote to developmental tasks (and other goals), rather than feeling compelled to invest it in fighting with their parents. For their part, of course, parents also need autonomy in relation to their children, so that they have sufficient space to take care of themselves and attend to their own needs.

The generational boundary establishes a hierarchy, which varies in its nature as children (and their parents) mature. In the best circumstances, and especially with older children, the hierarchy is less about control than about the parents claiming a position of leadership from which they can exercise authority and offer nurturance effectively.

When the generational boundary is not clear, parents may be looking to their children for support or meeting other needs inappropriately. The obvious examples are the extreme ones such as sexual abuse, but it occurs more subtly as well. For example, Maria Doyle is worried about her parents, and is unclear about what she wants out of a fear of hurting them. She needs to hear that it is not her job to worry about them or to protect them, and that she can trust them to take care of themselves.

This boundary can be blurred also when parents have different traditions or histories regarding parenting. This is normally the case, since we all have had somewhat different experience with being parented. Clarity comes when we can negotiate agreement about how to carry out the parenting role, supporting and complementing each other with regard to the joint functions of providing nurture and the security of clear structures and expectations. When there is unmanaged conflict over these tasks the results are different, with the tension of chronic disputes and pressures on the children to align with one parent or the other (triangulation) being common.

Unresolved trauma from the past can be played out in ways that blur the generational boundary as well. For example, a mother with a history of sexual abuse in her own childhood might have difficulty allowing her teenage daughter sufficient freedom to form relationships with young men, out of a fear for her safety. A father who was abusively treated as a child may, as a parent, have difficulty acting as a disciplinarian, vacillating between passivity and overreaction. In each case, issues that need to be dealt with by the parents are being made a problem for the child—a problem that the child will rarely understand and cannot solve.

As parents, a clear generational boundary allows us freedom to be more nurturing, or to discipline when necessary with firmness but not rejection.

Consider the following piece of the interaction between George, Connie, Connie's children, and Phil.

George: What brings you here today? Can I call you Connie?

Connie: Uh-huh. I am just having a really hard time understanding Matt.

George: Uh-huh, you are having difficulty with your nine-year-old son?

Connie: Yes, very much so.

George: What kind of difficulties?

Connie: Uh, I don't know. Everything I guess . . . like we just don't seem to click on our ideas.

George: Yes, okay. Can you tell me a little more about it?

Connie: Well, for one thing he is quite hyper and I just don't know how to cope with him anymore. I ask him to do something and he just does the opposite. I don't know. His moods seem to be up and down quite a bit. When I talked to Mrs. Davies, the principal at school, and I talked to his teacher, and he is like that, the same at school as what he is at home. And a couple of times when he has gone to Cubs he has left right in the middle of it because he has got upset and he has just walked out. The same with baseball, or anything he is involved in.

Connie's complaints are global and poorly differentiated, and they communicate her feelings of powerlessness—she does not see herself having a clear leadership position. Moments into the interview, it is apparent that a blurred generational boundary makes it hard for her to discipline without being rejecting and to nurture without feeling resentful.

George proceeded to ask Matt if he likes sports, and they talked about that for several minutes. This was an effort to join with Matt about something positive, focusing on his competence rather than on ways in which he was seen to be a problem. If Matt's first interaction with George were problem focused, their relationship would start on an adversarial footing.

Because of the process he has followed, George has also invited Connie not to complain about Matt, so when he returns to her concerns, she does not know what to say.

George: So what kinds of things, Connie, at home, cause you particular concern?

Connie: Oh, I don't know.

George [recognizing what he has done, turns to Matt]: Do you have a bad temper?

Matt: I guess so.

George: What upsets you at home, Matt?

Matt: Um—something. When she asks me to do one thing, then when I'm doing it she says to do another thing.

George: You're not even finished [with] that and then you are supposed to do another thing?

Matt: Yah.

George: Uh-huh.

Matt: When I'm right in the middle of the first thing.

Recognizing that Matt is inviting him into a pattern, as his mother did previously (a triangle where he is invited to join Matt against his mother), George changes the subject.

George: Uh-huh. Are there other things? How long have your mommy and daddy lived separately?

Matt: About seven years.

George: Seven years.

George: [to Connie, who is shaking her head]: It's not been that long?

Connie: No, three, four. No, maybe . . .

Matt [with annoyance in his voice]: Last time you said it was seven.

The confusion about when the separation occurred could be a comment on the feelings the mother has toward Matt, or a comment on her feelings toward her ex-husband, or both. In any case, it suggests an area of tension and unresolved issues worthy of further exploration. An understanding of boundaries allows George to develop, within minutes, a tentative working hypothesis. This hypothesis begins to guide the interview, with information being elicited in an organized fashion, and helps the social worker develop an understanding of the family's problems.

The Parent/Marital Boundary

Another focus for assessment and intervention respecting boundary clarity in family work is the parent/marital boundary. The deliberate use of this lens emphasizes that the adults in a family have a life that is separate from their role as parents.

Not uncommonly, when an intimate couple fails to negotiate a comfortable and gratifying relationship, the partners attempt to solve the problem by having children. Their struggle with each other is then deflected onto the children, transformed into conflicts over discipline or some other aspect of child rearing. Other couples may use career in the same way, with commitments to work providing distance and a reason for their unhappiness other than the more frightening possibility that the relationship itself is problematic. A different possibility is that sometimes when conflict between adult partners is reduced, parent-child conflicts become more severe.

When the parent/marital boundary is unclear, struggles in the marital relationship are played out in the parenting role. The need to negotiate distance and closeness as partners (and/or agreements about power and control) are expressed as parenting issues, and children are triangulated in matters that should not be their concern.

The Doyles, whom we discussed extensively in earlier chapters, are a family in which the generational boundary is unclear. Despite this they have a very strong marriage, which serves them well when they need to mobilize to change.

In contrast, when the parent/marital boundary is unclear, the same is normally also true of the generational boundary. When both boundaries are blurred, the clinical challenge is greater than with families such as the Doyles. Problems are more intractable, and the family is slower to change.

When Connie called for an appointment, she was invited to bring her ex-husband with her, and indicated she would do so. Instead, she brought Phil. This is a message to Phil about how she feels about him, and her desire for him to commit to her and her family. However, that invitation is given through Matt; it is his problem that brings Phil to the consulting room.

Here is a piece of dialogue illustrating boundary issues that can be understood using the parent/marital lens:

George: Are you upset that your mom and dad aren't living together?

Matt: A bit.

George: Yeah. Would you like to see them move back together again?

Matt: Uh-huh.

Phil [interrupting]: Does your dad talk to you at the top of his voice once in awhile or not? Does he talk louder than your mom to you when he asks you to do something, or does your mom talk louder to you?

George allows the interruption, wanting to see what position Phil will take.

Matt: My mom talks louder.

Phil: How come?

Matt: I don't know.

Phil [after another pause]: Would you respond more to her if she was to talk to you the same as I talk to you?

Matt: Uh-huh.

Phil: Would you be more helpful or do things more or would you be more interested in doing things for Mom if she would talk to you like I do or your friend? Does your friend holler at you to do something or does he talk nice to you?

Matt [scratching his head and appearing confused]: He talks nice.

Phil: So you do things for him in turn?

Matt: Uh-huh.

Phil: So, sometimes your mother talks to you in an ordinary voice and sometimes it doesn't work either, so if it has to come to a toss-up that way, that's—don't mind me speaking [turns to George]. I'm just talking for myself.

Phil's position now becomes clearer. He is distancing himself from Connie by criticizing her. Her bringing him to the interview is a request for greater involvement, but he is beginning to signal that he may not want that. However, like Connie, he is communicating about their adult relationship through Matt, which involves Matt in an issue that is not his concern.

George: Go ahead.

Phil: Connie doesn't maybe realize she is speaking to Crystal and Matt maybe through the top of her voice, you know, sometimes through habit.

George: Ahhh.

Phil: I mean I do things when I am talking through getting excited. I hesitate and trip over my words. I say to myself—well [if] I just slow down and think, I won't stumble over whoever I am talking to.

Phil is floundering, feeling confused and qualifying his previous comments, anxious about how Connie is reacting to what he has said.

George: Ahhh.

Phil: Or through excitement maybe I'll be talking about one subject and I'll zip through and start another one before I am finished [with] the first two.

George: Ahhh. So you feel that Connie . . .

George wants to invite Phil to take ownership of his comments. His question was going to be, "So you think that Connie would benefit by not speaking so loudly to her son?" Phil seems to sense where George is going and interrupts, again becoming more confusing, by qualifying his comments instead of clarifying them. Then, he distances himself further from taking ownership for his comments by changing the focus to his own family.

Phil [interrupting]: Well, it is up to . . . I mean it is up to the child and it's up to the children. It is up to the parent but who is responsible more or less—through experience. I have four of my own children.

George: Uh-huh.

Phil: The oldest is twenty-eight and the youngest is nineteen.

George: Uh-huh.

Phil: And I'm parted from my wife for now or whatever.

George: Are you divorced?

Phil: No.

George: Just separated?

Phil: Yes.

George: How long have you been separated?

Phil: It will be three years in February coming up, and she works at the fertilizer plant.

George: Uh-huh.

Phil: So I lived alone [a] while with my mother and brother, lived on the farm by myself. Batched for a year and a half to see what was— you know—and then after that time neighbors and friends suggested that I move around or mix with people or talk to people.

His change of focus continues his unwillingness to take ownership for his comments, but it does clarify his position in relation to Connie. He is separated "for now or whatever." His wife works at "the fertilizer plant," information that is not relevant to anyone else in the room, but does indicate where his own interest is—which is why Connie, at this point, moves in her chair to turn away from him. She is further displeased to hear that he is seeing her because "neighbors and friends suggested that. . . ." This all indicates his relatively weak investment in their relationship, and helps make sense of his criticism of her through Matt.

The confusion in the parent/marital boundary has now become apparent, with Connie and Phil attempting to work out their different needs for closeness and distance through Matt. All of this information is important to George, of course. Any treatment plan to help Matt should not give Phil a central role, since he would not follow through. More likely, he would only experience heightened ambivalence and this would encourage a continued lack of boundary clarity.

Personal Boundaries

In Chapter 1, we discussed how personal boundaries are essential to all of us at a very basic level, affecting our ability to maintain a coherent sense of self, to claim the space we need to grow, and to feel sufficiently safe in the world.

Not all families are equally good at encouraging and respecting optimal boundaries for their members as individuals. In some, boundary violations are frequent, and people do not feel permitted to think, act, or feel independently, or to solve their own problems. The result is that relationships involve ongoing control struggles. The emotional and cognitive consequence of disallowing differentiation is a degree of fusion, anxiety, emotional turmoil, and confusion.

When personal boundaries are violated, children and adolescents spend time struggling for clarification to maintain their identity. In extreme cases the struggle is primarily about survival, and very little energy is left for growth. When people cope with intrusions and violation of boundaries, little energy is left to explore one's world and the possibilities it presents, or to accept validation and support when struggling with difficulties.

Helping clients with creating, maintaining, and clarifying personal boundaries is a constant intervention in clinical work. Victims of abuse come easily to mind. Children who have been treated violently or women whose partners batter them benefit when we help them find ways to maintain the distance they need to be safe. John Doyle needs to learn to say "stop" effectively when his extended family is emotionally abusive to his wife and children.

In Connie's family, Matt's personal boundary vis-à-vis his mother has an aspect that is critical for his future well-being, which is that he is being assigned (and is enacting) an identity as a bad boy. Caught in conflicts and tensions originating with the adults in his life, he is learning to be their problem in ways that will inevitably cause him (and them) future pain. Thus, clarifying his personal boundary is an essential part of the treatment process. Let's observe how the personal boundary lens provides direction.

George: Uh-huh. Is it hard for you to talk to your mommy?

Matt: A bit.

George: Yeah. What makes [it] hard?

Matt: Sadness.

George: Sadness. Her sadness or yours?

Matt: Mine.

George: Your sadness? [to Connie] Could you find out what his sadness is all about? Maybe you could sit next to him. [Connie has been sitting with one chair between her and Matt. When George invites her to move closer Matt removes her purse, which Connie had previously placed on the chair between them, thus inviting his mother to move closer. George gets up from his chair and gets a box of tissues from the corner of the room, and hands them to Connie, inviting her to tune into Matt's emotional needs and nurture him.]

Matt's direct acknowledgment of his sadness is a lovely invitation for his mother to recognize his feelings, and George invites her to accept.

George: And if he wants to cry that's okay. [Connie takes the box of tissues and places them on the arm of the chair between them— thus creating a barrier between them, and she leans away from Matt.]

Connie: How come you're so sad?

Matt: About lots of things.

Connie: Can you tell me some?

Matt: When you get mad at me and when Crystal shouts at me, and when Crystal gets me in heck [pause] sometimes.

It would appear that Matt's anxiety got the better of him. Previously he was clear that his sadness related to his mother and father breaking up. Now, given the opportunity to talk about that by his mother, he shifts the focus, blaming her and triangulating his sister. Connie is unable to explore further and gets defensive.

Connie [after a long pause]: Uh-huh. [another pause] But why do I get mad at you then?

Matt: Because uh, Crystal always bugs me.

Connie: But what do you do to her sometimes though?

Matt [his voice changing pitch with anxiety]: I do it back and then she tells and then I get the heck.

Connie [irritation in her voice]: Sometimes you do it pretty good. [Connie is annoyed at Matt; she physically withdraws from him and looks away.]

The old pattern of Matt behaving like a bad boy, blaming mother and sister, and mother blaming Matt reemerges. The personal boundary between mother and son remains rigid.

George [gently to Connie]: Could you find out what else makes him sad before you help him understand it?

Connie [hesitates, then turns to Matt]: Is there anything else?

Matt [hesitantly]: Uh-huh. I think so.

Connie: What?

Matt: When I keep on thinking that it's my fault that you two split up.

Connie: Oh [pause]. I didn't know that you felt like that [pause]. You never told me [pause], and when you asked how come that we weren't living together I thought that I explained it to you lots of times.

Briefly, Connie seems to hear Matt's feelings, then she distances again and blames Matt: "You never told me."

Matt: But I didn't get it, what you meant.

Connie: Ummm. Is there anything else, beside me getting after you and Crystal or . . . ?

This is a shift in the pattern, with Connie taking a risk to explore further. She seems unsure how to do this, however. Perhaps she is struggling to decide which is the real Matt, the sad boy in front of her or the defiant boy she has experienced previously. George helps her take the next step.

Matt [after a long pause]: No.

George [pause]: Could you maybe find out what makes him think that it's his fault that you split up?

Connie: Why do you think that it's your fault that Mom and Dad split up, [that] we're not living together?

Matt [softly]: Because the only one that could get to talk to you was Crystal.

Again Matt slips into the pattern of triangulating Crystal.

Connie: Hmm?

Matt [close to tears]: Because the only one that could get to talk to you was Crystal when she was little.

Connie: Why couldn't you come talk to me, [pause] hmm?

Matt [very emotional]: Because I thinked you'd get mad at me.

George [after a long pause during which Connie is struggling with her emotions]: Can you find out what made him think that?

Connie: Why did you think that, Matt? That it was your fault? [Connie is clearly anxious and starts to speak quickly] I don't really know, I don't really understand you when you say you think it was your fault why Mom and Dad broke up. I don't know how you felt that or why you felt that.

Matt [crying]: Because [long pause during which he wipes away a tear] because you guys would make it hard on me.

Connie: You mean because for that little while, in the apartment, when I stopped Dad from coming to see you again?

Connie is becoming more aware of Matt's feelings, and it is increasingly difficult to see him as bad. The boundary separating her from him, which has been so rigid, becomes more open. Then her feelings escalate and she introduces her own explanation, triangulating Matt's father again.

Matt [clearly confused as he tries to follow his mother, letting go of his own issues]: When?

Connie: When you were seven; when you didn't see Dad for about six months, and right after that.

Matt [interrupting]: He had to pay.

Connie [interrupting Matt]: No. He had you for the whole weekend after that, then, instead of just Sunday afternoon.

Matt: And then Dad had . . . Dad said he had to pay to get us for the second week.

Connie: But I still don't know why you think it was your fault.

A very important shift in the pattern occurs here. For the first time, Connie catches herself and goes back to Matt, helping him to continue to clarify his personal boundary.

Matt: Because every time I asked you something you guys were sitting there arguing [pause] sometimes.

Connie [clearly distressed]: But that really . . . it wasn't about you.

Matt [very tearful]: And I thought you didn't like me.

Connie: Why did you think that?

Matt: Because you guys didn't answer me.

Connie [gives a long sigh of recognition]: Ooh.

Connie's insight into her son's plight is a big accomplishment, and it did not come easily. George was effective in assisting her and Matt in their struggle because his use of the personal boundary helped him stay very focused and goal directed in his intervention.

The Social Worker/Client System Boundary

When George interviews Connie, Phil, Matt, and Crystal, he is part of a five-person system and is subject to multiple powerful influences. The influences do not all come from the immediate situation either. Each person will pull on him with the story they tell, and will trigger memories and feelings in George of which they have no knowledge. Inevitably, their stories are received by George through his own personal lenses, shaped by his experience in his family of origin, his current family, his cultural background, gender, and so on.

Beginning clinicians often think they are dealing only with the stories the client presents, but this is never so—the situation is always more complicated than that.

As Figure 6.1 indicates, the stories and the emotions they carry influence the worker, but not without a degree of revision or interpretation. In part they are shaped and modified by what we have labeled personal lenses, and, in part, by what we have labeled professional lenses. To the extent that professional knowledge and theory are clear, and to the extent that we are self-aware and can distinguish personal from professional issues, we can be objective, see our clients clearly, and use our knowledge productively on their behalf—rather than letting our own issues, assumptions, and biases intrude in unhelpful ways.

FIGURE 6.1. The Clinical Social Worker's Filters

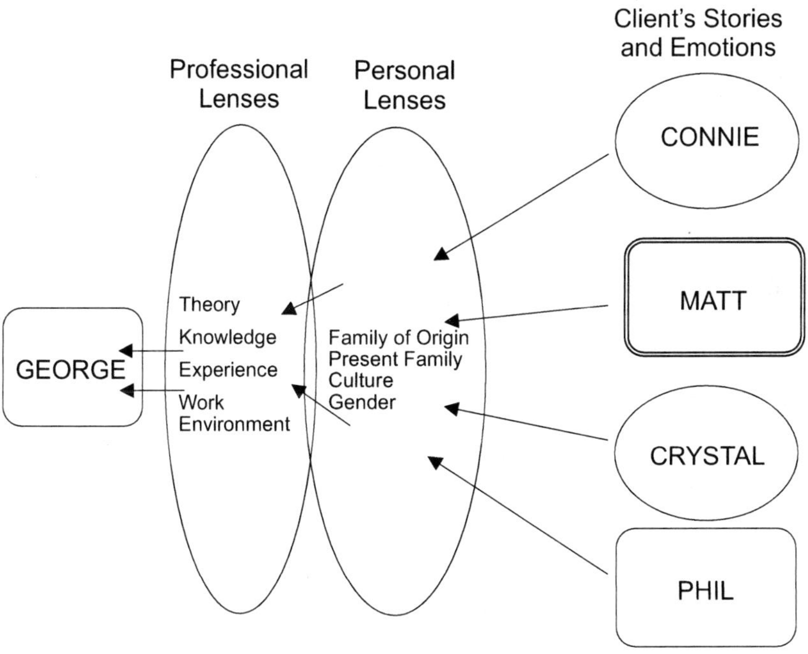

A primary focus for clinical workers throughout their contact with a family is on their personal boundaries in relation to their clients. It would be hard to overstate the importance of keeping this boundary clear, since doing so is a precondition for assuring that our motivation is to work toward what is best for our clients, uncontaminated by agendas rooted in our own needs or biases. When this boundary is not clear, a client can spend time struggling with the clinician (and vice versa) about differences in interpretation or priorities, rather than putting that energy into healing and growth.

Not long ago, George was seeing a fifteen-year-old boy who was severely withdrawn, and in considerable turmoil and at risk of suicide. His parents had separated five years earlier. The boy, Leo, had remained in the care of his mother, who quickly remarried. Her new husband was a rigid, organized, take-charge businessman, who related to Leo by imposing a high degree of structure on him.

Leo's stepfather's parenting priorities were a matter of some dispute between the parents, resulting in Leo feeling triangulated in their conflict. Worse, however, was the fact that his biological father and mother remained very angry with each other, and he was caught in two further conflicts: between his mother and biological father, and between his biological father and stepfather.

In an individual session with George, Leo expressed a desire to pose certain questions to his father. He wanted to know why he had been promised a snowboard for Christmas, but had received nothing. He also wanted to know why his father was neglecting to pay financial support to his mother on his behalf.

George offered to support him in raising these questions, and, with Leo's agreement, the father was invited to come to a subsequent session. He came, and Leo asked him about the snowboard. His father claimed he did not have enough money to buy him one. When Leo questioned him about how he could afford a new car and extensive travel, his father quickly changed the subject, focusing on his frustration with the financial settlement between himself and Leo's mother.

George asked the father to refocus on Leo's questions, and with this support Leo pressed the question why, given money spent on travel and so forth, his father was unwilling to pay child support. His father changed focus, discussing instead his future business plans.

Again, George pushed for attention to Leo's issues. Again, Leo asked his question. His father talked about a book he was writing that would provide a comfortable income and respectability when it was published.

For half an hour Leo posed variations on his question. Despite Leo's persistence, and George's consistent efforts to encourage him to respond to his son's issue, the father avoided answering. Finally, George caught Leo's eye and gently said: "Clearly, what you are hearing and feeling and thinking in your mind are very different than what your father is talking about."

Leo became very quiet and then started to cry. He asked to see George alone, and when his father left, he said: "Now I know why I've been feeling suicidal. What I think and feel is ignored so much I feel like I don't exist." He went on expressing both anger and relief, and finally interjected:

Leo: Oh, shit!!

George: What's the matter?

Leo: Did you know this before today?

George: No, but I knew if you talked with your father you'd get a better understanding of your feelings and what's going on for you. Why did you say "Oh, shit?"

Leo: Because I just broke up with my girlfriend a few days ago—she couldn't cope with me being suicidal.

In this example, George is helping a young man clarify boundaries between himself and his father. Using the personal boundary lens highlights the struggle Leo is engaged in as he makes the important distinction between his own needs and concerns versus his father's unwillingness to deal with them. Without clear boundaries, his father's evasiveness drove him to the conclusion that his concerns were invalid. He felt crazy, even as though he did not exist when his father refused to recognize him and his needs. With clarity of boundaries he could validate his own perceptions and concerns, while seeing his father's evasiveness as his father's responsibility. The result was a considerable sense of relief and empowerment.

An important aspect of this example is brought into focus as well when we use the social worker/client boundary lens. Leo wanted to know if George had been withholding important information from him, and that is a pertinent issue. We do not share all our perceptions and hunches with our clients all the time, and this boundary gives them space to draw their own conclusions more freely. In this case, Leo is questioning whether George had been withholding too much, keeping information to himself that Leo could have used to good effect in another important area of his life.

In this aspect of our work with clients, our relationship to them is a "laboratory," a metaphor suggesting that in dealing with us, they have an opportunity to experiment and learn, discovering options that can be transferred to other important relationships (Dozier and Tyrrell, 1998).

Clients (like everyone else) bring to their relationships a framework that shapes their expectations regarding how others will treat them, basic issues being whether it is safe to seek support and nurturance, and whether there will be reasonable freedom from entanglement as the relationship develops. To a significant extent, this framework has been acquired through experience with one's family of origin, and is therefore also linked to traditions promulgated by the family and culture.

Leo does not trust his father, for obvious reasons. The experience in George's consulting room is likely not entirely new to him, and it is reasonable to think that his framework about relationships impels him to believe that his perceptions and needs are not going to be received respectfully. Having achieved insight about this difficulty in relation to his father, is it any surprise that he then checks whether George has been treating him in a similar way, discounting him by withholding vital information?

Some theorists place this kind of work at the center of the therapeutic endeavor. Dozier and Tyrrell (1998), for example, offer a schema summarizing their model of therapeutic change (see Figure 6.2).

Some general issues will arise in helping relationships with great regularity, which have been recognized for many years. For example, when the social worker sets and clarifies boundaries with the client, defining the terms and limits of their relationship, the client may respond in many possible ways—some of them rooted in experience with past relationships. Traditionally, this has been referred to as *transference,* and it is a useful phenomenon to track. If the client's reaction is for any reason troubling, it is often useful to explore what has happened and what it means, using the helping relationship as a context to learn about the effects of past experiences on the present.

FIGURE 6.2. A Model of Therapeutic Change

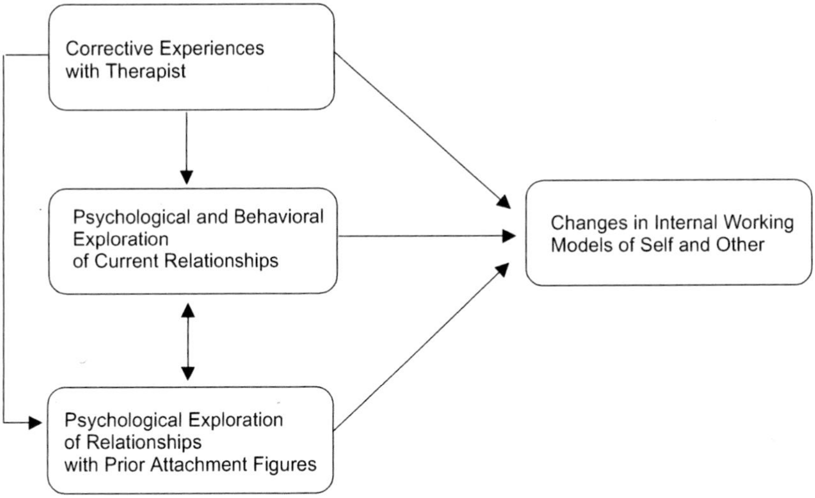

Source: Dozier and Tyrrell (1998), p. 223.

Workers also react to clients' boundaries (which is reminiscent of the traditional concept of *countertransference*). Sometimes we become angry if clients are not as forthcoming as we would like, and we label this behavior as resistance or denial as a way of expressing our displeasure. Part of our professional responsibility is to cultivate an awareness of such propensities and to be as clear as we can about what our reactions mean. If we suggest a client is avoiding something important and that is rooted in our perception of her or his needs at that time, fine. If the perception is rooted in our need for our clients to bolster our professional ego in some way, it is time for some honest reflection and/or a talk with a trusted colleague or supervisor.

Another slightly more complex variation on the countertransference theme is that when clients react to our setting boundaries, we react to their reaction. If a client becomes angry when we inform him or her that we have a holiday coming up and we will not be meeting for a time, what is our response? On a bad day, we might find ourselves feeling resentful and unappreciated; on a good day, we might recognize an opportunity to explore an important issue that could have ramifications for the client in other areas of her or his life.

CLARIFYING BOUNDARIES: AN EXTENDED EXAMPLE

It has been useful to extract relatively brief segments of the interview with Connie's family to illustrate particular points, but information is obviously lost (as are tone or flavor) by that practice. For this reason we finish the chapter with a more complete transcript—most of the first interview. This provides a much better appreciation of the struggle that boundary clarification entails, and of the utility of the flexible use of the various lenses we have discussed.

George: And you work too outside the home, don't you?

Connie: Uh-huh. Just part time in a bar.

George: In a bar? Where?

Connie: The Fraser Hotel.

George: The Fraser Hotel? How do you like it?

Connie: Pretty good. Yeah, Maybe it is because I work days all the time. I am home every day by the time the kids come home from school.

George: So you work from when to when?

Connie: Eleven to three-thirty p.m. or eleven to three p.m.

George: Oh, I see. Those are good hours for someone who is taking care of children.

Connie: Yeah.

George: What brings you here today? Can I call you Connie?

Connie: Uh-huh. I am just having a really hard time understanding Matt.

George: Uh-huh. You are having difficulty with your nine-year-old son?

Connie: Yes, very much so.

George: What kind of difficulties?

Connie: Uh, I don't know. Everything I guess . . . like we just don't seem to click on our ideas.

George: Yes, okay. Can you tell me a little more about it?

Connie: Well, for one thing he is quite hyper and I just don't know how to cope with him anymore. I ask him to do something and he just does the opposite. I don't know. His moods seem to be up and down quite a bit. When I talked to Mrs. Davies, the principal at school, and I talked to his teacher, and he is like that, the same at school as what he is at home. And a couple of times when he has gone to Cubs he has left right in the middle of it because he has got upset and he has just walked out. The same with baseball or anything he is involved in.

George: Do you like sports, Matt?

Matt: Uh-huh.

George: What is your favorite sport?

Matt: Baseball.

George: Baseball! What position do you play?

Matt: Pitcher.

George: Pitcher! How many games did you win?

Matt: Four. I almost won one a fifth.

George: Great stuff. Which team did you play on?

Matt: Hanover.

George: Hanover. Does the school have a team?

George focuses on Matt's strength, to connect with him and to avoid joining his mother in complaining about him—which would invite a relationship of pressure and irritation. They continue in this vein for a few more minutes, including Phil in the conversation briefly, after which George addresses Connie.

George: So what kind of things, Connie, at home cause you particular concern?

Connie: Oh, I don't know.

At the process level, George has suggested that Connie not complain about Matt, so now she does not know what to say. George recognizes what he has done and turns to Matt.

George [to Matt]: Do you have a bad temper?

Matt: I guess so.

George: What upsets you at home, Matt?

Matt: Um—something. When she asks me to do one thing, then when I'm doing it she says to get another thing.

George: You're not even finished [with] that and then you are supposed to do another thing?

Matt: Yeah.

George: Uh-huh.

Matt: When I'm right in the middle of the first thing.

Recognizing that Matt is inviting him into a pattern, as his mother did previously, triangulating him in his conflict with his mother, George changes the subject.

George: Uh-huh. Are there other things? How long have your mommy and daddy lived separately?

Matt: About seven years.

George: Seven years.

George [to Connie, who has been shaking her head]: It's not been that long?

Connie: No, three, four. No, maybe . . .

Matt [with annoyance in his voice]: Last time you said it was seven.

Connie: It must be close to six because Crystal was about a year and a half.

George: How old are you now?

Connie: She's seven.

George: She is seven.

Connie: It must be five or six.

George [to Matt]: Do you remember when—you are nine, right?

Matt: Uh-huh.

George: Do you remember when your mom and dad broke up?

Matt: Uh-huh.

George: Yeah. Did you miss your daddy?

Matt: Uh-huh.

George: Do you still see him?

Matt [with excitement in his voice, indicating that this relationship is important to him]: Uh-huh.

George: How do you get along with him?

Matt: Good.

George: Do you? Are you upset that Mom and Dad aren't living together?

Matt: A bit.

George: Yeah. Would you like to see them move back together again?

Matt: Uh-huh.

Matt's ability to be clear about a difficult issue is impressive. Connie is more anxious, and confuses the issue of how long ago her separation from her husband took place. Interestingly, Phil chooses this moment to interrupt.

Phil [interrupting]: Does your dad talk to you at the top of his voice once in awhile or not? Does he talk louder than your mom to you when he asks you to do something, or does your mom talk louder to you?

Matt: My mom talks louder.

Phil: How come?

Matt: I don't know.

Phil [another pause]: Would you respond more to her if she was to talk to you the same as I talk to you?

Matt: Uh-huh . . .

Phil: So, sometimes your mother talks to you in an ordinary voice and sometimes it doesn't work either, so if it has to come to a toss-up that way, that's—don't mind me speaking [turns to George]. I'm just talking for myself.

George: Go ahead.

Phil: Connie doesn't maybe realize she is speaking to Crystal and Matt maybe through the top of her voice, you know, sometimes through habit.

George: Ahhh.

Phil: I mean I do things when I am talking through getting excited. I hesitate and trip over my words. I say to myself—well, [if] I just slow down and think, I won't stumble over whoever I am talking to.

George: Ahhh.

Phil: Or through excitement maybe I'll be talking about one subject and I'll zip through and start another one before I am finished [with] the first two.

George: Ahhh. So you feel that Connie . . .

Phil [interrupting]: Well, it is up to . . . I mean it is up to the child and it's up to the children. It is up to the parent but who is responsible more or less—through experience. I have four of my own children.

George: Uh-huh.

Phil: The oldest is twenty-eight and the youngest is nineteen.

George: Uh-huh.

Phil: And I'm parted from my wife for now or whatever.

George: Are you divorced?

Phil: No.

George: Just separated?

Phil: Yes.

George: How long have you been separated?

Phil: It will be three years in February coming up and she works at the fertilizer plant.

George: Uh-huh.

Phil: So I lived alone [a] while with my mother and brother, lived on the farm by myself. Batched for a year and a half to see what was—you know—and then after that time neighbors and friends suggested that I move around or mix with people or talk to people.

George: Uh-huh. Are you living with Connie now?

Phil: No.

George: You two are just good friends?

Phil: Yes.

George: You feel that Connie would benefit if she didn't speak so loud to her son?

Phil: That I don't know. Ah, if the children don't respond to either way, well I guess like meaning the majority of people, if people don't respond to something they will pick up a higher pitch of voice. It don't matter whether it is a teacher, or if you are in the army or a policeman or whoever it should be.

George: Well, maybe we can talk about that a little more. [to Matt] You didn't quite finish your story before. You were saying that you would like your mom and dad back together again?

Recognizing that Phil is not committed to this family and that Connie is quite disengaged from Matt, George looks for a way to connect Matt and his mother, and invite them into a more supportive relationship with each other. George has a stronger connection with Matt at this point, so he starts with him.

Matt: Uh-huh.

George: Have you talked to your dad about that?

Matt: No.

George: Have you talked to your mom about that?

Matt: No.

George: Do you think they want to live together again?

Matt: I don't know.

George: What do you think?

Matt: When he picks us up they get along a little.

George: When he picks you up they get along a little, so that keeps you hoping, eh?

Matt: Uh-huh.

George: Have you ever talked to your mom about it?

Matt: I only mentioned it once. I said, "I want you and Dad to get together again." She said, "We can't sit down together and talk."

George: Ahhh. Have you talked to your dad about it at all?

Matt: No.

George: You haven't. Is he living by himself?

Matt: No.

Crystal: No.

George [to Crystal]: He is not living by himself?

Crystal: No.

George: He is living with someone else?

Crystal: Yeah.

George: Who is he living with?

Matt: Frances.

George: Another lady?

Matt: And Kirk and Willy are two children.

George: They are Frances' children? How do you get along with them?

Matt: Okay.

George: How about you?

Crystal: Good.

George: How about Frances?

Crystal: Good.

George: Do you like her?

Crystal [nods]: Yes.

George: What about you?

Matt: Uh-huh.

The children's openness and comfort discussing their relationship with their father's new partner, in front of their mother, and their freedom to acknowledge that they relate well to her suggest that neither parent wants to reconcile. This information is important in that it clarifies that the struggle between Connie and Matt is not connected to a possible attempt by either parent to use Matt to reunite them.

George [to Matt]: Why don't you talk to your mom and see if she thinks she would like to move back together with your dad? [Phil starts to interrupt, but George quickly overrides him] Do you want to do that?

Matt: Try it sometime.

George: Why don't you ask her now?

Matt [turning to his mother]: Do you?

Connie: No.

Matt: Why?

Connie: Because Mom and Dad tried to get along together and we just couldn't so we decided that it is better for us to live apart from each other.

There is a long silence, with Matt seemingly looking for something more. Phil, whose personal boundary is very weak, can't cope with the anxiety and gets pulled into the conversation.

Phil: Many times . . .

George [holding up his hand]: Just a minute Phil, let's finish this.

Matt [after a brief pause]: Any other reasons?

Connie: No, that is a good enough reason.

After another long pause Matt starts to cry. Connie looks away from him toward George, almost as if to say, "You made him cry—now you deal with him." The boundary between mother and son has obviously become quite rigid. Connie is unable or unwilling to hear Matt at an emotional level. It would appear that her perception of Matt as a bad boy blocks her from being attuned to him and offering emotional support. George labels Matt's feelings, to invite Connie to respond.

George [to Matt]: That makes you sad?

Matt: A bit.

Yet another long silence follows, with Connie making no move to comfort or talk to Matt any further.

George: Sure, lots of kids get sad when their mom and dad don't get together again. Do you think your mom understands your sadness?

Matt: I don't know.

George [after another long pause]: Do you ever talk to her about being sad that Mom and Dad aren't back together?

Matt: No.

George: You don't cry very often?

Matt: Once in a while.

George: Because you're sad or because you're angry?

Matt: Both.

George is struggling with how he will help Connie tune into her son's emotional needs and adopt a new story about her son as a sad boy instead of a bad boy. If Connie can accept that her son cries when he is sad as well as when he is angry, her image of him as a bad boy might loosen.

George: Both? [to Connie, after another long pause, during which she makes no move to respond to her son] Did you know that he was still very upset about your separation?

Connie: No. I knew that he was at first. And like I've sat down and explained to them why. I thought that they kind of understood because until recently, even when he came to get the kids we just didn't get along.

George: Uh-huh.

Connie: There was always bad words between us and so I thought they more or less could see for themselves why, what the problem was, and then when he started to live with this other woman he seemed to be a lot happier, so now I can—can't really sit down and have a real good conversation, but we can say a few words without getting into an argument, most of the time. The odd time we still do, but I didn't realize that it still bothered him that much.

George [to Matt]: Do you sometimes think it is your fault that they split up?

George introduces a universal theme for children of Matt's age when parents separate, still looking for something to connect mother and son emotionally.

Matt: Uh-huh.

George: What did you do?

Matt [after a long pause]: Because when I did the right things, I always got heck from him and when I do the bad things I get heck from her.

George: When you did the right things you got heck from whom?

Matt: My dad.

George: When you did the wrong things you got heck from Mom.

Matt: Uh-huh.

George: So no matter what you did it was always wrong?

Matt: Uh-huh.

George: That's pretty tough, isn't it?

Matt: Uh-huh.

George: So when they split up then you thought maybe it was your fault?

Matt: Uh-huh.

George: Did you ever tell your mom this?

Matt [after yet another long pause, during which Connie is unresponsive]: No.

George: Think maybe I could ask her if she thinks it is your fault?

Matt: Uh-huh.

George [to Connie]: Is it Matt's fault that you and your husband have split up?

Connie: No. It was just—we were two different people and we just couldn't make a go of it.

George: Was he to blame at all?

Connie: No, I wouldn't say he was.

George [to Matt]: Do you believe your mom?

Matt: Uh-huh.

George: Must have felt pretty bad thinking that you were to blame for your mommy and daddy not living together.

Matt: Uh-huh.

George [after a long pause, to Connie]: Did you know that he was concerned about that?

Connie: No—he holds everything inside.

Still unable to recognize Matt's feelings despite numerous opportunities, Connie talks about what she sees Matt doing wrong.

George: Is it hard for you to talk to him?

Connie: Very much so, because I ask him something and he won't answer. He just, ah, holds everything inside and he shows it in different ways.

George: Maybe that's why it is hard for him to cooperate sometimes, because he has so much inside of him.

Connie: Yes. Because he's been like this for a long time, and when he was in kindergarten I had taken him to Family Services because I was going through a bad time with him then, and she said, well—you know I went quite often at first. I can't remember just now exactly how often or how long of a time. She said she just couldn't get him to talk with me, so she didn't see any reason for me to come anymore.

George has continued to look for ways to reframe Matt's problems by suggesting that Matt is finding it hard to cooperate because he is hurting, not because he is rebellious. He is hoping Connie will change her story about Matt, seeing him as a boy who is more sad than defiant. Connie declines the invitation, introducing evidence that other people (even professionals) have found it hard to reach Matt. The problem as she sees it is still in Matt, not in their relationship.

George: Do you know what makes it hard for you to talk to him?

Connie: Well, I think it's . . . I ask him something and he just won't answer and I keep on repeating myself. I just don't get any answers.

George [to Matt]: Matt, do you know what makes it hard for you to talk to Mom?

Matt: No.

George: What does she do that makes it hard for you to want to talk to her?

Matt: Nothing.

George: Does she yell at you sometimes?

Matt: Once a day.

George: That's pretty good. Most kids get yelled at more than that.

Matt: Maybe sometimes twice.

George: Uh-huh. Is it hard for you to talk to your mommy?

This segment makes little sense at the content level, but George's protection of mother ("That's pretty good. Most kids get yelled at more than that.") seems to free up Matt to take another risk and to talk directly about his feelings.

Matt: A bit.

George: Yeah, what makes [it] hard?

Matt: Sadness.

George: Sadness. Her sadness or yours?

Matt: Mine.

George: Your sadness? [to Connie] Could you find out what his sadness is all about? Maybe you could sit next to him. [Connie has been sitting with one chair between her and Matt. When George invites her to move closer Matt removes her purse, which Connie had previously placed on the chair between them, thus inviting his mother to move closer. George gets up from his chair and gets a box of tissues from the corner of the room, and hands them to Connie, inviting her to tune into Matt's emotional needs and nurture him.]

Matt's direct acknowledgment of his sadness is a lovely invitation for his mother to talk to him about his feelings, which George encourages.

George: And if he wants to cry that's okay. [Connie takes the box of tissues and places it on the arm of the chair between them—thus creating a barrier between them, and she leans away from Matt.]

Connie: How come you're so sad?

Matt: About lots of things.

Connie: Can you tell me some?

Matt: When you get mad at me and when Crystal shouts at me, and when Crystal gets me in heck [pause] sometimes.

It would appear that Matt's anxiety got the better of him. Previously, he was clear that his sadness related to his mother and father breaking up. Now he shifts the focus and blames her, and triangulates his sister. Connie becomes defensive.

Connie [after a long pause]: Uh-huh. [another pause] But why do I get mad at you then?

Matt: Because uh, Crystal always bugs me.

Connie: But what do you do to her sometimes though?

Matt [his voice changing pitch with anxiety]: I do it back and then she tells and then I get the heck.

Connie [irritation in her voice]: Sometimes you do it pretty good. [Connie is annoyed at Matt. She withdraws from him and looks away.]

The pattern of Matt behaving like a bad boy, blaming his mother and sister, and of Connie blaming Matt reemerges. The personal boundary between mother and son remains rigid.

George [gently to Connie]: Could you find out what else makes him sad before you help him understand it?

Connie [hesitates, then turns to Matt]: Is there anything else?

Matt [hesitantly]: Uh-huh. I think so.

Connie: What?

Matt: When I keep on thinking that it's my fault that you two split up.

Connie: Oh. [pause] I didn't know that you felt like that [pause]. You never told me [pause], and when you asked how come that we weren't living together I thought that I explained it to you lots of times.

Briefly, Connie seems to hear Matt's feelings. Then she distances again and blames Matt: "You never told me," she says.

Matt: But I didn't get it, what you meant.

Connie: Ummm. Is there anything else, beside me getting after you and Crystal or . . . ?

This is a change from Connie, in that she is showing an interest in looking at Matt's feelings more deeply. Perhaps, however, she is torn between two images of Matt: the sad boy or the defiant boy. As a result she is uncertain what to do next, and George encourages her to go further.

Matt [after a long pause]: No.

George [pause]: Could you maybe find out what makes him think that it's his fault that you split up?

Connie: Why do you think that it's your fault that Mom and Dad split up, [that] we're not living together?

Matt [softly]: Because the only one that could get to talk to you was Crystal.

Again, Matt slips into the old pattern of triangulating Crystal.

Connie: Hmm?

Matt [close to tears]: Because the only one that could get to talk to you was Crystal when she was little.

Connie: Why couldn't you come talk to me, [pause] hmm?

Matt [strongly emotional]: Because I thinked you'd get mad at me.

George [after a long pause, to Connie, who is also showing deep feelings]: Can you find out what made him think that?

Connie [feeling anxious and speaking quickly]: Why did you think that, Matt? That it was your fault? I don't really know, I don't really understand you when you say you think it was your fault why Mom and Dad broke up. I don't know how you felt that or why you felt that.

As Connie becomes more aware of Matt's feelings the boundary that separates them becomes more open, and her narrative of him as a bad boy is challenged.

Matt [crying]: Because [long pause during which he wipes away a tear] because you guys would make it hard on me.

Connie: You mean because for that little while, in the apartment, when I stopped Dad from coming to see you again?

As Connie's boundary opens, her feelings become stronger and she tries to explain Matt's experience for him, triangulating his dad again.

Matt [long pause, in which he seems confused as he tries to follow what his mother is saying and loses touch with his own issues]: When?

Connie: When you were seven, when you didn't see Dad for about six months, and right after that.

Matt [interrupting]: He had to pay.

Connie [also interrupting]: No, he had you for the whole weekend after that, then, instead of just Sunday afternoon.

Matt: And then Dad had, Dad said he had to pay to get us for the second week.

Connie: But I still don't know why you think it was your fault.

This is a critical change. Connie could have become defensive again, but she refocuses on Matt, showing a genuine interest in what is happening for him and helping him to continue clarifying his personal boundary.

Matt: Because every time I asked you something you guys sitting there arguing [pause] sometimes.

Connie [distressed]: But that really . . . it wasn't about you.

Matt [very tearful]: And I thought you didn't like me.

Connie: Why did you think that?

Matt: Because you guys didn't answer me.

Connie [gives a long sigh of recognition]: Ooh.

Connie takes some time to struggle with her emotions but makes no move to respond to Matt, who is looking at her expectantly with tears in his eyes. Again, it seems Connie is recognizing that her story about Matt as a bad boy no longer fits. He has been helped to clarify his boundary and a new story has emerged too compelling to reject: Matt is indeed a sad boy feeling unloved instead of a bad boy wanting to defy his mother.

With Connie's silence, Phil is unable to contain his anxiety. Perhaps his own loneliness is too strong and his personal boundary too weak. Impulsively, he intrudes into Matt's space by entering the conversation. George had forgotten about Phil, becoming engrossed in the new story unfolding in front of him, and he neglects to protect the subsystem boundary around Matt and Connie.

Phil: Does it bother you, Matt, for me to come and visit you?

Matt [confused]: No.

Phil: Or was it—would it be—would you feel better if I stayed on the farm and phone—phoned you once in awhile to see how you were? How Crystal was? And how your mom was? Or you accept me coming to visit?

Phil is still in pursuit of his own agenda here, offering to help the family by removing himself from it. George recognizes that he needs to get the process back on track for Matt and Connie, and pulls his chair closer to Phil, preparing to interrupt him.

Matt: Uh-huh. Accept you to come visit us once in awhile—you come over and'stay.

Phil [interrupting]: And for you to go to the farm once in awhile? Do you enjoy coming to the farm?

Matt: Uh-huh.

George [to Matt]: Sounds like a nice thing. Maybe we can talk about that a little more. Sounds like you and Phil have a nice thing going. [to Connie] Do you begin to understand what's upset your son?

Connie: Uhm, I'm starting to. Ah, like I've known for a long time that . . . [She starts to cry. Matt leans forward and Phil folds his arms across his chest.]

George: Matt, can you give your mommy a Kleenex? [Matt reaches over and gives his mother a tissue. She takes it and wipes her eyes.]

Phil [still anxious, breaks the silence]: Connie's a bit disturbed too.

Phil wants to help Connie, but his method of helping changes the subject and could distract her from the feelings she had just discovered. George's priority is to use the opportunity to strengthen the emotional bond between Connie and her son; he has invited Matt to move closer to his mother physically.

George [holding up his hand to signal Phil to stop]: Why don't we just let her cry until she finds words to talk about herself? [Matt lifts one hand and pats his mother's back.]

George protects Connie's space and invites her to stay attuned to her pain, clarifying her personal boundary. There is a pause during which Connie is softly crying, during which Matt keeps his hand on her back.

Connie: You know, I think that Matt would be happier to live with his dad.

Connie expresses her pain by slipping back into the old pattern and triangulating Matt—thus again violating his personal boundary.

George [softly]: Why don't you check it out with him?

Taken off guard, George triangulates Matt instead of empathizing with Connie's pain.

Connie: I did. He won't answer me.

George: He what?

Connie [stress evident in her voice]: He won't answer me.

George: Maybe now that you have started to talk with each other, maybe now he will.

Connie: I don't know, I've asked him quite a few times. He just says,"Oh, there's nothing wrong—it's your problem." [pause] I tell him what goes on at school and he feels that his son, he doesn't do anything wrong.

Connie is demonstrating how difficult it is for her to see her ex-husband and her son as different people. Having begun to see Matt more clearly, she now needs to more clearly differentiate between him and the ex-husband with whom she remains angry. George needs to get back on track and clarify Connie's personal boundary instead of focusing on Matt or her ex-husband.

George: Who said?

Connie: His dad.

George: Uh-huh. [pause] Have you found it hard to be loving with your son?

Connie: Yes.

George: What's made that hard for you?

Connie [pause]: Because Matt is very much like his dad [pause] his moods, and the way he acts and the things he says [long pause].

Connie is again struggling with her emotions as she recognizes that some of her angry feelings toward her ex-husband have spilled over onto Matt. George helps her clarify her personal boundary.

George: So sometimes instead of trying to find out what he's feeling and thinking, you find yourself responding in old ways?

Connie: Yeah.

George: That happens a lot.

Connie's acknowledgment helps her take ownership and frees up George to be supportive.

Phil [interrupts, disturbed by George providing support at a time when he thinks a reprimand is needed]: If he was injured or had come across some sickness, would you be closer that way to him? Would you go to visit him in the hospital or would you feel close to him?

Connie: Yeah.

Phil: If he becomes sick?

Connie: Yeah.

Phil: Well, he—people have to accept the fact that he's . . . there's lots of good things along the way that he's . . .

George interrupts again, recognizing that Phil is admonishing her at a time when Connie needs support, and uses the opportunity to further clarify the boundary between Matt and his dad.

George: Yeah, but I think Connie is saying that sometimes she automatically finds herself responding in old ways even though she's got a new boy here. It's not Father—it's Matt. And I'm sure that Matt has learned some things from living with Father, about how to behave that way. But he's also a different person, and maybe sometimes by responding to him as though he were not Matt it makes it hard for him to be different [pause]. Does that make sense, Connie?

George introduces the reality that Matt's behavior is very much influenced by the way he is treated by his mother.

Connie [nodding her head]: Yes!

George [to Matt]: Sounds like your mommy's been sad at not being able to love you more too.

Matt: Uh-huh [long pause].

George [to Connie, who has been looking down and crying]: Can you talk about your sadness, Connie?

George now goes to Connie and invites her to clarify her personal boundary around the same theme of sadness that Matt introduced previously.

Connie [pause. Connie finally looks up and asks]: Me?

George: Uh-huh.

Connie [after a long pause, apparently lost in thought]: I think it's just trying to understand Matt, and I don't know how to cope with it anymore.

George: Uh-huh. Can you talk about that?

George, thinking Connie is going to talk about her pain, encourages her, but Connie reverts once again to the earlier pattern of triangulating Matt, and again illustrates how diffuse her boundary between father and son is.

Connie: I ask him to do something and he is saying, "No, I don't have to. My dad says I don't have to do this or that." Or if he wants something and I can't afford to get it for him he says, "Well, Dad gave you a hundred dollars."

George: Dad what?

Connie: Gave you a hundred dollars for us.

George: Uh-huh.

Connie: I send him to bed and he's still up fooling around for two hours at night, and everything I ask him or try to tell him or to explain to him he just does exactly the opposite.

George [changing the focus, wanting to reach Connie]: Uh-huh. Do you also feel guilty sometimes for not being able to love him more?

Connie: Yeah, very much so.

George: And how do you express that?

Connie: How do I express not loving him more?

George: No, the guilt.

Connie: Pardon?

George: How do you express the guilt?

Connie: I guess, uh, not having enough patience.

George: Pardon?

Connie: Not having enough patience.

George [gently]: By having less patience, by getting angry with him when you ordinarily wouldn't?

Connie [nodding]: Yeah.

George: By shouting at him rather than talking? [Connie nods her head.] You know, I have a hunch that maybe your son is trying to reach out for you to get more love, but he does it in such a way that it upsets you [Connie nods] and maybe you try to get him to listen . . .

Connie's willingness to take ownership encourages George to again reframe Matt's behavior.

Connie [interrupting]: In the wrong way.

George [long pause]: Did you ever think about that?

Connie [pause, during which she is reflecting]: No.

Connie's comment, "In the wrong way," and her acknowledgment that this is a new way of thinking about the problem indicate her willingness to accept the new story.

> **George:** Sometimes it's so hard when you are filled with so much pain, so much hurt, to hear yourself. [to Matt] Did you know that your mommy felt bad at not being able to love you more?
>
> **Matt:** No.
>
> **George:** When was the last time she put her arms around you and gave you a big squeeze?
>
> **Matt** [pause]: I don't remember.

A little later in the interview, after Connie has accepted George's invitation to hug her son, George invites mother and son into a new way of interacting to keep the changed pattern going.

> **George** [to Matt, after a long pause for Connie to wipe the tears from her eyes]: Sounds like maybe your mommy needs to talk to you about how it's not your fault that she and your daddy split up. Maybe you can show her when you want love by asking her for a hug rather than by telling her you won't carry out the garbage so she fights with you a lot. [pause] Hm?
>
> **Matt** [nodding]: Uh-huh . . . I think that's a good idea.

Matt's response indicates a willingness to try, and a new level of trust for his mother.

> **George:** You think it is? [to Connie] What do you think?
>
> **Connie** [nodding her head]: Much easier.

Connie reciprocates, and this indicates that the new approach has a good chance to succeed. Real progress followed, in fact, with Matt's behavior changing significantly, the changes being reinforced during subsequent sessions.

Toward the end of the fourth session, when Matt's behavior was no longer a preoccupation, Connie turned her attention to her relationship with Phil. She commented to George that she had taken note of the fact that Phil never introduced her when he took her to visit friends and relatives, and she wondered if that was significant.

Over time, Connie continued the work of differentiating between Matt and the ex-partner with whom she remained angry. The result was less pressure on Matt and much more room to be affectionate with him, and his behavior (understandably) steadily improved. In addition, increased clarity regarding Phil's ongoing investment in his previous marriage enabled Connie to acknowledge how little he had to offer her. Consequently, she saw his distancing for what it was, and disengaged from him as she developed other options for herself.

Chapter 7

Helping Vulnerable Families

*Go into the street and give one man a lecture on morality and
another a shilling and see which one will respect you the most.*

Samuel Johnson
from James Boswell, *Life of Johnson*

We have emphasized that creative clinical work entails flexibility,
so that whatever aspects of our professional framework we bring to
bear in a given situation are adapted to the client's unique needs. Respecting this dictum, we will now turn our attention to vulnerable clients and families, indicating how our ecological framework can be
employed differently with this group.

The Doyles, like Daniel and Rebecca and other families we have
discussed, are verbally accessible and relatively stable people. They
can respond to an approach to their problems that emphasizes verbal
exploration, analysis, and problem solving. Given sufficient skill on
the part of their social workers, they can take in ideas about their circumstances and options and can act on them. Not all clients are in a
place where they are ready to do this (at least not in the same way), and
we do them a disservice if we insist on such an approach at all times. In
fact, we may set them and ourselves up for failure.

THE CONCEPT OF VULNERABILITY

In the introduction, we indicated that an ecological perspective on
people and their environments has historically guided clinical social

work, and we suggested a framework emphasizing beliefs, competencies, demands, and resources as a way of thinking that is broad enough to honor our ecological assumptions. It may be helpful to refer to this discussion at this point, since our analysis of vulnerable clients and their needs will draw heavily on those concepts.

All of us are constantly using our resources (including our competencies) to meet the demands in our lives, and each of us has a unique way of understanding the demands we face and the resources at our disposal. The circumstances characterizing our lives are always a mix of independent realities and the narratives we associate with them (as Figure 7.1 illustrates).

Daniel was mistreated as a child. The bruises, the blood drawn, the instruction he received to be a disappointment and a failure—all these experiences are independent realities. To some extent, the experience of any other young person in the same situation would be similar. However, Daniel uses the traditions that were the context for his growth and his own capacities for creative meaning making to develop a narrative about himself and his history that is unique to him. Nobody else, in the same circumstances, would make sense of them in exactly the same way.

As a rough generalization, we can place demands and our interpretation of them on a continuum. Daniel, as a child being terrorized, faced demands such that he believed his survival was at stake—correctly or not, he thought that if his situation was not somehow dealt with he could

FIGURE 7.1. Independent Reality and Narrative Interpretation

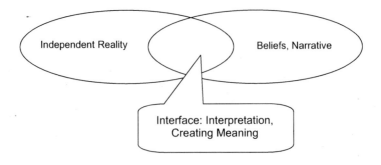

be seriously injured or even killed. Later, as an adult, he needs to find ways of relating to himself and others that take his remaining emotional needs—the residual effects of abuse—into account. The consequence, if he succeeds, is not survival so much as personal happiness.

The demands we face, under some circumstances, have implications for our basic comforts, stability, and even survival. In other situations they are construed differently; meeting or failing to meet them has consequences for our personal growth and happiness. The continuum, then, places demands somewhere at or between these two poles—those that we perceive as basic to our survival and stability, and those that we see as being important to our development (see Figure 7.2).

Another point will be helpful in clarifying the concept of vulnerability, which is that our responses to demands vary along with our perception of their implications for us (Rothery, 1999).

It is common to everyone's experience that we respond differently to demands at different times. When we are feeling competent, and see our resources as adequate to our needs, we respond to the demands in our lives creatively: we adapt, change appropriately, and grow as persons. A family such as the Doyles, coping with the developmental demands of the eldest child's adolescence, may respond by adapting creatively to this new reality. Boundaries are changed, rules modified, and relationships renegotiated to accommodate the teenager's ongoing needs for support coupled with more room to make independent choices.

The Doyles, as we know, were not successfully adaptive in their response to Maria's development. For reasons having to do with their own histories, John and Anita perceived Maria's growth as dangerous, and they responded by attempting to maintain the status quo—in effect, they wanted to keep her young. The goal is not to make adaptive changes so much as to maintain stability in the face of a perceived threat.

FIGURE 7.2. How Demands Are Experienced

Variations on the rigid position are very common in people or families who ask for help. A strategy for meeting a particular demand has become dysfunctional, and instead of adaptively trying something new, old approaches are maintained with increasing rigidity. People begin to experience pain because their needs are not being met by strategies that do not work, while more promising options go unrecognized.

It is important to note that the ability to maintain stability is a competency we need on a daily basis, and is not seen as inherently less valuable than the ability to change. In fact, we function best when we use a balanced combination of stability-maintaining and change-oriented skills (some theoreticians have labeled these *homeostatic* and *heterogenetic* functions). Problems tend to arise not from the use of stability-maintaining strategies per se, but from an overreliance on them and an underutilization of more creative options.

When we face demands that we perceive as likely to overwhelm our resources and competencies, so that even maintaining stability seems to be beyond our grasp, we may become increasingly disorganized or immobilized. The behaviors we employ make less and less sense from a problem-solving point of view, and increasingly look like the responses of someone who simply does not know what to do. Individuals who are extremely agitated or profoundly withdrawn or families in crisis may provide examples of such reactions. In fact we all exhibit them at times when stress is high and our resources are depleted.

It makes sense to observe that when demands are perceived as having implications for survival or basic needs, the situation is experienced as more serious than is otherwise the case. For this reason, such demands are more likely to invoke a stability-maintaining response, or to be disorganizing in their effects. If the Doyles fear for Maria's life because she has threatened suicide, they are less likely to be creative in their responses to her than if they see her needs as important but less drastic in their implications.

Finally, note that we have referred consistently in this discussion to peoples' experience and perceptions. As Figure 7.1 illustrates, the demands we confront are real, but they are also subject to interpretation, and it is our understanding of our circumstances that dictates how we will respond to them. Some real-life events are so extreme that the majority of people would become immobilized or disorganized by them (though some may still find the strength to respond in more adaptive ways). Other events are immobilizing for some people but not others, due to these factors: the resources at their disposal, and their perception of the severity of the demands they face.

The ideas contained in these three figures are helpful in clarifying the concept of vulnerability—which, in our view, represents *the extent to which a person (or family, or group) is inclined to respond to demands by becoming disorganized or immobilized.* Some people or families are described as being crisis prone, which means that almost any new demand is likely to elicit that kind of response. These people are vulnerable, while others whose resources and perceptions enable them to maintain stability and continue developing solutions are less vulnerable.

VULNERABILITY AND CLINICAL INTERVENTION

An important implication of the foregoing material is that people have different basic agendas, depending on how they perceive their circumstances. At times when we feel our safety, basic comforts, or survival are at stake, our goal is to achieve stability. We are not likely to have an interest in creative change or the discovery of new options in our lives—in fact, since change of that sort is inherently destabilizing to some extent, we will likely reject it as contrary to what we feel we need at the time.

When clients have become disorganized or immobilized in their functioning, it can be a serious mistake to attempt to engage them in efforts to implement new options. Indeed, if we do so we can be experienced as a threat, since our agenda will be seen as contradicting their need for safety and stability. At the point where Maria is actively suicidal, she and her family will not likely be interested in fresh insights into their family history and dynamics, or in discussion of how they might realign family boundaries. Understandably, they will be preoccupied instead with the threat to her survival. Later, when Maria's survival is not so immediate and pressing an issue, they can and do benefit from an exploration of new options and opportunities.

The same is true for all of us. There are times in our lives when we require support, protection, and nurturing more than anything else, and there are other times when we are able to proactively adapt and discover or create new options. Physical illness, extreme stress, serious emotional injuries, and traumatic events are all examples of experiences that can render us feeling vulnerable and in need of support from other people.

For vulnerable clients, then, our first task is often to find ways of shoring up their sense of safety and stability. Attempts to facilitate creative change and growth may be concurrent with this focus or may follow it—but the important principle is that unless these basic needs are somehow addressed it will be difficult for the client to engage in other kinds of problem solving.

Attention to Resources and Supports

The ecological model introduced in the introduction indicates that we all occupy an ecological "niche" in which our needs are met more or less well. Ecological thinkers refer sometimes to whether there is a "goodness of fit" between people and their environments. Operationally, this means that the demands the environment places on people or families are adequately balanced by the resources that are also present. When demands are excessive relative to resources, a goodness of fit is not present and some kind of symptom, pain, or dysfunction is frequently the result. All this is, as we have said, very much mediated by client competencies and narrative; however, the basic equation is a useful one.

It is well established now that the goodness of fit we experience with our environment is a powerful determinant of our well-being. Those of us who enjoy sufficiently rich and nurturing environments are happier, physically and emotionally healthier, and live longer than our less fortunate colleagues.

There are different ways of describing the kinds of supports and resources that make such a difference in our lives. One categorization identifies four types—it is not the only way of thinking about resources and supports available, but it will be sufficient for our purposes (Cameron and Rothery, 1985; Rothery, 1999).

- First, *concrete, instrumental supports* are services and material goods we use to cope with life's demands: food when we are hungry, or shelter when we are cold, for example.

- Second, *information supports* are knowledge and skills that help us cope with the demands in our lives. Education regarding the cycle of violence may be very important to someone in an abusive relationship, for example, or knowledge about the effects of alcohol on the central nervous system may improve the ability of a depressed person such as Daniel to make helpful lifestyle changes.
- Third, *emotional supports* are provided in relationships characterized by *understanding* and *safety*. When we can be open about our feelings and experience in a relationship where such self-disclosure is safe and will be respectfully understood, we are receiving emotional support. As an adult survivor of childhood abuse, Daniel will benefit from the opportunity to discuss the feelings of vulnerability, fear, and helplessness that often remain with people who have been unfortunate in this way—again, assuming this is met with empathy and credible assurances of safety.
- Fourth, *affiliational supports* are supports that come to us when we have access to meaningful social roles, and when we are validated as competent. Roles that we value provide both meaning and a sense of belonging. When others recognize our competence to perform our roles, that also enhances belonging and contributes to our sense of efficacy. The more Maria is validated as an increasingly independent, competent teenager, the less prone to self-doubt and depression she will be.

These are all supports and resources that come to us from a variety of sources: family, friends, neighbors, or professional helpers. Generally speaking, we are best off when we have diverse resources in our lives, and are not dependent on just one or two people to meet these kinds of needs when they arise:

> Each of us copes best in life when the demands placed upon us are manageable, and this is likely to be true (in part) when we have adequate supports of each of the four types described. . . . Also, it is a good thing if the sources from which we draw supports are relatively diverse, comprising a mix of formal and informal service providers—friends, social workers, educators, family, neighbors, doctors, churches, competent mechanics, and so on. The loss of one source of support will not have the same damaging effect for

someone with a rich diversity of sources of support as it would for someone who has been overly reliant on that one source and has not developed alternatives. (Rothery, in press)

VULNERABILITY AND BOUNDARIES

Vulnerability, we have suggested, is the frequency and quickness with which people or families (or other groups) tend to slip into disorganized or immobilized ways of responding to demands. Boundaries are a very important determinant of this. When a client is flexible and effective at the twin tasks of engaging and distancing, the ability to access both resources and safety is enhanced. When such is not the case, demands are more threatening, and vulnerability is increased.

The vulnerability of clients who have suffered severe abuse provides a clear example of this. The abuse experience teaches people that their boundaries are not secure, but can be violated at a whim with devastating consequences. For such clients, conflict with a partner or aggressive behavior by a friend or colleague may be a far more serious demand than would be the case for someone else. Having learned to believe they cannot maintain boundaries within which they are safe, they may become incapacitated by fear with a rapidity that surprises and perplexes others.

Daniel, the client introduced in Chapter 2, reported at one point in his work with Mike that he was likely to get depressed (and to drink too much) before and after visits to his parents. While he wanted to maintain family ties, he also found visits enormously stressful. On exploration he recognized that the visits frightened him, and they often triggered memories of particularly painful attacks he had experienced in the past. He also acknowledged that he could not describe his father's physical appearance, except with reference to the past. Somehow, he was managing not to look at him during his visits, keeping his eyes downcast and focused anywhere except on this person who had once terrorized him.

An intervention that proved important was to ask Daniel to begin learning about his father as he presently was, allowing himself to look at this once-fearsome person (with due respect for his need for safety) enough to take in new information (see Rothery, in press, for more detail about this work).

Daniel was surprised to discover that the man who had brutalized him as a child was now smaller than he was. He was still bitter and often belligerent, but he was not dangerous. This new information had to be amplified and integrated with some care, but it had many obvious benefits. At one point he had made an understandable decision to protect himself by enforcing extremely rigid boundaries, boundaries characterized by inflexible withdrawal. This strategy served an important purpose, but it was also costly, since it prevented him from taking in important new information—he missed the point at which his own growth made him strong enough that his father could no longer threaten him. By allowing himself to take in new information, he was able to feel more secure, and more free to explore options that previously would have been unimaginable to him. An equally important point is that had he been pressured by a well-meaning social worker to attempt changes in how he related to his family before his need to feel safe had been addressed, he may well have failed.

VULNERABILITY AND TRADITIONS

People come to relationships with traditions they have accumulated throughout life, and these will shape their response to the challenges that any new relationship represents. Rules about closeness and distance, about how to treat each other's vulnerability, about nurturing, support, feelings, power, having fun, food, sex, money, religion, holidays—these and many more are powerful determinants of the quality of our relationships.

These traditions, when they work well, nurture and sustain us. Sometimes, however, a family evolves traditions that work against people's needs being met. The Doyles' tradition of dealing with conflict by sacrificing one's needs, for example, does not equip them to respond well to Maria's adolescence. Daniel's propensity to withdraw in the face of conflict is understandable since conflict frightens him, but it is also a rule that makes it very hard for Rebecca to put demands to him; similarly, her inclination to interpret withdrawal as abandonment makes it hard for her to respond to his fear in a helpful way.

Traditions such as these leave us poorly equipped to cope with ordinary demands. Instead of problem solving adaptively, we may attempt to maintain stability by imposing rigid control over situations where we could be flexibly creative. Or, worse still, we may find that everyday problems leave us disorganized and immobilized. Under the stress of a disagreement about one small aspect of dinner, Daniel and Rebecca become painfully withdrawn, and each of them is dangerously depressed. The lack of traditions for coping with their needs for intimacy has made them vulnerable, and they become immobilized by an apparently trivial problem.

It also happens that families may be vulnerable not because traditions work against them so much as because they are missing. Members who have grown up bereft of opportunities to learn them may simply lack experience with rituals for engendering a sense of celebration or closeness, or collaborating over tasks, or nurturing children, for example. The everyday tasks that their neighbors handle with ease may render them vulnerable to crises because they have no fund of learned strategies to draw on. A temper tantrum by family A's two-year-old is dealt with effectively by parents whose histories have prepared them to work collaboratively, providing children with the limits they need to feel safe and grow. Family B, faced with the same demand, reacts more chaotically because they simply do not know what to do—the child is finally spanked excessively (without ceasing to throw a tantrum) and the parents become angrily critical toward one another.

The clinical response varies, hopefully, with the family's needs. Understanding and changing traditions that are inadequate to meet the demands of a particular task or stage in development can be important work. However, it is not a focus that will serve families where the main issue is a simple lack of traditions for responding to important life events. In the latter case, an educative approach to helping the family develop shared rituals will make greater sense than the more familiar focus on interpretation and change.

CASE EXAMPLE:
THE MCDOUGALLS

To illustrate work with vulnerable families, a new example is required. We have elected to introduce the McDougalls, residents of a small suburb in a Northwestern city. They are known to the social services systems in their area through involvements with financial assistance, mental health, child welfare, and juvenile justice agencies.

At the point where we visit the family, Francis McDougall, the father, had been hospitalized for psychiatric difficulties. Cheryl, the mother, was frequently physically incapacitated by arthritis, which made it hard for her to get around. Her health problems were exacerbated because their housing was substandard, as was their diet.

Francis and Cheryl had two children: thirteen-year-old Sherry and sixteen-year-old Floyd. Sherry had been seen by a child welfare worker a year earlier, when her teachers became concerned that she seemed inadequately dressed and fed, and was frequently absent. An investigation resulted in a report to the effect that the family was poor and was having difficulty coping, but was not abusive. A degree of neglect was described, but was not considered sufficient for Sherry to be declared at risk, and the file was closed.

Floyd had also had child welfare involvements in his younger days, over similar concerns. At sixteen, he had dropped out of school, and was unemployed. He continued to live at home, adding to the stress in his mother's life by having numerous friends visit at all hours, often for days at a time. These friends were, in Mrs. McDougall's opinion, undesirable. She thought most of them were unemployed like her son, and she had overheard enough of their conversations to believe that there were involvements with drugs and petty theft. Floyd had, in fact, been charged once with possession and twice with shoplifting. It was the possession charge that had led to him being suspended from school, and he had simply not bothered to return when the term of his suspension elapsed.

The hospital wanted to discharge the father and had determined that his chances of a successful return to the community would be enhanced if the marriage could be made stronger and more supportive. Mrs. McDougall, because she was asked to do so, was somehow making it to the hospital on a weekly basis to participate in marriage counseling, to improve communications with her husband. The social worker soon realized he and the McDougalls were getting nowhere. His note in the file expresses his frustration: "After six sessions, I think Mrs. McDougall is not really ready for counseling at this time. She says she wants to make things better for the two of them, and would like Mr. McDougall to come home, but she resists change by never following through on plans. There is a passive-aggressive quality to her responses, in that she agrees to everything and seems cooperative, but never follows through."

There are reasons why familiar clinical methods are not helping the McDougalls that have nothing to do with "resistance" or personality. The problem is one of seriously mismatching services and needs. The error is significant, since there are problems with the worker's model that are not only making him ineffective, but could lead to his doing harm.

EXPANDING OUR UNDERSTANDING: THE ECOMAP

An important tool for understanding the needs of vulnerable families developed by clinical social workers in recent years is the "ecomap." This is a way of visualizing people and their families in their ecological niche, summarizing information about the demands and resources they face (Hartman, 1978). Different authors offer different prescriptions for constructing ecomaps, one important variable being complexity. Some approaches are simple and basic (Meyer, 1995) and some attempt to capture a much greater amount of information, even employing computer programs to synthesize voluminous data and complex relationships (Lachiusa, 1996).

Our own prescription is, we hope, a pragmatic one. The degree of complexity to be observed in constructing an ecomap is a practical matter. Such diagrams cannot be complete; indeed, they are useful *because* they are somewhat reductionistic. The more we include, the more complicated and difficult to understand the diagram will become; on the other hand, we need to include enough information that we and our clients achieve a useful awareness of important contextual aspects of their problems and opportunities. A middle-of-the-road approach, similar to Johnson's (1998), is used here, but modified so that a systematic look at resources and demands is encouraged.

A FOCUS ON STRENGTHS

A very deliberate and systematic exploration of strengths is a useful initial intervention with vulnerable individuals and families. This is because such a focus is likely to be experienced as supportive in essential ways: an appreciation of existing strengths bolsters a sense of safety. Also, it engenders hope, which we have identified as a critical precondition for change. Finally, identifying strengths early in our work alerts us to resources present in the situation that we can utilize later, in the service of problem solving.

It is very often helpful to both client and clinician to summarize such information graphically, and engaging clients in the construction of an ecomap is a useful way to accomplish this. We can illustrate the process using the McDougalls as an example (see Figure 7.3).

First, draw a simple genogram and place it in a circle. Then invite the family to discuss how they help and support one another, and where they receive support from others in their community. With demoralized clients, this can be difficult at first; a good measure of determined encouragement from the clinician may be called for. It is not uncommon that clients have difficulty identifying strengths, but it is useful to consider that they are invariably present to be discovered.

This is not presented as the whole picture of the McDougalls' strengths and resources. Completeness is not required; the goal is rather to gain enough information that the family feels more hopeful and the exercise has uncovered resources that they can work with. One can always return to this and explore further if and when the need arises.

> Ecomaps are snapshots, frozen in time. Thus, they represent a piece of a client's reality at one point—they are necessarily incomplete and only temporarily valid. In fact, they are often redrawn at selected intervals as an aid in identifying and emphasizing changes as they occur. (Rothery, in press)

In exploring such questions with a family, it is often a useful exercise to go over the types of support we all require, systematically inquiring about relevant resources for each family member. Thus, we can explain what concrete supports are, and explore with people what needs are paramount and how they are meeting them. In both parents' cases, effective medical treatment is a very necessary concrete support; also, the whole family shares a sharp appreciation of the importance of being able to obtain adequate food and heat during the winter.

FIGURE 7.3. The McDougalls' Ecomap

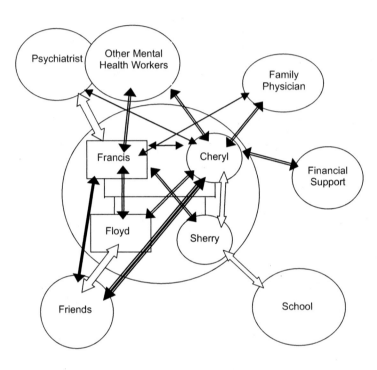

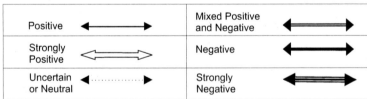

Note: Just as there is no standard practice for constructing ecomaps generally, there are no hard rules about how to diagram relationships within them. This is one system among many.

Similarly, each family member can talk about the need to have someone to talk to who will understand and respect his or her feelings (emotional support); each can discuss the kinds of information he or she needs— about mental illness, arthritis, or drug abuse, for example. Finally, one considers the roles each family member occupies: do they have social roles in which they feel welcome and validated?

If we return to the ecomap with this kind of detailed thinking as our guide, we will consider further avenues to explore. Who talks to Sherry and Floyd about the effects of having a mentally ill father, for example, or about what it is like to be poor in a community where most of their peers are more economically comfortable? Does Cheryl have all the information she needs about treatment options for ameliorating the effects of her arthritis? Her feelings about her family doctor are mixed because she likes him and thinks he has handled Francis well. On the other hand, she feels he does not want to be "bothered" much with her arthritis, implying to her that nothing can be done about it except to accept it and cope stoically.

Often, depth and detail are added to this discourse with clients if we encourage attention to each of the important roles in their lives. We have noted that we all require access to meaningful roles in which we feel validated. Francis can be complimented for his endurance in the face of a difficult mental illness (his role as patient), but it would almost certainly be instructive to ask him also about his roles in the family. Does he receive validation for what he does as a father, for example? Or his husband role? To be sure he has, like many mental health clients, been marginalized and therefore has limited access to meaningful roles; this makes it doubly important for his clinical social worker to work hard at helping him identify the roles he does occupy (in addition to "patient") and to explore with him the supports he needs to derive gratification and a sense of competence from them.

The same can be said of Cheryl. Her role as parent is important to her, and she is a consumer of health services. She is also a partner to her husband. These are roles to which she has brought as much competence and energy as she can muster, for which she deserves and will appreciate applause.

The reader is invited to think about each of the children in this family: what roles do they occupy, and what kinds of instrumental, informational, emotional, and affiliational supports do you expect would be important to you if you were in a similar position?

IMPLICATIONS FOR SERVICE

It is quite possible that Cheryl and Francis McDougall's marriage could benefit from improved communication, and that this would improve the odds of Francis returning successfully to his family. The mistake associated with seeing them to work on marital communications was not in this focus per se so much as in timing and context.

This is a vulnerable family. Some of the demands they face have to do with basic comforts and the stability of their family. Francis's medical difficulties have resulted in his removal from the family, and Cheryl's affect her ability to cope on a daily basis. Also, though there was never consideration of apprehending either child, child welfare has been involved, and this could easily be perceived as a threat to the family.

It is, as we have noted, an error to make change a priority if needs for stability and safety are unattended. Well intended as it was (and however skillfully delivered), the effort to improve marital communication was not experienced as help so much as a threat—offering a drowning person swimming lessons when she only wanted something to keep her afloat. Cheryl responded by becoming immobilized, and the social worker expressed frustration by labeling that as "resistance."

Help with the marriage might be received differently if it were offered, not as a single, isolated service, but in the context of a more comprehensive *service package* (Cameron and Rothery, 1985). This principle has been known to social workers serving vulnerable populations for many years (Wood and Geismar, 1989) but has recently been developed and popularized by such approaches as "wraparound services," especially in children's services and mental health (Clark and Clarke, 1996: note that this is the lead article in an issue of the *Journal of Child and Family Studies* devoted entirely to the subject of wraparound services). Similar discussions of theory, research, and practice with vulnerable families have appeared in recent years in the literature on family preservation and family support (Cameron and Vanderwoerd, 1997).

The McDougalls will benefit most from an integrated set of services tailored to their specific needs. The design of this service package is driven by their unique needs and circumstances (not by the predilections of service providers, or by any other consideration).

Assessing those needs is enhanced by consulting the ecomap (Figure 7.3). We can think, for example, about steps that might be taken to improve the medical care they are receiving—the picture is not all negative, but Cheryl's physical care could be improved, as could her relationships with the mental health workers serving her and her husband.

Since Sherry has a positive relationship with the school, it may be that interventions could connect her parents with the school in positive ways, to reinforce and build on her success, and to provide the parents with validation for their competence in raising a child with strength in this area.

Children with a mentally ill parent need to come to grips somehow with the implications of this. If the condition has resulted in negative parenting in the past, some discussion of that and efforts to repair the damage could be helpful. If Sherry and Floyd are ashamed or embarrassed by their father's condition, and have therefore distanced themselves from him, those feelings may be a focus for work. It would be nice to see, in a later ecomap, more positive relations between Francis and his children (and more validation for Francis in his parenting role). Presently, Francis's most positive relationship is with his psychiatrist, and this can be supported at the same time as we look to strengthen his ties to other sources of support.

Relative to the children in this family, we note a particularly troubling issue in the ecomap. Floyd's friends are his only unambiguously positive relationship, which makes them very powerful, especially given his age. At the same time, they are a strongly negative factor in Cheryl's life, and they are openly contemptuous of Francis because of his illness. The dilemma is that the family requires stronger boundaries to reduce the negative impact of these young people, but Floyd will be unwilling to cooperate in establishing those boundaries. This may change if he can be connected with better options: a strength-based assessment of his interests and needs might well suggest ways in which he could be helped to feel validated and successful in more prosocial ways. A less happy scenario is that the family may need to consider distancing from him along with his friends if no other resolution can be found.

This is not exhaustive, but examples that help to make the critical point, which is that a service package addressing a number of needs stands a better chance of making a real difference to the McDougalls than a single clinical intervention such as marriage counseling. The principles associated with the development and delivery of such a package follow from our understanding of ecological thinking and vulnerable families.

First, we have emphasized that it is a mistake to attend to needs for growth and change without assuring that needs for safety and stability are also addressed, either before or concurrently.

Second, the approach suggests teamwork by a number of professionals and other resource providers. Coordinating a package of services is a demanding task, and good collaboration by different service providers is necessary if it is to be successfully carried out. Common wisdom has it that one person should accept the role of team coordinator, with overall responsibility for the services to the family.

It is also accepted that an essential part of the team is the family itself. The McDougalls can (and normally should) be involved in assessing their own needs (participating in the construction and analysis of the ecomap, for example) and determining what the priorities are. To succeed in a full "buy in" by the family, the professionals in the team will have to be unceasingly respectful of the family, and tireless in identifying and supporting its strengths and successes.

A further point about the development of service packages is that the supports mobilized should be as diverse as possible. It is usually unfortunate if the resources supplied come primarily from formal, professional services. A mix is preferred: the long-term needs of the McDougalls will be met more consistently and completely if they are met by a combination of friends, extended family, neighbors, peers, and colleagues as well as social workers and health professionals. This work has a community development aspect that is not associated with clinical intervention as we traditionally think about it. A degree of humility may be required of clinical workers as they accept a role in the family's life that seems, at first, less central than the role we customarily see for ourselves—we are one person among many working on the family's behalf, and our contribution may be less important in the long run than the support offered by a pastor, employer, grandparent, or good friend.

Finally, the hallmark of good work with vulnerable families such as the McDougalls is the same as in all clinical endeavors. While it is informed by the disciplined and intelligent application of sound theory, it is always ultimately creative. The social worker's framework is as sophisticated as she or he can make it, but it is always open. Respect for the McDougalls requires a constant willingness to hear the ways in which their story is unlike any other, deserving a response that is unique to their needs and priorities.

Epilogue

Future Creative Challenges

Memory truly counts only if it holds together the imprint of the past and the plan for the future, if it allows one to do things without forgetting what one wanted to do.

Italo Calvino
Why Read the Classics?

Clinical workers in the helping professions lack a well-developed sense of history. We tend to proclaim each innovation to be a radical change departing fundamentally from what has gone before, rendering the hard work of earlier helpers obsolete. This can be inefficient, if time and energy are consumed rediscovering useful knowledge that was previously developed and forgotten. It can also be dangerous if we lose the "imprint of the past" and forget the core values that motivated those whose path we follow.

Choosing to commit a few final pages to predictions about what issues will engage our professions in the near future, we step into territory that may be relatively new to us but would not have looked at all strange to practitioners and scholars fifty or more years ago.

In 1949, Father Swithun Bowers published a three-part meditation on the meaning and nature of social casework (which, in today's parlance, would include clinical social work) (Bowers, 1949a, 1949b). Having analyzed all available published definitions from earlier decades, Bowers concluded that social casework was *"an art in which knowledge of the science of human relations and skill in relationship are used to mobilize capacities in the individual and resources in the community appropriate for better adjustment between the client and all or any part of his total environment"* (Bowers, 1949b, p. 417, emphasis in the original). Gendered language aside, this definition sounds strikingly modern and very congruent with the ecological point of view with which we began this book. It is also remarkable that Bowers' emphasis on client, client context, and relationship is, more than half a century later, being validated by current clinical outcome research. When he refers to the clinical enterprise as an "art," he points to the fact that though we must use the "science of human relations" to guide our practice, there is always an element of creativity in making general principles responsive to the unique needs of particular clients.

An ongoing issue for clinicians in the coming years, we think, will be the need to continue the development of useful practice frameworks while diversifying these to meet the needs of different clients. There is growing interest in integration of core ideas from different models, but a tendency to market specialized approaches in a "one size fits all" spirit continues as well. The need to be responsive to diverse clients' needs and priorities requires that we be skeptical of our favorite models and willing to stretch them and break their rules when client interests suggest this is necessary. A holistic analysis of client issues is accepted as desirable; at the same time, specialized theoretical commitments, important as they can be, often lead to reductionism.

Although the struggle may be old news, the need to be as holistic as possible in our understanding of clients' needs and creative options will continue to challenge us and provoke us to grow. This is especially true in our efforts to help clients who are often marginalized: those affected by poverty, oppression, homelessness, mental illness, addictions, and a myriad of other difficulties that can be daunting to the most experienced clinician. It is not by accident that our closing chapter is about work with vulnerable families, since we think work with highly needy populations will be an area in which we will be challenged to innovate and grow in coming years.

Our work has another dimension that Swithun Bowers anticipated and that is demanding increasing attention at the present time. This is the recognition that clinical work is always, at its core, in part an enactment of values. In the quest for scientific validity that has preoccupied us in recent decades, this fact has been lost, but is reemerging as a critical issue. Try as we might to claim a scientific objectivity in our work, the ethical dimension remains and demands our attention.

The issue of values is not an easy one, which is why the profession has yet to find a completely satisfactory way of addressing it. Originally, the work of our predecessors was explicitly value based: it expressed and was motivated by a desire to help people be better citizens in a society that was more just and equitable. Standards of good citizenship and what makes a desirable society are necessarily value based.

The problem that was soon identified was (and remains) that the values of our profession espouses concerning a just society and the responsibility of its members to the common interest are not necessarily the values that will be held by members of diverse races, cultures, and socioeconomic groups. The profession was accused of cultural imperialism, whereby middle-class Western mainstream values were imposed on people to whom those values were foreign, and the criticism stung because it had validity.

One attempted solution was simply removing the clinician's values from the helping situation. The clinician was expected to set her or his values aside, to remain neutral, and the theories that supported our work fit this goal nicely. Psychodynamic, behavioral, and family systems theories were highly influential and each was extremely deterministic: they proposed that forces for which people were not ultimately responsible caused their problems and triumphs, and therefore no rational basis existed for making value judgments about clients' choices. A pragmatic assessment as to whether a given action was functional or not (worked to meet needs in the sense of meeting needs without causing avoidable pain) was undertaken, but this was seen as objective and value free. With such assumptions in place, an ersatz neutrality is available to clinicians, who can assume that scientific objectivity rather than personal or professional values drives decisions.

Psychoanalysts could therefore support the metaphor of the "therapist as mirror" (Greenson, 1967); family therapists could prescribe, for themselves, a neutral stance in which they had no preferences regarding the outcomes their interventions might generate (these being the family's choice) (Selvini Palazzoli et al., 1980); enormously influential humanists such as Carl Rogers similarly maintained that the clinician's job was to listen to the client. Deep and skilled understanding, it was argued, led to self-exploration and personal growth, which should be uncontaminated by the clinician's own priorities or agendas.

If deterministic theories seem to offer an escape from the values dilemma, so too do the recently popular constructivist and narrative perspectives (which inform much of what we have written in this book). These are not inherently deterministic, but they offer a different rationale for neutrality in the form of a highly relativistic approached to values. If what really matters about reality is our interpretation of it, and if all interpretations are equally valid, the idea that actions may be absolutely right or wrong is what we agree to denounce. From a strictly narrative point of view, there is no basis to maintain that some actions (at an individual or societal level) are better than others, regardless what the individual or collective may believe. It is hard to see how a thoroughly committed constructivist can negatively sanction someone who truly believes his sexual exploitation of children is an expression of love, or declare an Eichmann's atrocities to be wrong despite the fact that they were committed in a social context that defined them as noble. One construction of reality is as valid as any other.

Neither the deterministic nor the relativistic approach to the values dilemma has worked, and the clinician's dilemma remains. On the one hand, we see the dangers of cultural imperialism and wish to avoid imposing our own values on people who may construe life differently. On the other hand, what do we say to an abusive partner whose patriarchal belief system truly supports the subjugation of women? Do we accept harsh punishments of children if the abusive parent honestly thinks this is the right way to rear the young (citing biblical authority to support the case)? Do we silence ourselves about such matters as the genital mutilation of female children, or female infanticide, or compelling eighteen-year-old boys to serve in the military (sending them off to kill other young men) on the basis that these decisions are made by one culture or society and no one else's business?

Imposing values is dangerous; current scholarship on cultural diversity makes this abundantly clear. However, it seems equally clear that a strict determinism or relativism will not work either. We are confronted daily with situations in which we perceive actions that we see as wrong (though we may not use that word) despite the fact that the actor views them as proper—and in which effective work requires a belief in peoples' capacity for choice and responsibility. When Mike interviews a couple in which the wife is depressed and her husband's analysis is that she should be investing more energy in ironing his socks, Mike's response to the husband's lack of compassion is rooted in a value position emphasizing equity and mutual respect. The fact that the gentleman is from a patriarchal culture helps Mike to understand and respond respectfully, but it does not lead to the conclusion that the belief is acceptable. Since Mike believes that this man could (and should) manage his marriage differently, he also invokes values regarding individual choice and responsibility. In this, as in most clinical situations, there are distinct limits to how far we can take moral relativism and determinism; these solutions to the values dilemma have usefulness, but they are insufficient.

Quite possibly, what we will see as we grapple with values in professional practice is an effort to work out a more complex position. This position will, we think, incorporate the understanding that true neutrality is impossible, as well as the need to identify certain core values that are absolute, distinguished from others that are mere expressions of cultural, personal, or professional practices. The impossibility of complete neutrality derives from the fact that values imbue everything we do: as Arthur Koestler (1969) commented, they are like water to a fish—so much a part of their world that we may be unaware of them much of the time. Pretending to be entirely neutral when we cannot can lead to dishonesty, and a better, more realistic alternative may be to accept a professional responsibility for a lifelong struggle to be as aware as we can of our values and how they affect our work. Needless to say, part of discipline associated with clinical work is to monitor how our values affect our response to a given family and to assure that we use such knowledge to the family's benefit. Since perfection in the face of such demands is unlikely, it is also important to develop techniques for repairing potential damage when we slip up.

Differentiating absolute from relative values promises to be a perennial problem that belies a final solution. Examples of each are easy enough to identify: nobody would argue that torture, rape, murder, or sexual exploitation of children are ever acceptable. The values that proscribe such behavior are absolute, independent of culture. On the other hand, such issues as the amount of time family members spend together, how they express affection or anger, how often the dishes are washed, and a myriad of other choices vary freely across families and cultures and should be left to do so. The difficulty is the gray area where absolute and relative values overlap (and this area is disconcertingly large). When does strict parenting become abusive? When does role differentiation between adult partners become exploitive and constraining? When do normal efforts to influence one another become destructively controlling? All these are areas where the clinician's values often diverge from the client's, and determining what to do with that difference—set it aside or act on it somehow—will always be an important but difficult decision.

Recent work in philosophy does support an effort along these lines, and it may prove possible to identify, in general, what the acceptable basis for making absolute value judgments should be (Taylor, 1989). On what basis do we say one narrative is better than another (Dean and Rhodes, 1998)? However, applying such general principles to the specific situations that arise in practice will remain challenging, and the process of moral reasoning required of the practitioner is, we think, likely to be an important focus for scholars and educators in the coming years.

In the Swithun Bowers articles referred to earlier, another important challenge is identified that has been reemerging as a critical issue for social workers. The point he makes is that if we accept that some values are absolute, we are then faced with the problem of where they come from. As a devout Roman Catholic, his answer was rooted in his faith:

> There can be no standards of adjustment of adaptation to an environment, there can be no bad, better or best, there can be no measure or evaluation, without an answer to the fundamental question: To what end does man live in this or any environment? . . . Essentially, this is a religious question, and ultimately social work must find the answer in the sphere of religion. For try as we will, we cannot divorce the ultimate objectives of society from the question which is basic to all religion: what is man? Where lies his destiny? (Bowers, 1949a, pp. 374-375)

The helping professions, however, have been largely secular in the past half century: as a consequence, we have not developed clarity as to how to respond to spiritual issues.

In his work with Daniel (see Chapter 2), Mike was encouraging him to talk about his feelings of alienation as they contributed to his being depressed. Daniel, recalling a period in his life when things were truly awful for him (he was about ten years old), remembered feeling abandoned. A child with strong spiritual needs and instincts, what caused him the most anguish was not the failure of his family and community to sustain him, but coming to the awful conclusion that he had been abandoned by God. Mike, having little expertise in such matters, did not know how to respond, except to return the focus to Daniel's familial experience.

Another helper, someone with both spiritual and psychological insights, might respond more effectively. Jean Vanier (1998), for example, writes compellingly about how profound loneliness can lead to depression but can also provoke spiritual growth.

We cannot be all things to all people, of course, but the point is that spiritual needs are part of the experience of a great many of our clients, and because the majority of clinicians have been trained in secular traditions, we have little preparation for responding effectively to those needs. Historically, we have even been strongly ambivalent about whether to consider them valid.

Ironically, while the advantage of secularism is that we reduce the risk of violating a client's spiritual beliefs by promoting our own, *denying* the importance of spiritual issues can be a different, equally damaging imposition. Whereas respect for cultural diversity requires that we do not proselytize for our own worldview, if that means avoiding confronting spiritual problems we will inadvertently be guilty of cultural insensitivity when clients come from a culture that ascribes fundamental importance to spiritual realities. Aboriginal clients are often mentioned in this regard (Voss et al., 1999; Weaver, 1999).

The schism between spiritual and secular helping is over 200 years old (Ellenberger, 1970), and it is deep. However, there is currently a growing understanding of how spiritual needs and understandings affect the everyday issues that clinicians confront—family, violence, addictions, and child abuse, for example, all evoke themes such as forgiveness, obligation, redemption, and the quest for meaning for many clients. For such people, the interface between spiritual and psychosocial issues is very real, and the fact that the helping professions have worked so assiduously to separate them is problematic. For this reason the work of such scholars as Becvar (1997, 1998) and others is potentially so important, and represents another focus that will require our respectful (and creative) attention in coming years.

References

Introduction

Cameron, G. and Vanderwoerd, J. (1997). *Protecting children and supporting families: Promising programs and organizational realities.* New York: Aldine de Gruyter.

Ellenberger, H. E. (1970). *The discovery of the unconscious: The history and evolution of dynamic psychiatry.* New York: Basic Books.

Frank, J. D. and Frank, J. B. (1991). *Persuasion and healing: A comparative study of psychotherapy* (Third edition). Baltimore: Johns Hopkins University Press.

Gardner, H. (1982). *Art, mind, and brain: A cognitive approach to creativity.* New York: Basic Books.

Gardner, H. (1997). *Extraordinary minds: Portraits of four exceptional individuals and an examination of our own extraordinariness.* New York: Basic Books.

Gilgun, J. F. (1996a). Human development and adversity in ecological perspective, Part 1: A conceptual framework. *Families in Society: The Journal of Contemporary Human Services 77*(4), 395-402.

Gilgun, J. F. (1996b). Human development and adversity in ecological perspective, Part 2: Three patterns. *Families in Society: The Journal of Contemporary Human Services 77*(5), 459-476.

Greenson, R. J. (1967). *The technique and practice of psychoanalysis,* Volume 1. New York: International Universities Press.

Gurman, A. S., Kniskern, D. P., and Pinsoff, W. M. (1986). Research on the process and outcome of marital and family therapy. In S. Garfield and A. Bergin (Eds.), *Handbook of psychotherapy and behavior change: An empirical analysis* (Third edition) (pp. 525-623). New York: John Wiley.

Haley, J. (1963). *Strategies of psychotherapy.* New York: Grune & Stratton.

Kohut, H. (1977). *The restoration of the self.* New York: International Universities Press.

Miller, S., Hubble, M., and Duncan, B. (1995). No more bells and whistles. *The Family Networker* (March/April), 53-63.

Nichols, M. (1987). *The self in the system: Expanding the limits of family therapy.* New York: Brunner/Mazel.

Richmond, M. (1922). *What is social casework?* New York: Russell Sage Foundation.

Rothery, M. (1999). The resources of intervention. In F. J. Turner (Ed.), *Social work practice: A Canadian perspective* (pp. 34-47). Scarborough, Ontario: Prentice-Hall Allyn & Bacon Canada.

Rothery, M. (in press). Ecological-systems theory. In P. Lehmann and N. Coady (Eds.), *Theoretical perspectives in direct social work practice: An eclectic generalist approach.* New York: Springer.

Rothery, M. and Tutty, L. (in press). Client-centered theory. In P. Lehmann and N. Coady (Eds.), *Theoretical perspectives in direct social work practice: An eclectic generalist approach.* New York: Springer.

Selvini Palazzoli, M., Boscolo, L., Cecchin, G., and Prata, G. (1980). Hypothesizing—circularity—neutrality: Three guidelines for the conductor of the session. *Family Process 18*(1), 3-12.

Stern, D. N. (1985). *The interpersonal world of the infant: A view from psychoanalysis and developmental psychology.* New York: Basic Books.

Tomm, K. (1984). One perspective on the Milan systemic approach: Part II. Description of session format, interviewing style and interventions. *Journal of Marital and Family Therapy 10*(3), 253-271.

White, M. (1995). *Re-authoring lives: Interviews and essays.* Adelaide, South Australia: Dulwich Centre Publications.

Wood, K. and Geismar, L. (1989). *Families at risk: Treating the multiproblem family.* New York: Human Sciences Press.

Young, P. (1935). *Interviewing in social work: A sociological analysis.* New York: McGraw-Hill.

Chapter 1

Bateson, M. (1994). *Peripheral visions: Learning along the way.* New York: HarperCollins.

Becvar, D. and Becvar, R. (1993). *Family therapy: A systemic integration* (Second edition). Boston: Allyn & Bacon.

Boszormenyi-Nagy, I. (1965). A theory of relationships: Experience and transaction. In I. Boszormenyi-Nagy and J. Framo (Eds.), *Intensive family therapy: Theoretical and practical aspects* (pp. 33-86). New York: Harper and Row.

Bowlby, J. (1988). *A secure base: Parent-child attachment and healthy human development.* New York: Basic Books.

Byng-Hall, J. (1995). *Rewriting family scripts: Improvisation and systems change.* London: Guilford.

Erwin, E. (1997). *Philosophy and psychotherapy: Razing the troubles of the brain.* Thousand Oaks, CA: Sage.

Glover, J. (1988). *I: The philosophy and psychology of personal identity.* London: Penguin.

Golding, W. (1959). *Free fall.* London: Faber and Faber.

Nichols, M. and Schwartz, R. (1995). *Family therapy: Concepts and methods* (Third edition). Needham Heights, MA: Simon & Schuster.

Sapolsky, R. (1995). Ego boundaries, or the fit of my father's shirt. *Discover 16*(11), 62-67.

Shapiro, D. (1981). *Autonomy and rigid character.* New York: Basic Books.

Stern, D. (1985). *The interpersonal world of the infant: A view from psychoanalysis and developmental psychology.* New York: Basic Books.

Watzlawick, P., Beavin, J., and Jackson, D. (1967). *Pragmatics of human communication.* New York: W. W. Norton.

Chapter 2

Bowen, M. (1961). Family psychotherapy. *American Journal of Orthopsychiatry 31*(1), 40-60.

Bruner, J. (1986). *Actual minds, possible worlds.* Cambridge, MA: Harvard University Press.

Byng-Hall, J. (1995). *Rewriting family scripts: Improvisation and systems change.* London: Guilford.

Kerr, M. and Bowen, M. (1988). *Family evaluation.* New York: W. W. Norton.

L'Abate, L. (1990). *Building family competence: Primary and secondary prevention strategies.* Newbury Park, CA: Sage.

McClure Goulding, M. and Goulding, R. (1979). *Changing lives through redecision therapy.* New York: Brunner/Mazel.

McGoldrick, M. and Gerson, R. (1985). *Genograms in family assessment.* New York: W. W. Norton.

McGoldrick, M. and Gerson, R. (1989). Genograms and the family life cycle. In B. Carter and M. McGoldrick (Eds.), *The changing family life cycle: A framework for family therapy* (Second edition) (pp. 164-189). Boston: Allyn & Bacon.

Satir, V. (1983). *Conjoint family therapy* (Third edition). Palo Alto, CA: Science and Behavior Books.

Chapter 3

Aylmer, R. (1989). The launching of the single young adult. In B. Carter and M. McGoldrick (Eds.), *The changing family life cycle: A framework for family therapy* (Second edition) (pp. 191-208). Boston: Allyn & Bacon.

Bowen, M. (1966). The use of family therapy in clinical practice. *Comprehensive Psychiatry 7*(2), 345-374.

Bowen, M. (1978). *Family therapy in clinical practice.* New York: Jason Aronson.

Bowlby, J. (1988). *A secure base: Parent-child attachment and healthy human development.* London: Routledge.

Bradt, J. (1989). Becoming parents: Families with young children. In B. Carter and M. McGoldrick (Eds.), *The changing family life cycle: A framework for family therapy* (Second edition) (pp. 235-254). Boston: Allyn & Bacon.

Carter, B. and McGoldrick, M. (Eds.). (1989). *The changing family life cycle: A framework for family therapy* (Second edition). Boston: Allyn & Bacon.

Carter, B. and McGoldrick, M. (Eds.). (1999). *The expanded family life cycle: Invididual, family, and social perspectives* (Third edition). Boston: Allyn & Bacon.

Erickson, E. (1968). *Identity: Youth and crisis.* New York: W. W. Norton.

Garcia-Preto, N. (1989). Transformation of the family system in adolescence. In B. Carter and M. McGoldrick (Eds.), *The changing family life cycle: A framework for family therapy* (Second edition) (pp. 255-283). Boston: Allyn & Bacon.

Gardner, H. (1997). *Extraordinary minds: Portraits of four exceptional individuals and an examination of our own extraordinariness.* New York: Basic Books.

Goldner, V., Penn, P., Sheinberg, M., and Walker, G. (1990). Love and violence: Gender paradoxes in volatile attachments. *Family Process 29*(3), 343-364.

Kegan, R. (1982). *The evolving self: Problem and process in human development.* Cambridge, MA: Harvard University Press.

Levinson, D. (1978). *The seasons of a man's life.* New York: Knopf.

Mahler, M., Pine, F., and Bergman, A. (1975). *The psychological birth of the human infant.* New York: Basic Books.

McCullough, P. and Rutenberg, S. (1989). Launching children and moving on. In B. Carter and M. McGoldrick (Eds.), *The changing family life cycle: A framework for family therapy* (Second edition) (pp. 285-309). Boston: Allyn & Bacon.

McGoldrick, M. (1989). The joining of families through marriage: The new couple. In B. Carter and M. McGoldrick (Eds.), *The changing family life cycle: A framework for family therapy* (Second edition) (pp. 209-233). Boston: Allyn & Bacon.

Rosen, H. (1988). The constructivist-developmental paradigm. In R. Dorfman (Ed.), *Paradigms of clinical social work* (pp. 317-355). New York: Brunner/Mazel.

Walsh, F. (1989). The family in later life. In B. Carter and M. McGoldrick (Eds.), *The changing family life cycle: A framework for family therapy* (Second edition) (pp. 311-331). Boston: Allyn & Bacon.

Walsh, F. (1999). Families in later life: Challenges and opportunities. In B. Carter and M. McGoldrick (Eds.), *The expanded family life cycle: Individual, family, and social perspectives* (Third edition) (pp. 307-326). Boston: Allyn & Bacon.

Chapter 4

Bandura, A. (1977). Self-efficacy: Toward a unifying theory of behavioral change. *Psychological Review 84*(1), 191-215.

Biestek, F. (1957). *The casework relationship.* Chicago: Loyola University Press.

Coady, N. (1999). The helping relationship. In F. Turner (Ed.), *Social work practice: A Canadian perspective* (pp. 58-72). Scarborough, ON: Prentice-Hall Allyn & Bacon Canada.

Frank, J. D. and Frank, J. B. (1991). *Persuasion and healing: A comparative study of psychotherapy* (Third edition). Baltimore: Johns Hopkins University Press.

Goulding, R. and McClure Goulding, M. (1978). *The power is in the patient.* San Francisco, CA: TA Press.

Kramer, R. (1995). The birth of client-centered therapy: Carl Rogers, Otto Rank, and "the beyond." *Journal of Humanistic Psychology 35*(4), 54-110.

Menaker, E. (1982). *Otto Rank: A rediscovered legacy.* New York: Columbia University Press.

Rogers, C. (1959). A theory of therapy, personality and interpersonal relationships as developed in the client-centered framework. In S. Koch (Ed.), *Psychology: A study of a science* (Volume 3). New York: McGraw-Hill.

Rogers, C. (1961). *On becoming a person: A therapist's view of psychotherapy.* New York: Houghton Mifflin.
Rogers, C. (1980). *A way of being.* New York: Houghton Mifflin.
Rothery, M. and Tutty, L. (in press). Client-centered theory. In P. Lehmann and N. Coady (Eds.), *Theoretical perspectives in direct social work practice: An eclectic generalist approach.* New York: Springer.
Seligman, M. (1989). Explanatory style: Predicting depression, achievement, and health. In M. Yapko (Ed.), *Brief therapy approaches to treating anxiety and depression* (pp. 5-32). New York: Brunner/Mazel.
Smalley, R. (1967). *Theory for social work practice.* New York: Columbia University Press.

Chapter 5

de Shazer, S. (1985). *Keys to solution in brief therapy.* New York: W. W. Norton.
de Shazer, S. (1988). *Clues: Investigating solutions in brief therapy.* New York: W. W. Norton.
Goulding, M. (1990). Getting the important work done fast: Contract plus redecision. In J. Zeig and S. Gilligan (Eds.), *Brief therapy: Myths, methods and metaphors* (pp. 303-317). New York: Brunner/Mazel.
Hamill, P. (1995). *A drinking life.* New York: Little, Brown and Company.
O'Hanlon, W. and Weiner-Davis, M. (1989). *In search of solutions: A new direction in psychotherapy.* New York: W. W. Norton.
Prochaska, J. (1995). An eclectic and integrative approach: Transtheoretical therapy. In A. Gurman and S. Messer (Eds.), *Essential psychotherapies: Theory and practice* (pp. 403-440). New York: Guilford.
Tutty, L. (1999). The setting of objectives and contracting. In F. Turner (Ed.), *Social work practice: A Canadian perspective* (pp. 132-145). Scarborough, ON: Prentice-Hall Allyn & Bacon Canada.
Watzlawick, P., Weakland, J.H., and Fisch, R. (1974). *Change: Principles of problem formation and problem resolution.* New York: W. W. Norton.
White, M. and Epston, D. (1990). *Narrative means to therapeutic ends.* New York: W. W. Norton.

Chapter 6

Dozier, M. and Tyrrell, C. (1998). The role of attachment in therapeutic relationships. In J. Simpson and W. S. Rholes (Eds.), *Attachment theory and close relationships* (pp. 221-248). New York: Guilford.

Chapter 7

Cameron, G. and Rothery, M. (1985). *An exploratory study of the nature and effectiveness of family support measures in child welfare.* Toronto: Ontario Ministry of Community and Social Services.

Cameron, G. and Vanderwoerd, J. (1997). *Protecting children and supporting families: Promising programs and organizational realities.* New York: Aldine de Gruyter.

Clark, H. and Clarke, R. (1996). Research on the wraparound process and individualized services for children with multisystem needs. *Journal of Child and Family Studies 5*(1), 1-7.

Hartman, A. (1978). Diagrammatic assessment of family relationships. *Social Casework 59*(4), 465-476.

Johnson, L. (1998). *Social work practice: A generalist approach* (Sixth edition). Boston: Allyn & Bacon.

Lachiusa, T. A. (1996). Development of the graphic social network measure. *Journal of Social Service Research 21*(4), 1-35.

Meyer, C. (1995). The eco-systems perspective: Implications for practice. In C. Meyer and M. Mattaini (Eds.), *The foundations of social work practice* (pp. 17-35). Washington, DC: NASW Press.

Rothery, M. (1999). The resources of intervention. In F. Turner (Ed.), *Social work practice: A Canadian perspective* (pp. 34-47). Scarborough, ON: Prentice-Hall Allyn & Bacon Canada.

Rothery, M. (in press). Ecological-systems theory. In P. Lehmann and N. Coady (Eds.), *Theoretical perspectives in direct social work practice: An eclectic generalist approach.* New York: Springer.

Wood, K. and Geismar, L. (1989). *Families at risk: Treating the multiproblem family.* New York: Human Sciences Press.

Epilogue

Becvar, D. (1997). *Soul healing: A spiritual orientation in counseling and therapy.* Toronto, ON: Harper Collins.

Becvar, D. (1998). *The family, spirituality, and social work.* Binghamton, NY: The Haworth Press.

Bowers, S. (1949a). The nature and definition of social casework.: Part II. *Social Casework 30*(9), 369-375.

Bowers, S. (1949b). The nature and definition of social casework.: Part III. *Social Casework 30*(10), 412-417.

Dean, R. and Rhodes, M. (1998). Social constructivism and ethics: What makes a "better" story. Families in Society: *The Journal of Contemporary Human Services 79*, 254-262.

Ellenberger, H. E. (1970). *The discovery of the unconscious: The history and evolution of dynamic psychiatry.* New York: Basic Books.

Greenson, R. (1967). *The technique and practice of psychoanalysis* (Volume 1). New York: International Universities Press.

Koestler, A. (1969). Ethical issues involved in influencing the mind. In Canadian Broadcasting Corporation, *The ethics of change.* Toronto, ON: Canadian Broadcasting Corporation.

Selvini Palazzoli, M., Boscolo, L., Cecchin, G., and Prata, G. (1980). Hypothesizing—circulatory—neutrality: Three guidlines for the conductor of the session. *Family Process 18*(1), 3-12.

Taylor, C. (1989). *The making of the modern identity*. Cambridge, MA: Harvard University Press.

Vanier, J. (1998). *Becoming human*. Toronto, ON: Anansi Press.

Voss, R., Douville, V., Little Soldier, A., and Twiss, G. (1999). Tribal and shamanic-based social work press: A Lokota perspective. *Social Work 44*, 228-241.

Weaver, H. (1999). Indigenous people and the social work profession: Defining culturally competent services. *Social Work 44*, 217-225.

Index

247

HAWORTH Social Work Practice in Action
Carlton E. Munson, PhD, Senior Editor

THE WITNESS STAND: A GUIDE FOR CLINICAL SOCIAL WORKERS IN THE COURTROOM by Janet Vogelsang. (2001). "A must-read for defense attorneys and their investigators. Vogelsang has very succinctly put in writing what social workers need to know about: preparing for a case for trial, how to work with the attorneys and investigators, and how to testify." *Stephen J. Gustat, MS, BS, Criminal Defense Investigator, Adjunct Professor, Department of Criminology, University of Tampa, Florida*

CLINICAL PRACTICE WITH FAMILIES: SUPPORTING CREATIVITY AND COMPETENCE by Michael Rothery and George Enns. (2001). "Make a number of significant contributions to the field of family therapy. . . . Reflects an appreciation for the complexities of practice that is often missing in books on family therapy." *Nick Coady, PhD, Associate Professor, Wilfrid Laurier University, Waterloo, Ontario, Canada*

SMART BUT STUCK: EMOTIONAL ASPECTS OF LEARNING DISABILITIES AND IMPRISONED INTELLIGENCE, REVISED EDITION by Myrna Orenstein. (2001). "A trailblazing effort that creates an entirely novel way of talking and thinking about learning disabilities. There is simply nothing like it in the field." *Fred M. Levin, MD, Training Supervising Analyst, Chicago Institute for Psychoanalysis; Assistant Professor of Clinical Psychiatry, Northwestern University, School of Medicine, Chicago, Illinois*

SOCIAL WORK THEORY AND PRACTICE WITH THE TERMINALLY ILL, SECOND EDITION by Joan K. Parry. (2000). "Timely . . . a sensitive and practical approach to working with people with terminal illness and their family members. I recommend this book to anyone who wants to meet the challenge of working with the terminally ill and their survivors." *Jeanne A. Gill, PhD, LCSW, Adjunct Faculty, San Diego State University, California, and Vice President, Southern California Chapter, AASWG*

WOMEN SURVIVORS, PSYCHOLOGICAL TRAUMA, AND THE POLITICS OF RESISTANCE by Norma Jean Profitt. (2000). "A compelling argument on the importance of political and collective action as a means of resisting oppression." *Gloria Geller, PhD, Faculty of Social Work, University of Regina, Saskatchewan, Canada*

THE MENTAL HEALTH DIAGNOSTIC DESK REFERENCE: VISUAL GUIDES AND MORE FOR LEARNING TO USE THE DIAGNOSTIC AND STATISTICAL MANUAL (DSM-IV-TR), SECOND EDITION by Carlton E. Munson. (2000). "A carefully organized and user-friendly book for the beginning student and less-experienced practitioner of social work, clinical psychology, or psychiatric nursing . . . . It will be a valuable addition to the literature on clinical assessment of mental disorders." *Jerrold R. Brandell, PhD, BCD, Professor, School of Social Work, Wayne State University, Detroit, Michigan and Founding Editor, Psychoanalytic Social Work*

HUMAN SERVICES AND THE AFROCENTRIC PARADIGM by Jerome H. Schiele. (2000). "Represents a milestone in applying the Afrocentric paradigm to human services generally, and social work specifically. . . . A highly valuable resource." *Bogart R. Leashore, PhD, Dean and Professor, Hunter College School of Social Work, New York, New York*

SOCIAL WORK: SEEKING RELEVANCY IN THE TWENTY-FIRST CENTURY by Roland Meinert, John T. Pardeck, and Larry Kreuger. (2000). "Highly recommended. A thought-provoking work that asks the difficult questions and challenges the status quo. A great book for graduate students as well as experienced social workers and educators." *Francis K. O. Yuen, DSW, ACSE, Associate Professor, Division of Social Work, California State University, Sacramento*

SOCIAL WORK PRACTICE IN HOME HEALTH CARE by Ruth Ann Goode. (2000). "Dr. Goode presents both a lucid scenario and a formulated protocol to bring health care services into the home setting. . . . This is a must-have volume that will be a reference to be consulted many times." *Marcia B. Steinhauer, PhD, Coordinator and Associate Professor, Human Services Administration Program, Rider University, Lawrenceville, New Jersey*

FORENSIC SOCIAL WORK: LEGAL ASPECTS OF PROFESSIONAL PRAC-TICE, SECOND EDITION by Robert L. Barker and Douglas M. Branson. (2000). "The authors combine their expertise to create this informative guide to address legal practice issues facing social workers." *Newsletter of the National Organization of Forensic Social Work*

SOCIAL WORK IN THE HEALTH FIELD: A CARE PERSPECTIVE by Lois A. Fort Cowles. (1999). "Makes an important contribution to the field by locating the practice of social work in health care within an organizational and social context." *Goldie Kadushin, PhD, Associate Professor, School of Social Welfare, University of Wisconsin, Milwaukee*

CLINICAL WORK AND SOCIAL ACTION: AN INTEGRATIVE APPROACH by Jerome Sachs and Fred Newdom. (1999). "Just in time for the new millennium come Sachs and Newdom with a wholly fresh look at social work. . . . A much-needed uniting of social work values, theories, and practice for action." *Josephine Nieves, MSW, PhD, Executive Director, National Association of Social Workers*

SOCIAL WORK PRACTICE IN THE MILITARY by James G. Daley. (1999)."A significant and worthwhile book with provocative and stimulating ideas. It deserves to be read by a wide audience in social work education and practice as well as by decision makers in the military." *H. Wayne Johnson, MSW, Professor, University of Iowa, School of Social Work, Iowa City, Iowa*

GROUP WORK: SKILLS AND STRATEGIES FOR EFFECTIVE INTERVEN-TIONS, SECOND EDITION by Sondra Brandler and Camille P. Roman. (1999). "A clear, basic description of what group work requires, including what skills and techniques group workers need to be effective." *Hospital and Community Psychiatry* (from the first edition)

TEENAGE RUNAWAYS: BROKEN HEARTS AND "BAD ATTITUDES" by Laurie Schaffner (1999). "Skillfully combines the authentic voice of the juvenile runaway with the principles of social science research." *Barbara Owen, PhD, Professor, Department of Criminology, California State University, Fresno*

CELEBRATING DIVERSITY: COEXISTING IN A MULTICULTURAL SOCIETY by Benyamin Chetkow-Yanoov. (1999). "Makes a valuable contribution to peace theory and practice." *Ian Harris, EdD, Executive Secretary, Peace Education Committee, International Peace Research Association*

SOCIAL WELFARE POLICY ANALYSIS AND CHOICES by Hobart A. Burch. (1999). "Will become the landmark text in its field for many decades to come." *Sheldon Rahan, DSW, Founding Dean and Emeritus Professor of Social Policy and Social Administration. Faculty of Social Work, Wilfrid Laurier University, Canada*

SOCIAL WORK PRACTICE: A SYSTEMS APPROACH, SECOND EDITION by Benyamin Chetkow-Yanoov. (1999). "Highly recommended as a primary text for any and all introductory social work courses." *Ram A. Cnaan, PhD, Associate Professor, School of Social Work, University of Pennsylvania*

CRITICAL SOCIAL WELFARE ISSUES: TOOLS FOR SOCIAL WORK AND HEALTH CARE PROFESSIONALS edited by Arthur J. Katz, Abraham Lurie, and Carlos M. Vidal. (1997). "Offers hopeful agendas for change, while navigating the societal challenges facing those in the human services today." *Book News Inc.*

SOCIAL WORK IN HEALTH SETTINGS: PRACTICE IN CONTEXT, SECOND EDITION edited by Toba Schwaber Kerson. (1997). "A first-class document . . .It will be found among the steadier and lasting works on the social work aspects of American health care." *Hans S. Falck, PhD, Professor Emeritus and Former Chair, Health Specialization in Social Work, Virginia Commonwealth University*

PRINCIPLES OF SOCIAL WORK PRACTICE: A GENERIC PRACTICE APPROACH by Molly R. Hancock. (1997). "Hancock's discussions advocate reflection and self-awareness to create a climate for client change." *Journal of Social Work Education*

NOBODY'S CHILDREN: ORPHANS OF THE HIV EPIDEMIC by Steven F. Dansky. (1997). "Professional, sound, moving, and useful for both professionals and interested readers alike." *Ellen G. Friedman, ACSW, Associate Director of Support Services, Beth Israel Medical Center, Methadone Maintenance Treatment Program*

SOCIAL WORK APPROACHES TO CONFLICT RESOLUTION: MAKING FIGHTING OBSOLETE by Benyamin Chetkow-Yanoov. (1996). "Presents an examination of the nature and cause of conflict and suggests techniques for coping with conflict." *Journal of Criminal Justice*

FEMINIST THEORIES AND SOCIAL WORK: APPROACHES AND APPLICATIONS by Christine Flynn Salnier. (1996). "An essential reference to be read repeatedly by all educators and practitioners who are eager to learn more about feminist theory and practice: *Nancy R. Hooyman, PhD, Dean and Professor, School of Social Work, University of Washington, Seattle*

THE RELATIONAL SYSTEMS MODEL FOR FAMILY THERAPY: LIVING IN THE FOUR REALITIES by Donald R. Bardill. (1996). "Engages the reader in quiet, thoughtful conversation on the timeless issue of helping families and individuals." *Christian Counseling Resource Review*

SOCIAL WORK INTERVENTION IN AN ECONOMIC CRISIS: THE RIVER COMMUNITIES PROJECT by Martha Baum and Pamela Twiss. (1996). "Sets a standard for universities in terms of the types of meaningful roles they can play in supporting and sustaining communities." *Kenneth J. Jaros, PhD, Director, Public Health Social Work Training Program, University of Pittsburgh*

FUNDAMENTALS OF COGNITIVE-BEHAVIOR THERAPY: FROM BOTH SIDES OF THE DESK by Bill Borcherdt. (1996). "Both beginning and experienced practitioners . . . will find a considerable number of valuable suggestions in Borcherdt's book." *Albert Ellis, PhD, President, Institute for Rational-Emotive Therapy, New York City*

BASIC SOCIAL POLICY AND PLANNING: STRATEGIES AND PRACTICE METHODS by Hobart A. Burch. (1996). "Burch's familiarity with his topic is evident and his book is an easy introduction to the field." *Readings*

THE CROSS-CULTURAL PRACTICE OF CLINICAL CASE MANAGEMENT IN MENTAL HEALTH edited by Peter Manoleas. (1996). "Makes a contribution by bringing together the cross-cultural and clinical case management perspectives in working with those who have serious mental illness." *Disability Studies Quarterly*

FAMILY BEYOND FAMILY: THE SURROGATE PARENT IN SCHOOLS AND OTHER COMMUNITY AGENCIES by Sanford Weinstein. (1995). "Highly recommended to anyone concerned about the welfare of our children and the breakdown of the American family." *Jerold S. Greenberg, EdD, Director of Community Service, College of Health & Human Performance, University of Maryland*

PEOPLE WITH HIV AND THOSE WHO HELP THEM: CHALLENGES, INTEGRATION, INTERVENTION by R. Dennis Shelby. (1995). "A useful and compassionate contribution to the HIV psychotherapy literature." *Public Health*

THE BLACK ELDERLY: SATISFACTION AND QUALITY OF LATER LIFE by Marguerite Coke and James A. Twaite. (1995). "Presents a model for predicting life satisfaction in this population." *Abstracts in Social Gerontology*

BUILDING ON WOMEN'S STRENGTHS: A SOCIAL WORK AGENDA FOR THE TWENTY-FIRST CENTURY edited by Liane V. Davis. (1994). "The most lucid and accessible overview of the related epistemological debates in the social work literature." *Journal of the National Association of Social Workers*

NOW DARE EVERYTHING: TALES OF HIV-RELATED PSYCHOTHERAPY by Steven F. Dansky. (1994). "A highly recommended book for anyone working with persons who are HIV positive. . . . Every library should have a copy of this book." *AIDS Book Review Journal*

INTERVENTION RESEARCH: DESIGN AND DEVELOPMENT FOR HUMAN SERVICE edited by Jack Rothman and Edwin J. Thomas. (1994). "Provides a useful framework for the further examination of methodology for each separate step of such research." *Academic Library Book Review*

CLINICAL SOCIAL WORK SUPERVISION, SECOND EDITION by Carlton E. Munson. (1993). "A useful, thorough, and articulate reference for supervisors and for 'supervisees' who are wanting to understand their supervisor or are looking for effective supervision." *Transactional Analysis Journal*

ELEMENTS OF THE HELPING PROCESS: A GUIDE FOR CLINICIANS by Raymond Fox. (1993). "Filled with helpful hints, creative interventions, and practical guidelines." *Journal of Family Psychotherapy*

IF A PARTNER HAS AIDS: GUIDE TO CLINICAL INTERVENTION FOR RELATIONSHIPS IN CRISIS by R. Dennis Shelby. (1993). "A welcome addition to existing publications about couples coping with AIDS, it offers intervention ideas and strategies to clinicians." *Contemporary Psychology*

GERONTOLOGICAL SOCIAL WORK SUPERVISION by Ann Burack-Weiss and Frances Coyle Brennan. (1991). "The creative ideas in this book will aid supervisors working with students and experienced social workers." *Senior News*

THE CREATIVE PRACTITIONER: THEORY AND METHODS FOR THE HELPING SERVICES by Bernard Gelfand. (1988). "[Should] be widely adopted by those in the helping services. It could lead to significant positive advances by countless individuals." *Sidney J. Parnes, Trustee Chairperson for Strategic Program Development, Creative Education Foundation, Buffalo, NY*

MANAGEMENT AND INFORMATION SYSTEMS IN HUMAN SERVICES: IMPLICATIONS FOR THE DISTRIBUTION OF AUTHORITY AND DECISION MAKING by Richard K. Caputo. (1987). "A contribution to social work scholarship in that it provides conceptual frameworks that can be used in the design of management information systems." *Social Work*

R.D. Michaels
your expectation of touch heals
> dogs
> acceptance